Praise for *Rez Rules*

"Some people have said there is racism in Canada but there is no systemic racism in Canada. To those people I say, clearly you have not read the Indian Act, because it reeks of racism. Chief Louie has spent a lifetime trying to rid Canada of such racism."

—The Right Honourable Brian Mulroney PC, CC, LLD

"In his own straight speak, Chief Louie provides a compelling and no-holds-barred exposé into what it is really like to be an elected Chief on an Indian reserve in Canada. Without concern for the political correctness of someone who has never actually lived on a reserve, lest try to govern one effectively under the Indian Act, Chief Louie tells it like it is and provides an important and timely contribution during this period of Indigenous nation rebuilding. Never apologetic, always practical, my 'good buddy's' reflections, advice and political musings around Osoyoos finding economic prosperity, despite ongoing challenges, is a must read."

—The Honourable Jody Wilson-Raybould

"A remarkable book by a remarkable man. By the time I had finished the first few pages I had already placed an order for fifty copies for friends and family."

—David Chilton, author of *The Wealthy Barber*

"Chief Clarence Louie is a friend of mine but don't hold that against him! He's a miracle worker. He created the 'miracle in the desert' in the Okanagan, and now he's got his sights set on creating a 'miracle of reconciliation' in Canada that we all want to see happen. We all *want* to see reconciliation, Chief Louie wants it too, the difference is he delivers, and here's his plan."

—Peter Mansbridge, former chief correspondent, CBC News

"Chief Clarence Louie, a highly successful Indigenous leader, offers a raw and honest perspective on First Nations leadership and what it takes to create a thriving and long-lasting Indigenous nation amidst colonialization and its fallout. His book is definitely worth reading."

—Manley Begay, Jr., former co-director,
Harvard Project on American Indian Economic Development

"The Canadian government has created the poverty conditions that make it far more likely for First Nations children to be separated from their families and Nations. What is required is blunt truth telling like Chief Louie's book, confronting Canada's systemic racism and economically empowering First Nation communities."

—Cindy Blackstock, executive director,
First Nations Child & Family Caring Society

"Chief Louie has captained the Osoyoos Indian Band to unparalleled success in business based on the long-standing Indigenous values he learned from his ancestors. His support for the rights of his people and the Blackhawks logo reflect the same type of tenacity I always expected from a member of the Hawks. I am proud to have worn a jersey that a respected Native chief like Clarence loves as much as I do. His book is a testament to the type of no-nonsense leadership we all long to see more of nowadays."

—Chris Chelios, NHL Hall of Fame defenseman
and former Chicago Blackhawks captain

"Chief Clarence Louie shares stories of his early years and how those years taught him real leadership principles and led him to a lifetime of great achievements and a humility that endears him to all who meet him. He is a wise man, and his book will be endearing and entertaining to all who take the opportunity to share his experiences with him."

—Jim Pattison, CEO, The Jim Pattison Group

REZ RULES

CHIEF CLARENCE LOUIE

REZ RULES

MY INDICTMENT OF CANADA'S

AND AMERICA'S

SYSTEMIC RACISM

AGAINST INDIGENOUS PEOPLES

McClelland & Stewart

Library and Archives Canada Cataloguing in Publication data is available upon request.

ISBN: 978-0-7710-4833-3
ISBN: 978-0-7710-0206-9 (signed edition)
ebook ISBN: 978-0-7710-4834-0

Interior text design by Andrew Roberts
All photographs are courtesy of the author unless otherwise noted.
The cartoon on p. 3 of the photo section is by John Larcher. (Reproduced
by permission of Western Standard New Media Corp.)
Jacket Art: Courtesy of the author
Back jacket images: Beaver pelt courtesy of Garry Oker;
Crown: Den Rozhnovsky / Shutterstock; Bill: Jeff Kingma / Getty Images,
image used with the permission of the Bank of Canada.
Typeset in Leitura News by M&S, Toronto
Printed in Canada

McClelland & Stewart,
a division of Penguin Random House Canada Limited,
a Penguin Random House Company
www.penguinrandomhouse.ca

1   2   3   4   5   25   24   23   22   21

I dedicate this book to my kids and grandkids (Vern, Clarissa, Sarenna, Darian, and Zenaya), the mother of my children Sandra (Sam), Brenda, my spouse, and my "mean Rez mom"—everyone calls her "Lucy." Also to all past, present, and future Osoyoos Indian Band members and all our "cuzzins" throughout Indian Country—Rez country on both sides of the Canada–U.S. border. That foreign colonial border continues to divide my people, but it did not divide our ancestors, who could not speak, read, or write English or French. I continue to think of the Aboriginal people of Australia and the Maori of New Zealand who asked me to speak on their lands and who have also suffered from colonial racism. May all the "Rezskins" one "Indian Magic" day in the future wake up and fulfill the prophecies and dreams of our ancestors that we remain a distinct people with our own language and the unshackled pride of 10,000 years of heritage and culture on our traditional territories. Look at the old black-and-white historical pictures of the "Hostiles & Savages," the old Indian frontier photos (Chief Sitting Bull, Chief Joseph, etc.). I hang the old frontier pictures of those two Chiefs above my desk for a reason. I see in their eyes the look of prisoners of war, a once-free, economically independent people. But most important, in their eyes I do not see a conquered people. Read the words of our ancestors as they spoke up against the racist treatment by the leaders of the Canadian and American governments. Our spiritual knowledge keepers have been asking our people to wake up for a long, long time. I may not be around when our communities finally fully wake up and rid ourselves of the colonial traps, like the Indian crab syndrome and drug and alcohol abuse, but I see the signs of our people reuniting with their Tribal past and becoming stronger and taking our rightful place as economically sovereign leaders and protectors of our traditional lands and waters. Our core principles must never change—regardless of the new challenges of climate change and pandemics, our people, present and future, must look to their ancestral past for guidance and, no matter what, must never forget how to "Indian up!"

Soon after this my father sent for me. I saw he was dying. I took his hand in mine. He said: ". . . . Always remember that your father never sold his country. . . . A few years more, and white men will be all around you. They have their eyes on this land. . . . This country holds your father's body. Never sell the bones of your father and your mother."

—Chief Joseph (Nez Perce)

CONTENTS

FOREWORD

This is an important book for all Canadians. I may not agree with some of the opinions stated here, but this is a book that should be read and considered, as it is a look at who we are and how we got here by one of the country's most significant Indigenous leaders. For far too long, Indigenous voices have been underrepresented in our country's dialogue, making this kind of book long overdue.

I like Clarence Louie, and we have known each other for several years. I respect his opinions even when we differ, which happens. However, it is important that he is able to express his views, even the harsh ones.

The accomplishments of the Osoyoos Indian Band of British Columbia under their long-time chief are remarkable. This First Nations reserve in the South Okanagan Valley has rightly been called a "Miracle in the Desert."

This band went from near bankruptcy and Depression-level unemployment to a thriving, self-sustaining community that contributes significantly to the local and provincial economies. Where once there was next to no work on the reserve, today there are almost twice as many jobs as there are band members. The Osoyoos band runs a five-star resort and owns a championship golf club. They are involved in a racetrack, an RV park and campground, a gas bar, and stores. They have their own prestigious winery, Nk'Mip Cellars, which is known across the country—truly, a Miracle in the Desert!

In 2016, when Chief Clarence was vested as a Member of the Order of Canada, the highest civilian honour our country awards, the citation read:

> Clarence Louie has brought prosperity to his community. Elected chief of the Osoyoos Indian Band at the age of 24, he was driven to improve living standards for his people. To this end, he formed a development corporation to foster business relationships and entrepreneurship. Over the past three decades, his efforts have helped revitalize the community with the establishment of a cultural centre and several businesses, including a winery, a golf course and a commercial centre. In addition, he has been instrumental in safeguarding the Okanagan language and cultural heritage for future generations.

Being able to build a sustainable Indigenous economy is critical when it comes to proper reconciliation between those who *were* here and those who *came* here. Like Chief Clarence, I believe absolutely that there can be no reconciliation without fairness and a strong Indigenous economy.

When I became prime minister in 2003, top among our priorities was a series of agreements that became known as the "Kelowna Accord." Many of the ideals of the Kelowna Accord are happily alive and well in Osoyoos. The notion that young mothers need support, that youth need every educational opportunity, that teachers and principals need proper resources, that post-secondary education be made readily available—all are so very important. They cannot remain ideals; they must become reality.

Chief Clarence Louie is a passionate collector of quotes. Sprinkled throughout this powerful book you will find the wise words of Chief Sitting Bull, Martin Luther King Jr., Nelson Mandela, Muhammad Ali, and Canada's own Chief Dan George.

Mark my words—future books will be quoting Chief Clarence Louie.

—The Right Honourable Paul Martin

ACKNOWLEDGEMENTS

I first want to thank the hundreds of Osoyoos Indian band members who had faith in me to serve as their Chief when I was still a youth of 24 to now being in my 60s. To Roy MacGregor (my pilgrim buddy), who accepted my request to make this book happen. I know I made him "circle the wagons" a few times with my choice of words. I talk and write like a Rez Indian. I don't believe in being politically correct. A big thanks to my publisher—McClelland & Stewart and especially editor Jenny Bradshaw, who worked with me to edit and re-edit. I also want to thank Bruce Westwood and Meg Wheeler at Westwood Creative Artists.

I am deeply grateful for all the words (quotes) and stories from all the teachers I have had throughout my life. My brother Arnie was a far better writer than I can ever hope to be. He asked me to put these words on his headstone: "To Write Is To Be Remembered."

The words and stories I treasure come from my love of books and listening to speeches of the greats in sports, business, and politics, as well as from reading every Native non-fiction book I could find. I thank the many successful people I have met—my network of contacts—as my words are really their words said my Rez way.

I want to thank businessman Peter M. Brown from Vancouver and Peter Mansbridge (the voice of Canada's national news for decades) who, among others, nominated me, as the first "First Nations" inductee into the Canadian Business Hall of Fame (2019). History proves (through archeological evidence) that it was the First Nations who were Canada's and America's first entrepreneurs.

As Native people, we are so lucky to have ancestors who learned from nature and brought nature's laws into our decision making. My people's university was "Mother Nature." My gramma Christine once pointed to the moon and said, "That's your gramma." The so-called "uneducated savages" had knowledge that the world needs today. The old Indians were as wise as any professor. I now realize that teachers can come in all shapes and sizes. I am so grateful for all the reserves and reservations I have been on, as that is where most of my teachings come from. There is still so much to learn (especially from nature), and from the "little people"—the kids of all races—I know I will always be a life-long student. "*Limlmt*"—thank you in my language (Nsyilxcǝn / Okanagan) to all my teachers past, present, and future!

REZ RULES

INTRODUCTION

Indian policy in Canada and the United States—from termination to assimilation and now reconciliation

"White settlers succeeded in building a society with all the features of the modern world. . . . But this development occurred at the expense of the Indian population. As a society they could only be characterized as a dependent, impoverished, diseased and illiterate people, prone to alcohol and appearing to lack in ambition. White success was built upon Indian dispossession."

Okanagan historian Duncan Duane Thomson, thesis, "A History of the Okanagan: Indians and Whites in the Settlement Era, 1860–1920."

A book from a Chief is rare. Over the last fifteen years or so, I have been asked by many people, both Native and non-Native, "When is your book coming out?" I have written many articles and have given hundreds of keynote speeches all over North America, as well as speeches in Australia, New Zealand, Germany, and France, but when people asked me about putting my thoughts and what I have learned over those many years of leadership down on paper, I never gave it more than a casual thought.

It took a child to change my mind.

Back in December 2016 I received a letter from Siera, a little girl I had never met. Her grade four class was doing a project on leadership, and at the suggestion of her dad, she had selected me as someone to interview. I imagine her dad had heard of the Osoyoos Indian Band and me through the many media reports on the success of our economic and business development. The Osoyoos Indian Band (OIB) has more businesses and joint ventures on a per capita basis than any other First Nation in Canada, a fact that has turned us into an economic power in the South Okanagan Valley of British Columbia.

In Canada there are over three thousand federal Indian reserves. Some are very small (only a few acres), and the biggest is the Blood Tribe in Southern Alberta, which sprawls over some 350,000 acres. In the United States there are 326 federal Indian reservations, with the largest being the Navajo Nation, at sixteen million acres. White people in the U.S. call where Native people live "reservations." In Canada, white people say "reserve." We who live there call it simply "the Rez."

My Rez, the Osoyoos Indian Band, is one of those rare First Nations that has more jobs than it does band members (540 members, with more than a thousand jobs). We own a golf course, cement company, cultural centre, RV park and campground, two gas bars, winery, vineyard, sewage and water utilities, and forestry operations, plus thousands of acres of leased property in vineyards, a hotel, preschool and grade school, and commercial and residential properties. We have gained national attention through such highly visible business projects as our joint venture with Arterra Wines, Canada's biggest wine producer. We had Canada's most famous race car driver, Jacques Villeneuve, build his signature racetrack here on the Osoyoos Rez.

The Osoyoos Indian Band has focused on putting what I call the original "treaty relationship," based on business and economic and social independence, into action. Not long ago, a *Globe and Mail* article called it "The Miracle in the Desert." In a way, it is exactly that. The Osoyoos Indian Band proves that when a First Nation is not dependent (in a welfare state) but independent (in a business state) while contributing to the local, regional, and national economy, it is good for all of Canada and the United States.

In her own little-girl handwriting, Siera asked me five questions, and she said she hoped that I would respond in writing. Now, I had received requests like this before, from students of all ages from across the country. I'm always deeply honoured and I make sure to free up time to accommodate such requests. I have also written multi-page personal thoughts and feelings that I have shared from time to time with Osoyoos Indian Band staff and members. But this was different.

Siera's questions were excellent. They reminded me of something often said by leadership expert John Maxwell: "Good leaders ask great questions." I decided to answer the five questions in far more detail than a grade four student would need, as I also wanted to share my answers with my own kids as well as with members and staff of the Osoyoos Indian Band, of which I have been Chief for over thirty-five years. I answered the little girl's questions on leadership in many pages, and after my grown daughter Sarenna read my answers, she said, "Dad, you really should write a book." That gave me the push I needed.

Recently, I received a surprise phone call from former prime minister of Canada Brian Mulroney. He told me, "The only thing that lives on in history are books. So write a book so your children and grandchildren can read the words you leave behind." This book is not a biography, but it is about my time as Chief of the Osoyoos Indian Band. It is about the leadership path I have been on since I started organizing sports teams as a teenager, and that continued later as I became a lifelong student of Native issues throughout North America. Most importantly, though, it's going to tackle issues that have and continue to confront North America's Native population (racism, multi-generational trauma, economic disparity), and it's going to do so with some tough talk . . . it's not always going to be pretty or popular or politically correct, but it's going to be the truth, from someone who lives the Rez experience every day.

As anyone in their fifties knows, time flies once you get over forty. And keeps flying faster and faster. I hadn't paid much attention before to the "write a book" request, but after being chosen by a little girl for her class project on leadership and having my own daughter tell me a few weeks later what I had heard many times before but ignored, I had a change of heart. I thought, *I'm now in my last quarter, and I don't have many years left in me. It's time. I have a "Chief duty"— some may call it a leadership duty—to pass on what I have learned to First Nations, to the various levels of government and to corporate Canada and corporate America, and more importantly, to any little Native girl or boy on and off the Rez!*

Like Chiefs everywhere, I have had the honour and duty of serving my people through the good and the bad. I have witnessed hundreds of Osoyoos Indian Band youth become adults. It's mind-blowing to me that all OIB youth under the age of thirty-five have a memory of only one Chief—and that's me. That's a very heavy burden, but at the same time such a huge honour and responsibility. I have also had to go to hospitals or band members' homes in order to be there for my people when they were on their death beds. Being there for my people at all ages, even when they might be so weak they cannot talk and can barely breathe, is a duty and responsibility at the highest level. I have to be there.

A few years ago, I visited with Thelma, one of my people who had stage 4 cancer. She was one of our best employees—hard-working, never late, always paid her bills, never asked the band for anything but a career opportunity. That's the way all our people should be. I knew Thelma was in a lot of pain and could see that she had lost a lot of weight. Yet she was so happy to see me and spoke in such an upbeat tone, even though she knew she had only days left. Some would say I went to see her to comfort her, but the truth is I was the one comforted by her inspiration.

I have said many times that the Chief and council are not the only leaders on a Rez. Anyone who collects a paycheque on behalf of a band or tribe holds a leadership position. That position, that job, either makes the community better or worse. And the old, those who have retired and "earned their rest," are also leaders. Thelma had worked at our gas station and store for years, and she said to me many times one of the most important sentences anyone can say to me, words I love hearing from my people—"*I love my job!*"

"I love my job" is one of the most fulfilling, life-changing statements a person can make. And that's why job creation and job training and development is one of the most important responsibilities of all the leaders on the Rez. I just wish the government bureaucrats who collect their middle-class and higher paycheques and pensions for jobs that are intended to improve the lives of Indian people would care about providing Indian people with paycheques and pensions equal to the ones they pocket each month.

Thelma reminded me of how a real leader thinks. She was dying and she knew she didn't have much time left. She did not talk of her cancer or the pain she was going through but of her hope for her family and the Osoyoos Indian Band. During my last visit with her she talked very seriously to me and thanked me for providing her with a job, a career that she had loved. Then, with a smile that never left her face, she took my hand and said, "You are the only Chief that I had gotten to know, and I'm really worried. Not for me—I have had a good life because of the job I loved—I am worried for my family. Especially my kids and grandkids." She stopped and kept on smiling. I had heard the same concerns before from others. But then, in the nicest tone I have ever heard, she gave me a kick in the rear. One that I needed.

Thelma was acting as real leaders do. Real leaders look beyond their own needs and put the future of their community ahead of everything else. This was true Indian "seventh-generation" thinking. "You are not going to be Chief forever," Thelma told me, still smiling. "You have to protect the future of the band. We have many businesses that will have to be protected for the future generations. We need more hard-working leaders who will sacrifice and think always of the future. It's up to you to work with the youth to pass on your knowledge to train and develop more *real* leaders, not phony leaders. Like me, you have to think of the future. What youth do you think have real leadership potential to one day be Chief?"

It was a tough question for me to answer, so I listened as Thelma named some youth who she thought could eventually take over as Chief. We both agreed OIB has some good-hearted, hard-working youth who do have Chief potential. Today I see many diligent, educated, and culturally motivated youth. Some have picked up the drum (*dang*, we got some good traditional singers!). Some have become very good hunters and fishers. Some are learning much more of the Okanagan language than I know myself. Some are going on to university and college. I believe Native youth need to balance contemporary education with our own Native heritage and culture. There are several young men and women who I hope will one day outperform me and raise the Osoyoos Indian Band up and beyond what was accomplished during my thirty-plus years.

This was to be the last conversation I had with Thelma. But it was also the conversation that gave me a final nudge to begin working on this book. After thirty years, the time has come to pass on my knowledge and my recommendations on what it takes to be a Chief and a leader on the Rez. I need to do this not only for my own community but for all First Nations, all bands and tribes, all Indian/

Aboriginal/Indigenous—whatever term you use—people. All those terms are of course English words used by government to identify my people. I personally choose to use the English term "Indian," as that is what I have been called by my white buddies since grade school. I take no offence, nor do I consider it racist to be called an Indian. Just as white people should take no offence or consider it racist when I call them white people—'cause that is what they are. I believe in race, and everyone should be proud of their skin colour. The oldest Elder on my Rez (Jane), who turned ninety in 2020, has said, "I was born an Indian and I will die an Indian." My mom actually hates the terms "Aboriginal" and "Indigenous" being applied to us.

The Canadian Constitution identifies three distinct groups of Indigenous people—Indian (First Nations), Inuit, and Métis. Only First Nations people were relegated to federal Indian reserves/reservations (although most First Nations in the Far North do not have Indian reserves).

In this book, I will explain why I have a lot of distrust, anger, and disappointment toward Canada and the United States. I also want it clearly understood that I love the two countries that now occupy my First Nation's territory. However, I despise how those two countries historically treated my ancestors. I despise how they continue to deny justice and reconciliation for all that followed the broken treaties and land rip-offs, as my people were forced onto reserves in Canada and reservations in the United States. My love/hate relationship with Canada and the United States is rooted in the core historical facts of how those new countries were founded on systemic racism toward the original people of this land. The newcomers colonized my peoples' territory and thereby denied all First Nations the socio-economic right to live the so-called Canadian and American dream.

Words can be powerful, dangerous, inspiring, comforting, maddening, and confusing. They can be good and they can be bad. Throughout this book, I'll include some of my favourite quotes from my book collections and my personal notes. I believe the phrase "leaders are readers" truly applies in the modern context. When I am in a successful person's office or home, no matter if they are a prime minister, premier, or a multimillionaire successful business person, I first look for their bookcase. I want to know what this leader read that helped them get to where they are today.

Spoken words don't last as long as written words, just as former prime minister Brian Mulroney said. But I have never been involved in a book before. It's all new and unexplored territory for me. I do buy most every non-fiction book about Indians that I hear about. I am very proud of my personal library, and I encourage young leaders to start their own book collection. What you read or don't read says a lot about you. I read somewhere that "The two major influences in your life are the people you meet and the books you read." Years ago, in a used bookstore, I bought a book called *Chief: The Fearless Vision of Billy Diamond*. I had heard about the James Bay Cree and their fight against the Quebec government back in the 1970s, when I was a Native studies student. In 2001, I was asked to be a keynote speaker at the James Bay Cree's annual general meeting in Northern Quebec; I got to meet Grand Chief Billy Diamond and get the book signed. That book, *Chief*, sits in my office and is one of my most prized books. It was written by Roy MacGregor, but I never paid attention to that name. I was only interested in the Chief.

In September 2006, I was again a keynote speaker, this time at a non-Native conference in Fort McMurray. I explained to the gathering that I don't speak like many Chiefs who act like phony politicians, the same white politicians who they claim oppress and disappoint them. Politicians speak to their base and toe the party line. Politicians change their tone depending on who is in the room or what the polls say. I'm not a politician, I'm a leader, and I'll stand alone on an issue if I must. I don't speak for votes or to please whoever is in the room. I speak the truth and sometimes Natives don't like what I say. That's okay, because I'm not a politician.

One of the greatest business leaders of all time, Walt Disney, said, "The road to failure is to try and please everyone." I don't expect or demand that everyone agree with me. Sometimes my own mom doesn't agree with me! In a real democracy, it's okay to disagree and still be on the same team. I told that meeting in Fort McMurray that there are a few simple truths we all know but too often forget. One of them is that in business you must start on time. You can't run a business or make money with slackers—"lazy asses," as the Elders call them. Everyone, including management, must show up on time. You can't run a business and make money on "Indian time." Heck, every kindergarten teacher must start on time. If a kindergarten teacher showed up late, the parents would be pissed—and rightly so. A teacher who shows up late gets fired. Yet still today most Native meetings don't start on time.

I said a few things at that meeting that caught the ear of one of the white reporters in the audience. I later got to meet Roy MacGregor, the author of *Chief: The Fearless Vision of Billy Diamond.* Then, a few days afterwards, he wrote an article about my Fort McMurray speech and titled it "Indian Time." That article appeared in the *Globe and Mail* on September 21, 2006, and all these years later I still get emails about it. That one little newspaper article really made its rounds in "Indian Country" on both sides of the border.

So, it was only fitting that I contacted Roy in 2017 to ask him if he would like to help with a book about another Chief. It would be the book that Siera, Sarenna, and Thelma inspired. It would be a book from the

Rez, about the Rez culture, about leadership, about the lies of the founding fathers on both sides of the border and the continuing dishonour of the Crown. It would be about First Nations economic development and the benefits of such business and community development to corporate Canada and corporate America. It would talk about how the American Bureau of Indian Affairs (BIA, which Natives say stands for "Boss Indians Around") and the Canadian Department of Indian Affairs (DIA, which I say stands for "Department against Indians Achieving") must change their systemic racism and failed formulas and programs that have created Third World conditions in two of the wealthiest countries in the world. To a shocking extent, the Canadian and American economies were built on racist policies and programs, the suffering of Indigenous people, and the theft of tribal nations land. So much for the treasured founding concepts of freedom and justice for all.

Clearing the land now called Canada and the United States of Indians to allow for white settlement and resource development has always been at the heart of federal, provincial, and state government Indigenous policy. It's time for Canada and the United States to face up to their racist past and honour the treaties and give back (reconcile) Indian land it stole.

I believe the Canadian and American societies do have much good in them and that they are now wrestling with the systemic racism woven into the fabric of their flags and institutions. The vast majority of the new generations of Canadians and Americans do want to build a new business relationship with the original people of this land, one that is based on *real* truth and reconciliation. But, in order to go forward, we must clean up the historical injustices and reconcile the racist past with settlement money and land, not just apologies. The outstanding land question has always been the founding fathers' unfinished business.

I set out to write a book because I truly want our people to act and live like hard-working people as our ancestors once did, and to be as independent and self-supporting as our ancestors were long before the European empires of Britain and France and Spain planted their racist colonial flags on our territories. This book is a first step. It calls out some hard truths and makes recommendations that will help achieve this goal.

One day, not far off, my name will be included with the ancestors'. All real leaders, when they get to the time in their life when they realize their leadership time is setting, have a deep inner feeling of the past, present, and future. One quote that goes to the very core of my time as Chief, and why I felt it was time to write this book, is from one of the best writers of all time, Mark Twain: "The two most important days in your life are the day you are born and the day you find out why."

I don't know the exact day I found out why I was born, but I do remember the incident. While still a teenager in the mid-1970s, I heard a speech on an 8-track car stereo while driving my aunt Tilly's Mustang. The album playing was *Plight of the Redman*, by a Native American rock band called "XIT." Included on the concept album was a speech that I have listened to a thousand times since then, and that I still listen to today. Every time I hear the speech, I know why I was born.

> *The Indian has been out there on the ghetto of the reservation*
> *for a long, long time.*
> *We have existed without adequate food, clothing, shelter or*
> *medicine to name but a few.*
> *In their place we have been given malnutrition, poverty, disease,*
> *suicide and bureaucratic promises of a better tomorrow.*

*Your America has not been the land of your proclaimed equality
and justice for all.*

*The treatment of our people has been a national tragedy and
disgrace*

*The time has come to put an end to that disgrace—Alcatraz, Fort
Lawton—whatever necessary,*

*We must now manage our own affairs and control our own
lives.*

And through it all,

We are made to be the true Americans.

Real reconciliation must start with all the outstanding land questions.

CHAPTER 1

"INDIAN MAGIC"

"Sometimes the magic works—sometimes it doesn't."

—Chief Dan George in the movie *Little Big Man*

A lot changed for me when I turned sixteen. The big dream for many kids on a reserve is to have your own "Rez ride" so you can go on road trips to other Rezes with your buddies. For me, it meant not having to ask for a lift from my poor mom. Having your own ride is really your first taste of freedom—and also your first big responsibility.

Most Rez youth back in the 1970s didn't have a vehicle, and the few who did drove "Rez bombs"—uninsured vehicles that are really just pieces of junk held together with duct tape. Some Rez bombs even had names—like "The Convict," a four-door boat of a vehicle that could "Indian squeeze" eight Rez boys. Those cars might have a broken windshield or no muffler, but their owners will still sometimes drive them to town hoping not to get pulled over by the cops (the Queen's Cowboys).

I never set my bar so low as to own a Rez bomb. If you're going to own something, it should be something you can own with pride. When I was sixteen, I got a full-time summer job off the Rez, saved up my paycheques, and got myself a pretty nice vehicle: a 1968 Ford pickup. In the public high school I went to, that ride was one of the better rigs. The first addition to my rig, naturally, was to save up for some "tunes." A good ol' 8-track and speakers and I was off to the next Rez!

That year, 1976, was also the first year I ever went off the Rez to work or live. I left to work at Kootenay National Park, which is a long way away from the Okanagan. There was a job-opportunity contest put on by Parks Canada. They had a program where they would pick eight sixteen-year-old boys and eight sixteen-year-old girls and place them in a national park for the summer. The National Parks Service summer-student work experience was the very best summer job I ever had. To win one of the jobs, you had to write an essay on the importance of national parks. I wrote my essay and sent it in, and then, in May, I was notified that I was one of the kids who had been picked.

It was nice to know they'd liked my essay, but when I heard that I'd been picked for one of the jobs, I didn't want to go, even though a summer job on the Rez meant labouring in the hot vineyard. My mom would hear nothing of this, though, and she forced me to leave the Rez and take that job with Parks Canada. How's that for some old-school "tough love"? "You're going, and that's it!" she said. I am forever thankful my mom was tough on me and forced me to "get off the Rez and get a job."

It can be life-changing to be forced to do something and go somewhere you don't want to go. Today they say youth need to get out of their comfort zone. My mom got her sister, my aunt Tilly, who had a nice '68 Mustang, to drive me seven hours away to Radium Hot Springs, where Kootenay National Park begins. Aunt Tilly dropped me off at the trailer camp where I'd be staying and left to drive back to the Rez. There were other youngsters there, all looking as lost as I felt. A counsellor took us all aside. "I can tell you all want to go home," he told us. "You're homesick. Well, halfway through the summer you'll all change your minds and wish you never had to go home. I can promise you that." None of us kids believed him, but it turned out he was 100 per cent right. By the end of August, none of us wanted the national park job experience to end. We learned to love our job and the experience.

Part of that experience was opening my first bank account so that Parks Canada could put my pay in each week. We couldn't spend much money because we were always in the mountains and rarely got to town. For the first time in my life, and at sixteen years old, I had saved up over a thousand dollars.

I had worked summers before. As kids we were lucky (though I never looked at it that way at the time) that our reserve, unlike most, had its own business—a vineyard. Inkameep Vineyard, the Osoyoos Indian Band's first business, started in 1968. For most OIB youth in the 1970s, working in the vineyard was our first summer job. When kids were twelve or thirteen we were considered old enough to work. We had to get up at 4 a.m. get to the field by 5 a.m., and we would work until 1 p.m. By early afternoon in the Okanagan, it gets too hot to work. I was paid two dollars an hour and I also learned another adult responsibility—paying bills. When I got my first cheque my mom took half of it for gas and food. More "tough love." I learned pay-your-bills responsibility real fast.

Kids should learn at an early age to work hard and should also pitch in to help pay the bills. As youth, we worked hard in the summer, and the vineyard provided a tough job-training ground for many OIB members. That's why most of our people are very hard-working. The Osoyoos also learned to do outside hard labour jobs such as ranching, orchard work, logging, and working in the sawmills. Living off grants or federal transfer dollars and working easy hours in a heated and air-conditioned office was never an option for most of my people.

When I got back to the Rez after that summer working in Kootenay National Park, I immediately got my driver's licence and bought that '68 Ford truck. I was the only youth around my age with a nice pickup that wasn't a Rez bomb, and it got me a lot of attention from the Rez crowd. I got to meet and hang around more Rez people (the older ones) because I was one of the few sixteen-year-olds with his own licensed vehicle. I could go to town or cruise the Rez. I could travel to sports tournaments and powwows throughout the Okanagan territory. It was my first big step into freedom and pride of ownership. A driver's licence is an adult responsibility that can become a big help in holding a real job. If you get driving offence fines, pay them off—and don't get any more!

A year or so later I somehow talked my mom into buying a '66 GTO, a "muscle car," and we did an "Indian trade"—she took over my truck. Now I had the best hot rod in the entire high school. Southern Okanagan Secondary School in Oliver had around eight hundred students, and you could count the ones from the Rez on one hand. So, through my love of sports and, later, cars and pickup trucks, I had no problem fitting in with teenagers both on and off the Rez. When you're driving around in a red classic GTO with an 8-track, powerful pipes, and music blaring, it's easy to make friends.

I graduated from high school in 1978 (barely), and I soon found myself hanging around non-Indians less and less. Having a driver's licence and a nice set of wheels has its positives and negatives. I was happier being with the "skins." I got the "Rez bug," and most every weekend the Rez boys I liked to hang with wanted to saddle up and get away to another Rez in the valley. Somewhere we could party and "snag" (find a honey for the night).

There's something very special, a kind of feeling only Rez people get, when you're on your own Rez or a different Rez. It's that ancestral connection—to the historical strength every Rez has and to the oppression they went through. The good, the bad, and the ugly. All First Nations reserves have basically the same history and connection. It's like being in the old Montreal Forum, Maple Leaf Gardens, or the old Yankee Stadium. All sports fans know what I mean. Those sites weren't just another hockey rink or baseball park. There was a special feeling in those old cathedrals of sports. They talk about the "hockey gods" in sport, but when I pass the imaginary line of being *on* the Rez and *off* the Rez—even when I'm in a different tribal territory—I feel that the ancestors from that Rez are there. I can sense how those ancestors fought and struggled against the DIA or the BIA.

The Rez is kind of our stronghold, our last piece of land to hold out against Canadian and American assimilation. The Rez wasn't designed for this purpose, of course. The governments saw it as an assimilation tool—a concentration camp, if you like—where they could control and manipulate Indians. But what I call "Indian Magic" (and others call karma) works in strange ways, and the government Rez assimilation system actually helped in some ways to protect Native identity. Indian Magic turned the Rez system into something opposite of what was intended. It was something that even the local racist "Indian agents" couldn't see coming. It gave us a strong identity and a connection with all other Rezes throughout Canada and the United States.

I appreciate that there are Natives, especially in the Far North, who don't have reserves and can't understand why southern Indians (in both countries) will defend the Rez system and promote the inclusion of more lands within the Rez. We don't *want* to be "brown municipalities," and we don't want to be under provincial or state land status. But our legal, historical relationship is with the federal governments, "for better or worse, till death do us part."

"Indian reserve" or "Indian reservation" is a federal government legal designation for an area of land managed jointly by an Indian band or tribe under the federal bureaucracy that was in the past officially called, and is still most often referred to as, Indian Affairs. In Canada today, the bureaucracy is called Indigenous Services. The Rez system was created to keep Native people off the lands the white settlers wished to have, pure and simple.

From 1966–2017 Indian Affairs and Northern Development were one ministry, though with a few name changes, including most recently Indigenous and Northern Affairs Canada. Then, in 2017, Prime Minister Trudeau dissolved INAC and replaced it with two new departments: Crown-Indigenous Relations and Northern Affairs Canada (often called CIRNAC) and Indigenous Services Canada (ISC).

In 1851, the United States Congress passed the Indian Appropriations Act, which created the American reservation system. Reserves in Canada were already being created before Confederation in 1867. In creating this system, the main goal of both the Canadian and American federal governments was to bring Native Americans under government control—to minimize conflict between Indians and settlers and assimilate Indian kids to take on the ways of white people, religion included. Any band of Indians not forced onto a Rez was declared "hostile" by the federal government, and the cavalry was sent after them. As more settlers came into a region and began to intrude on Rez land, the government merely stole land set aside for Indians by breaking treaties. Once the governments were able to move Natives onto a reserve or reservation, the U.S. and Canadian departments of Indian Affairs, through racist Indian agents, were able to control every aspect of Rez life—even down to when an Indian could or could not leave their Rez.

To me, the Rez is hallowed ground and is the foundation of our fiduciary relationship with the federal government. My great-grandfather, Chief Manuel Louie, said back in the 1960s, in an interview with the *Oliver Chronicle*, "Our original reserve lands, the boundary was the Okanagan River, Indians on this side, and Whites on that side."

Rez Indians love their reserves and reservations. The Rez is our historic territorial stronghold, with all its faults and dysfunctions, and we love it as family. We owe a lot to our ancestors, who truly suffered when the reserves and reservations were first established, and I am thankful every time I can step on and feel the spiritual history of any Rez.

There are a few basic Rez rules I learned from those years of sports and summer jobs on the Rez and from eventually leaving the Rez for work and school. They are:

- Stay in school. (In fact, no matter what your age, always be a student.)
- Get a job, especially off the Rez. Summer jobs are very important as a youth. As an adult, your employment record says a lot about you.
- Get active in sports as a player, an organizer, or a fan.
- Coach a kids' sports team at least once in your life. Some of your best adult memories will come from a kids' locker room. Kids' non-political support of each other is a big lesson for adults.
- Attend community functions, especially cultural ceremonies.
- Get a driver's licence and protect that licence.
- Save money to purchase your own "iron horse." Don't hitchhike or bum rides. And please—no Rez bombs!
- Pay your bills! Especially your rent. Paying bills keeps your name in good standing.
- Practise personal growth and development. Read, listen to podcasts or tapes, attend seminars and lectures. Find smarter people to hang around. Hang around hard-working people and get away from the lazy asses.

- Pay your child support, unconditionally. Any self-respecting man or woman must own up to parental responsibility. You might not be raising your own kids, but they are still your kids and need your financial support.

It was tough leaving for university, but my mom had the old Rez rule, "Go to school, get a job—or get out!" Labour jobs didn't bother me. I didn't feel entitled to a cushy band office job. No matter what summer job I had, I seldom missed work or showed up late. I had a vehicle to support and places I wanted to go. Like most of the working Osoyoos Indian Band members from the 1960s and 1970s, I would put my attendance record at work up against anyone's. Most OIB members were hard-working labourers. We got down and got dirty in the heat, cold, wind, and rain. I have a high degree of respect for workers who earn a living working outside. Everyone should, at least once in their life, work outdoors so they have the personal experience of what it's like to make their living working outside.

If I wanted to keep my car on the road, I had to earn a paycheque every two weeks. I didn't have parents to pay for my gas or car maintenance, and there was no land claim, casino, or oil money per-capita Rez payments back then. I also knew getting a full-time job on the Rez was difficult. Back then, OIB didn't have many job opportunities for young people. This, of course, is the biggest problem that still exists today on most reserves: lack of career and job opportunities, and the sad fact that, far too often, dirty Rez politics determines who gets hired for or fired from whatever jobs there are.

So, at nineteen, I knew I wanted more than an entry-level labour job and I left the Rez for the second time in my life. I got on my first plane, flew east over the mountains to the prairies, and landed in

Regina, Saskatchewan. I enrolled in Native American Studies at the Saskatchewan Indian Federated College, later to be renamed First Nations University of Canada. The distance from home was tough, and I brought the most important thing I owned (other than my GTO): my hockey gear. I was hoping to find a Native hockey team.

At the University of Regina library, I fell in love with the large collection of books on Native history. For the very first time, I was reading the old stories and quotes from the famous Chiefs—Sitting Bull, Crazy Horse, and Chief Joseph. I couldn't afford to buy books, so sometimes I would go to the library and handwrite out almost an entire Native book. In class, hearing about the historic and legal significance of treaties was life-changing for me. For the first time, I was getting a chance to learn about my people and our struggles against the Canadian and American governments. The school was in Cree territory, and the Cree students I met were Rez kids no different from me. It was fantastic. I loved the Native American Studies program.

I had never before had the opportunity to study Indians. For a Rez kid to be in a university where we read, wrote, and talked about Natives' issues in every class—*wow*, bring it on! I remember one of the professors questioning my essay, saying that I was maybe too harsh in lumping all white people together as racists who were against Indians and their land rights. He thought perhaps I was too "pro-Indian." He told me Indians are not all necessarily good and trusting people. I was at that time very naive about Rez politics, and I later found out that my professor was right: not all Natives are trustworthy, and some do not live by the "Rez code."

But I still remember defending my "pro-Indian" position. The professor had long grey hair and I was a teenager. After debating him, I remember thinking, *The way he talked, did that guy even grow up or spend any time on the Rez?* Maybe he was book smart, but not Rez smart, one of those "urban academic" Indians? There is a difference—a big difference.

The following semester I transferred to the University of Lethbridge, where, once again, my major was to be Native American Studies. It was very tough being a "starving student," barely getting by on the $550-a-month "Unit 1" post-secondary living allowance from Indian Affairs. Most Native students receive no financial support from their families, as their families can't afford to send any money. It was no different for me. I was broke all the time, and, in the end, I didn't finish my degree at Lethbridge. While I was there, however, I learned everything I could about North American Indian issues from some of the best Native professors, people like Leroy Little Bear, Marie Smallface Marule, and Thomas King.

At university, my three "happy places" were Native Studies classes, the gym (working out), and the library (looking for books and papers on Native issues). A gym (weight room) is still one of my main hangouts; it's where I go to get some real healing and wellness. Real healing and wellness is not just mental, emotional, and spiritual; it must also include the physical, as every doctor keeps telling us. If you're not feeling good, get some exercise. If you want to get healthy, go to a gym. It's very good medicine. I find it crazy that most Native healing and wellness meetings and conferences never talk about simply getting your butt into a gym or starting a regular exercise program. How can that be?

Now, another place to get some real healing and wellness is a library or bookstore. At the University of Lethbridge, it was awesome to find book after book on Natives—and, for the first time, to read Native newspapers. Native news: that's what I love. I loved to read the *Akwesasne Notes* every chance I could. That is a Native newspaper from the Mohawk Rez of Akwesasne, which is a one-of-a-kind Rez that straddles both sides of the St. Lawrence River near the Ontario-Quebec border and extends into Upper New York State. It was the first time I had ever come across a Native-controlled news publication.

I loved to read about the "Indian resistance" and the Native civil rights protests of the 1960s and '70s. I remember reading about the American Indian Movement (AIM) and being in awe. AIM organized protest marches such as the Trail of Broken Treaties caravan to Washington, D.C., in 1972. They went to the U.S. capital to remind America of the 372 treaties that had been broken. Their occupation of the Bureau of Indian Affairs building was an awakening not only in the U.S. but in Indian Country in Canada as well. The seventy-one-day occupation and military standoff at Wounded Knee in 1973 made national and international headlines. Canadians and Americans were shocked to learn that, contrary to their beliefs and hopes, the "Indian Problem" had not been bureaucratized away.

As poor as I was as a student, I ordered the book *Voices from Wounded Knee*, which remains part of my prized book collection. In 2006, when I helped organize the Osoyoos Indian Band's first Economic Development Conference, I wanted as a guest speaker Russell Means, the former leader of the American Indian Movement— and I got him! We had a budget for the conference and I wanted to bring him to Osoyoos to talk about the American Indian Movement and Rez leadership.

Russell Means, like most Native leaders, came with some baggage, but he still had been there, in person, in the trenches at so many Native American protests. I picked him up at the airport in Spokane, Washington, and asked him many questions about the Native civil rights movement of the '60s and '70s on our long drive back. It was a fascinating few hours.

AIM was not a perfect organization. Like all Native groups, it suffered from the Rez culture—internal jealousy, suspicion, and, at times, a lack of leadership and proper organizational structure. Yes, AIM did some dumb shit, made some major mistakes, and had some big internal struggles that led to a few very tragic deaths. But, as Dennis Banks observed in his book *Ojibwa Warrior*, AIM was, and remains, fundamentally important to the Native movement:

> We were the prophets, the messengers, the fire-starters. Wounded Knee awakened not only the conscience of all Native Americans, but also of white Americans nationwide. We changed an attitude of dependence on the B.I.A. and the government. . . . We resurrected old beliefs and ways of life, blending them with the demands of modern life. . . . We have not achieved all that we wanted. We only have made a dent in solving our many problems. As the FBI and the marshals at Wounded Knee found out we are still a strong people.

We are a strong people for sure, but sometimes we have to be lucky as well. I truly believe in what I have been calling "Indian Magic"—how some things happen out of the blue and don't make any sense but still make you wonder in amazement. *How and why did that just happen?* I believe some things are more than just a coincidence. Some unexplained incidents actually change your life journey. Sometimes Indian Magic moments are very spiritual in nature to me.

When I was first elected Chief, my first major purchase was a 750 Honda Shadow motorcycle. I had never owned a new ride. I got my bike licence and rode that iron horse for a few years, but I was still playing sports and didn't ride much and eventually sold the Honda. At the time, I didn't know why my first major purchase when I became Chief was a motorcycle. Like most Rez boys I had never even ridden a dirt bike. Decades later I had paid my house off (Indians don't get free housing, no matter what you may have heard) and decided to get back into motorcycles. In 2009 I bought my first Harley-Davidson. On the surface, that purchase had absolutely nothing to do with Native culture or spirituality. Yet that first Harley would take me on many awesome Native cultural and spiritual journeys. Yeah, Indian Magic can be anywhere, at any time, through any means—even on two wheels.

Only a few months after buying that Harley, I found out about the Wounded Knee Memorial Motorcycle Run—an annual honour ride to preserve the memory of the more than 250 Lakota people who suffered and died at the Wounded Knee Massacre on December 29, 1890. The ride starts on Chief Sitting Bull's Rez in North Dakota, the famous Standing Rock Reservation, and it ends at the site of the biggest mass shooting (massacre) on North American soil: the Wounded Knee gravesite on the Pine Ridge Reservation in South Dakota. The white media forgets the truth—the what and where—of the biggest mass shooting in America. The Lakota motorcycle riders are creative; they take their love of "iron horses" and use that passion to remember one of the worst tragedies committed against Indian people. So now I think back and connect the dots. I believe Indian Magic led me to my motorcycle purchases. Going on Native motorcycle honour rides is a match for any cultural, heritage, and spiritual gathering I have ever attended.

First, like all Native cultural gatherings, no drugs or alcohol! Native motorcycle rides are not a party. They are serious cultural gatherings that use motorcycles to bring people together, both Native and non-Native. There are "Sweats," smudging, drumming, spiritual and historical speakers, and lots of ceremony. The amount of Indian land you see is second to none, and the brotherhood and sisterhood connections made on Native motorcycle rides are on par with those made at any Native cultural and spiritual gathering.

From the Wounded Knee Memorial Motorcycle Run, I quickly found out that many other Natives have taken the "iron horse" into the cultural/spiritual realm on other motorcycle honour rides, like the Cherokee Trail of Tears Commemorative Motorcycle Ride, the Navajo Hopi Honor Run, and the Apache Run to the Rez Ride. A tribal nation to the north of me does the yearly Shuswap Nation Motorcycle Ride. All these rides are awesome, with organizers genuinely committed to the "Indian way." I tell people I don't play sports anymore and I don't go to hockey or ball tournaments (unless it's for kids). Those are nice events, nice to hang around—but for me, sports gatherings are nothing compared to Native motorcycle honour rides.

As I've said, a Rez motorcycle ride is not a party. It's not a leisure cruise and there's no five-star treatment. It's about honouring the sacrifice of our ancestors and war veterans and connecting with the heritage and culture of the host nation. Sitting Bull and Crazy Horse are two of my heroes, and my Harley brings me to Lakota country every year on the first weekend in August for the Wounded Knee Run. It is a profoundly spiritual experience riding the sacred Black Hills, which the Lakota still legally own even as the U.S. federal government continues to dishonour the treaties the government itself drafted.

The Navajo Hopi Honor Run in the middle of May honours all veterans, and especially the sacrifice and memory of Lori Piestewa, who, during the war with Iraq in 2003, became the first female Native American to be killed in combat. The event is sometimes called the "Ride for Lori." Navajo is the biggest Rez in the world: six million acres and 300,000 members. This four-day ride through the Navajo/Hopi Rez, which includes meetings with "Gold Star" families who have lost family members to war, is very emotional and worth the time and expense. The Navajo code talkers, who helped win the Second World War, are an example of the second-to-none military sacrifice of all North American tribes.

Most Canadians and Americans don't realize that during both world wars and the Vietnam War, First Nations people volunteered at a higher rate than any other race. At the time, First Nations people in Canada did not even have the right to vote, as the government's racist attitude was that Indians were not citizens of Canada. Even after all the broken treaties and massacres, the cultural genocide and Rez land rip-offs, no other people stepped up more to enlist during the wars—no matter that their ancestors were forced at gunpoint and by starvation onto federal Indian reserves and reservations. That's the ultimate proof of the Native warrior spirit. Native motorcycle rides are for a historic cause, and I give a loud and proud shout-out to all the organizers of Native motorcycle honour rides! To me, those rides are a true example of Rez leadership.

One important Rez rule for all Native leaders is to incorporate some traditional spiritual practices into your leadership. I realize we have to organize ourselves within a modern business structure, complete with organizational charts, balance sheets, and profit and loss statements. Yes, we need the proper financial numbers and good legal and human resources advice, but no tribe or band should go 100 per cent corporate or municipal. As Native people, we must incorporate some of our heritage and culture into all of our organizations and into all the programs and services on the Rez.

Before the colonial forces slammed their flag onto Indigenous land, our ancestors had good governance models and rules and procedures and protocols between tribes. Our forebears were not perfect, but over thousands of years (as opposed to a few hundred) they had developed systems of governance and economic trade that worked for them. We need to look into our own culture regularly for governance and corporate guidance—to spend some time on the Native side of the scale.

Every year, a leader should be able to say that they participated in a traditional ceremony, or attended a cultural site to gather strength and seek guidance in decision-making. If you're a Native who goes to church, that's your personal choice, but if you're going to claim to be Indian, then do something Indian! Don't just carry a status card or tribal membership card. To me, spirituality is very important, and no one religion is better than another. How and to whom you pray is no one's business but your own. Most of my inner circle never hears me talk of what I do on the spiritual side—where I look for spiritual guidance, where I go for contemplation. First Nations didn't have missionaries. We didn't go around preaching and trying to convert others. Most Indians don't publicly preach about their spirituality, and neither do I. I just know it's needed and that it's a requirement of core Rez leadership.

Leadership takes time to develop. There is no such thing as an instant leader. My first involvement in Native activism was in 1980, while I was still at the University of Lethbridge. Some of the Rez boys from the Blood Tribe west of Lethbridge organized a demonstration treaty run from Blackfoot Crossing, site of the Treaty 7 negotiations back in 1877, all the way to Ottawa. In Ottawa there was going to be a special meeting of the National Indian Brotherhood (later renamed the Assembly of First Nations), which would involve Chiefs from all across Canada and representatives of the federal government, including then prime minister Pierre Elliott Trudeau. For the first time in Canada, a treaty bundle would be carried by Native runners from Treaty 7 across most of Canada—it was called "The Run," which stood for "Treaties Honoured Entirely—Reservations Under Natives."

Some of the Native Studies students, especially those from the Blood Tribe and the Piikani (Blackfoot Confederacy Bands), were going to join in. I don't remember who asked me to join, but as my major was Native American Studies and I had been reading and writing term papers about Native issues and Canada's broken treaty promises, I did not hesitate. "Count me in," I told them.

I knew I had to get back home and find a summer job. I wanted to get back on the ball diamond and catch up with all my friends and family on my own Rez. But The Run was far more important. I even phoned one of my cousins, Jarvis, back in the Okanagan (Westbank First Nation) and told him to get on the next bus and come and be one of the runners. He left immediately.

The Run took place in early April, after our classes were over. Other University of Lethbridge Native American Studies students also dusted off their old moccasins (Mike Bruised Head, Esther Tailfeathers, Pat Twig, Narcisse Blood) and joined the Run. It took about twenty-two days for the treaty bundle to be relayed to Ottawa. Mile by mile, runners—waiting in Rez bombs (old cars and trucks)—were spread out along the Trans-Canada Highway; each one would receive the bundle from the runner before them and, in turn, they would carry and pass it on to the next runner waiting up the road. I was worried about how many of the Rez bombs would make it to Ottawa and back. Johnny Blood's car was held together with sinew and duct tape. It didn't have air conditioning but at least it had a cassette deck. It was my first great cultural experience, and I will always be indebted to the Blackfoot people and the grassroots Rez boys and girls who put up their own money and sacrificed their Rez bombs to pick up runners all the way to Ottawa and back.

The Run was not only a political demonstration about broken treaties but also a very spiritual event. We often camped along the highway, and every morning and every night, a medicine man (Tiny Man from the Blackfeet Rez in Browning, Montana) would lead the runners in a smudge and prayer and song. On that run I also I saw real Rez leadership, which I had never known before. I realized you don't need to be elected to Chief and council to be a leader. You don't need a boardroom, papers, or an "I care" speech in a community hall to show real Rez leadership.

Most of the Rez boys on the run were not athletic, did not play sports, and surely did not exercise or run. I went to the gym most every day in university and had been a long-distance runner in high school, and I could tell on my first day of The Run that many of the boys were pretty out of shape and were not regular joggers. Regardless they all did "Indian up!"

Admittedly, there were some slackers, some guys who, after running a mile, would claim bad knees or pulled muscles and would have to join the "cripples" in a car or pickup truck that would be sent ahead to set up camp. The leaders of The Run had rules (as all good leaders do), and if you were not going to run you still had to pitch in. The Rez humour was awesome along the way, and guys would "Indian squeeze" into vehicles and wait alongside the road arguing about whose turn it was to run. It all reminded me of Rez sports. We were truly a team, with a lot of laughs and a few disagreements. And of course, as the days went by, "Indian politics" crept in between some of the boys. Sometimes the older guys, the organizers like Dennis and Sheldon First Rider, would call a "circle" and give us a kick in the rear. Usually, we deserved it.

Along the way we were greeted by many reserves. Again, there are many good points to the Rez culture, and one of them is sharing and helping out other Natives in times of need and protest. The reserves along the Trans-Canada Highway would send people out to greet us, feed us, and sometimes put us up in their Rez community centre. Other runners would join up, and we eventually had some very good runners. But Dennis and Sheldon First Rider knew we were still falling behind schedule. We had to do some twenty-four-hour runs to meet our schedule. Most of the crew would camp for the night while a few (the best runners) would be asked to run all night, in the dark in the middle of nowhere.

The first all-nighter was somewhere in Ontario. A local Rez was setting up to host the runners, providing a nice meal and place to sleep. I remember Dennis going around to every vehicle asking for volunteers. We were all young guys in our late teens or early twenties and very few of us wanted to volunteer, especially after hearing a Rez was going to host us. Most of the boys wanted to head to the Rez and hang out, eat, and check out the Rez girls. When no one in the vehicle I was in volunteered, the leader of The Run looked directly at me and asked me to run all night, but I turned him down. I wanted to chill and take it easy.

I learned an important lesson about leadership in that moment: a real leader does not take it easy or rest when an important job needs to be done. A real leader carries not only his own load but, at times, the load of the group. I remember genuinely feeling bad as I shook my head when asked to stay and continue running. I noticed the other guys didn't feel bad at all. In fact, they were quite pleased with their decision to take the easy way out. There can be big differences in how individuals commit to a team or cause. Some give 50 per cent, a few more give 75 per cent, and the rare few give 100 per cent. A leader always takes on extra responsibility and does things a majority of people don't want to do.

The other difference between a leader and other people is how they feel inside after a decision. That day on The Run, the sun was going down, and as I sat in the car listening to the teasing and joking I glanced back and saw the few who were staying behind in the middle of nowhere—the few who volunteered to give up a hot meal and a comfortable rest and a chance to meet some Rez girls. My conscience got to me, and I began to feel bad about the decision I'd made to say no to our team leader. I don't remember exactly what came over me. I just remember asking the driver to stop and let me out. My buddies all looked at me in shock and said, "Stay in the car. We're going to the Rez to have some fun." The other guys in that car could easily live with their decision not to volunteer, but I couldn't. At the time I didn't think or look at it as a leadership decision. I just said to the driver, "Stop. I'm getting out and staying." I told my friends to have fun and that I would see them in the morning.

As I walked back to the lone vehicle and watched the lineup of cars and trucks leave for the Rez, I was at first upset. Damn, I really wanted to go to that Rez! So did the others who were staying, it turned out. We joked for a few minutes about saying *To heck with this job, volunteering sucks, let's just pile in and head to that Rez*. But once the treaty bundle was put on our back, all that mattered was to run and run, to make up as many miles as we could through the night.

It was getting dark. Remember, we had no cellphones back then, or any other way of communicating with the rest of the group. We picked who would run first and the rest squeezed into a single truck. Because it was pitch dark and we had no clue where we were, the truck stayed behind the runner with the lights on him. There were no houses, no street lights around, and very little traffic. And with only a handful of runners, we switched quicker than usual throughout the night. When you weren't running or driving the pickup truck, you tried and tried to get some sleep by resting your head on your buddy next to you.

It was a long, tough night, but we all felt proud to "Indian up!" and stay behind and carry the treaty bundle on our back through the darkness. I remember toward daylight taking my shift driving behind the runner, the truck lights on his body, nothing but darkness all around, the other guys sleeping or resting with their eyes closed, no one talking near the end of the night run. I was mesmerized by the runner's feet going up and down, so slowly, and I thought I could be somewhere else, taking it easy, but that *this* was where I belonged— with the few, not with the crowd. I would rather be there toughing it out for an "Indian cause" than anywhere else in the world.

Thinking back, that's one of the best leadership examples I can share. And yeah—no one, including me, even noticed the leadership lesson at the time. Our small group of volunteers continued to run well into daylight—we didn't worry about when the others were going to get there to relieve us. I don't think any of us even owned a watch. We would get woken up to get out and do our shift to either drive the truck or run. When the support crew did catch up to us, the night runners all piled into Leroy Little Bear's van and found the best spot to sleep. It was one of the best sleeps I've ever had.

Leroy Little Bear was a professor and head of the Native American Studies program at the University of Lethbridge, and he had joined The Run after exams. He had a nice blue "hippie van," no Rez bomb, and I've always thought that for him and his wife, Amethyst, to volunteer their nice vehicle and time to join the cause said a lot about them. Some Indians can have university educations and live and work in the city but never forget their "Rez roots," and they will step up to the plate when needed. Leroy's van took quite a beating on that trip, but personal sacrifice is what Rez leaders do. Leroy never once told any of the runners to be extra careful in his fancy van. He sacrificed his vehicle for the cause just like those who brought their Rez bombs did.

I remember late in the next day getting back in the car with my buddies who had gone to the Rez and listening to them talk about all the fun they had had. They told me I should never have volunteered, that I should have gone with them instead. I didn't say much, because I knew they wouldn't understand. I knew taking it easy was fine within their mindset, but I'd been where I belonged during the night. Not with the take-it-easy crowd but with the hard-working, sacrificing few. There are times when real leaders have to get away from the take-it-easy crowds, the crew, and the staff and go it alone.

I loved the Native American Studies program at Lethbridge. Reading and studying and listening to some of the best leaders in Indian Country was, and still is, a passion of mine. As Eleanor Roosevelt once said, "Great minds discuss ideas; average minds discuss events; small minds discuss people." I was fascinated by ideas. I wanted to do something that would involve ideas.

In the early 1980s, a job came up at the Okanagan Tribal Council in Westbank, and I ended up being an assistant to the administrator. For the first time, I was working in the trenches, representing the Okanagan Bands on tribal issues. Sitting in the same room with the Chiefs and council members, and watching and listening to our land claim and programs and services struggles against the federal government was putting my education to work. While I was working for the Okanagan Tribal Council, one of the old Chiefs said to me, "If you're really interested in Native issues and causes, the very best training grounds is to get elected to Chief and council." I had never thought about running for Chief or council before that moment.

This conversation changed my life. I don't remember who nominated or seconded me for Chief of the Osoyoos Indian Band back in the fall of 1984, but I do remember that many of the older people were not surprised and were supportive of my decision to run for Chief at the age of twenty-four. Even though I had been away at university for eight months out of every year for the past few years, many of the older people knew my organizational skills and leadership in sports, that I was a good worker who held jobs on and off the Rez, and that I was one of the few young guys who owned and looked after a nice vehicle. Through running for office, I got to know many of the older people on a personal level.

Building business and personal relationships is one of the most important things any individual can do in life, especially with their own people. I don't remember why so many older people had faith in me to run for Chief rather than to first run for council, but I do remember that not one person told me "You're too young and inexperienced to run for Chief." I had proved myself to be a good worker and a good sports organizer. I had left the Rez to go to university, but I didn't talk differently after university or act like a high-society, fast-talking, educated Indian and hang around white people. I was a Rezskin and proud of it!

I won my first election for Chief in December 1984.

CHAPTER 2

REZ CULTURE

"Every reserve has one. The place where hidden agendas thrive, and personal interests are served. It's a centralized, hypocritical vacuum—confusion is rampant. It's a place where 'Me-First' politics thrive. It's also the number one employer in most communities. Welcome to the Band Office."

—My brother, Arnie Louie, Osoyoos Indian Band, Okanagan Nation

When I speak of the "Rez culture," I am not speaking of our traditional Native culture. Traditionally, no First Nation peoples had federal Indian reserves or reservations. Therefore, there was no "Rez." No elections, no Indian Act, no Indian Affairs, no band office, no membership cards, no land allotments, no treaties, and no Canadian or American colonial maps drawing arbitrary lines across Indian territory and separating our traditional land into provinces and states.

The Rez culture is what I and every First Nation person raised on a Rez have grown up under. One of my grammas lived to be over one hundred, and she was born well after the reserves and reservations were established in the 1870s. So it's safe to say that no one who belongs to a Rez today has a living experience of what life was like before there was a Rez. The Rez culture is interwoven with over 150 years of colonial cultural genocide, and like most things, it is both good and bad.

Historian Keith Thor Carlson has written that the B.C. reserve creation essentially boils down to "the government's attempt to skirt its political and legal obligations to negotiate with Aboriginal people and to provide compensation for alienated land and resources. In effect it was to extinguish Aboriginal title through administrative and bureaucratic means."

In the 1860s, reserves in the territory that would become the province of British Columbia had barely been established before officials moved to reduce them in size under the pretense that Indians did not need so much land and that white settlers would make better use of that land. Hence today's federal "Specific Land Claims," whereby First Nations receive money settlements for past Rez land rip-offs. Fact is, we don't want settlement money—we want our Rez lands back. All over Canada and the United States, bands and tribes have been fighting court cases not only over the size of the original reserves/reservations (whereby white settlers got more acres per family than Native people) but over the outright theft of land assigned to the original reserves/reservations.

It's ironic (and good karma) that the very government program meant to assimilate Indians in the mid-1800s—the creation of Indian reserves/reservations—actually helped First Nations maintain some of their heritage and culture by being forcibly separated from the dominant society. Having a separate land base managed differently from provincial or state land gave a distinct uniqueness to federal Indian reserves/reservations that continues to this day. Every band/tribe seeks to increase its Rez size. In Canada, there is a federal policy known as "Additions to Reserve" that allows for land to be taken out of municipal or provincial status and given Indian reserve status. The Rez system has actually backfired on them—Indian Magic at its strongest—by creating a stronghold where we can reconcile its past injustices while building on an ancestral spiritual hallowed ground that we now call "the Rez."

In his recent book *First Nations Self-Government*, former Blackfoot Chief Leroy Wolf Collar gives a reality check into the existing Rez culture, noting:

> Many internal issues get in the way of creating healthy political, economic, and social environments within First Nation communities. We have too many unhealthy leaders at both the political and administrative levels. These unhealthy leaders often get in the way of progress due to their lack of leadership competencies, the excess baggage they carry as a result of intergenerational trauma, and the dysfunctionality of the governance system. These people in positions of delegated powers often find themselves in situations that put them in constant conflict of interest. Some spend their entire term of office micromanaging their Band administration's programs and services. Band administrations can be toxic at times because of daily practices of favoritism, nepotism, personal vendettas, bullying, lateral violence, and other types of unethical conduct practiced by elected leaders, managers, and front-line employees.

I have never lived or worked on a Blackfoot Rez, but what happens in their office and businesses is also happening on Osoyoos and every other Rez. I always say, "There is the way it oughta be—then there is the way it is."

A big part of today's Rez culture is the white concept of private land ownership. Historically, Natives did not believe in individual land ownership, only tribal ownership—people ownership. For thousands of years before Indian reserves and reservations were established by government there were no land allotments or Certificates of Possession (CP) that today allow for private land holdings on Indian reserves/reservations. Indian Affairs archives show that the white concept of private ownership of land was part of the Rez assimilation process pushed by federal Indian agents to crush tribalism and get Indians to think "me-me" rather than "we-we." Colonial history proves that's how you assimilate tribal societies: you first break down their core beliefs around land.

At the heart of the Canadian and American dream is private land ownership. Many European migrants were wooed by the Canadian and American government to come to the "New World" on a promise of private land ownership—all on the backs of Indian tribal land. Destroying tribalism, the core concept that all of a tribe's land is owned equally by all the people, was one of the Canadian and American government's major anti-Indian policies.

Traditional Chiefs such as Sitting Bull resisted breaking up Rez land into individual self-serving allotments. Speaking against the Bureau of Indian Affairs policy on the allotment of reservation land among tribal members, Chief Sitting Bull declared, "I wish all to know that I do not propose to sell any part of my country. The whites will try to gain possession of the last piece of ground we possess. Let us stand as one family as we did before the white people led us astray." Chief Joseph of the Nez Perce Tribe in the Pacific Northwest of the United States added to that when he said, "My father claimed that no man owned any part of the earth and a man could not sell what he did not own." Simply put, but strongly stated.

At the San Carlos Apache Reservation in Arizona, the band has posted this statement in a display in their museum: "Attempts to end Apache culture—with the establishment of the San Carlos Indian Agency in 1872. . . . Under the reservation system the Federal Government adopted a policy of assimilation such as private land ownership, cash-based agriculture, and Christianity."

Christianity was the federal governments' "spiritual sword," used to attack the Indian spirit through residential or boarding schools. In the United States, the Dawes Act of 1887 was deployed to push the land allotment policy, while in Canada the Certificate of Possession was used to attack and break up the tribal concept of "we" ownership of Rez land and turn it into "me" ownership.

On almost every Rez, the biggest internal fights and divisions have been caused by this government brainwashing regarding private land ownership. Often, members would fight against each other or with the band council over who should own what land. The arguments have usually been along these lines: "Fences are in the wrong place," or "Back in the fifties or sixties my family was supposed to have been allotted that land that is wrongly recorded as band/community land."

As Natives began to "decolonize" their thinking and governance in the early 1970s, many of those "me" policies were ripped up and a tribalism sense of "we" began coming back among the young people. I am not against private land ownership. Today, no First Nation or tribe continues the land allotment system. That land grab system, encouraged by the Indian agents, created "haves and haves-nots" on the Rez and was neither fair nor sustainable. If land allotments were continued, there would be no band or tribal land left for future generations. As a result, all bands and tribes, including those in the Okanagan Nation, have therefore abandoned this system. The only remaining type of land allotment on Osoyoos is a house allotment, no bigger than an acre. What's left of Rez land (outside of individual housing) is kept for the use and benefit of *all* the membership. This is traditional thinking, exactly what the pre-reserve/reservation ancestors believed in.

One sad reality of the history of Rez culture is alcohol abuse. And today, drug abuse is often even worse than alcohol abuse. Why is there so much alcohol and drug abuse on most reserves/reservations? When the reserves and reservations were established in the late nineteenth century, Native communities did not have a drug and alcohol problem. Alcohol abuse started with the fur traders who pushed whisky on Natives as part of a strategy to get Indians drunk so they could rip them off at the trading posts or forts. On the prairies, the major job of the Royal Canadian Mounted Police (RCMP) was to stop the "whisky trade." The Natives' alcohol problem started with the fur trade, and then expanded to land issues. Just before the Rez system was forced upon us, smallpox and other foreign diseases decimated some First Nations communities by upwards of 80 per cent. Around the 1870s most First Nations were suffering huge population losses and were starving or being attacked by military force. After the reserves and reservations were established, Natives were not allowed to leave the Rez in search of food or to continue their economic livelihoods. Dependence on government rations became the lifestyle. Racist cultural genocide was Canada's and America's solution to the "Indian Problem," and alcohol was a colonial trap. It is still the number one problem on most Indian reserves.

In the book *Firewater: How Alcohol Is Killing My People (and Yours)*, Harold R. Johnson, a Cree from Treaty 6, writes, "We have to ask ourselves: Are we drunks because we are poor, or are we poor because we drink? Do we drink because we don't have a job, or do we not have a job because we drink? Do we drink because our communities are fragmented, or are our communities fragmented because we drink? Do we drink because we come from broken homes, or do we have broken homes because we drink?"

I highly recommend Johnson's book, as he addresses a core problem of the Rez culture. I grew up around alcohol abuse but I am no expert on it. Some of the Rez kids (my cousins) I grew up with became alcoholics, and there was a time most deaths on my Rez were tied to alcohol abuse. Today the 80/20 rule applies to problem drinking on the Rez: 80 per cent of my people don't have a drinking problem, but the 20 per cent who do cause 80 per cent of our problems. The 20 per cent who can't hold a job have serious addiction issues. And now there is the added problem of drug abuse—coke, crack, meth, and heroin. Before the turn of this century, I had never heard of discarded needles on my Rez, but today discarded needles are a new danger for Rez children. When I was young and went to Rez parties I never once saw coke, crack, and meth being used, but now I hear it's as common as drinking. The Osoyoos Rez now has a few drug dealers, and drugs are more of a problem than alcohol—the mental damage seems more severe and the connected violence has gone beyond the odd drunken fistfight. Today there are drug dealers on most Rezes, and the drug dealing has caused intense violence and arguing between families. Many community members are trying to stand up against drug dealers at great personal risk.

I want to salute the treatment centres and those who work to address addictions. Many of my people have thrown the bottle away after going to treatment, and many have quit on their own. On the Rez, we have to be very careful of the "sober drunks"—those who have sobered up and quit their alcohol abuse and who announce it every chance they get. The fact is most were drunken idiots and they're now sober idiots who think they walk on water. To me it takes more than being sober to be a good leader.

The Chief and council of Osoyoos have committed thousands of dollars of our own business revenue toward the ongoing war on drug and alcohol abuse. It is heartbreaking to see the damage. "Lock them up!" is what most of my people want to do to Rez drug dealers—family or not. The court system has become too soft, and today it often seems the criminals have more rights than the victims. Sleazy lawyers who get paid with drug money to represent drug dealers should also be locked up! It makes a mockery of justice when these predators get acquitted on some small technicality taken advantage of by a high-priced, immoral lawyer. Most judges and lawyers never see with their own eyes the carnage in the streets or on the reserves that drug dealing causes. The cops and Rez Indians see it and live with it every day of every week. If Canadians and Americans want justice, then one thing everyone should agree on is that the drug dealers who are getting our people addicted to meth, coke, and heroin should be locked up! Many First Nations have called for banning all drug dealers from their Rez—including their own people. We all need to get tougher on drug dealers and continue the war on drugs.

Traditionally, we had no band or tribal office. Traditionally, Natives had no Indian status cards or tribal cards. Another major difference under the Rez culture as opposed to a First Nations traditional culture is elections. Indian Affairs brought in and forced the election system as another major part of "civilizing" Indian societies. In the early years of the reserve system, the Indian agent and the church held a dominating and controlling social and political status on every Rez. The traditional people resisted as best they could. Many Native ceremonies went underground, and many people refused to vote in the early Chief and council elections. The political and social unrest caused by the Indian agent and the church caused many of the divisions that still exist today on many reserves.

I tell off-Rez mayors and council members, "You guys got it easy when it comes to politics. On the Rez, elections and politics is truly a 'blood sport.'" On the Rez most people know each other and grew up with each other, and that alone can cause some divisions that go very deep. Old divisions often hang around from one generation to the next. So, for those who have grown up or worked on the Rez, the Rez culture has always been a dominating force, like some alien virus for which we can't seem to find a cure. Jealousy, bitterness, and infighting plagues every Rez. "Internal cannibalism" is what the great Cree Chief Billy Diamond called it, and I agree with him.

In the late 1800s, Indian agents created this internal fighting by playing political favourites with those Chiefs and councils who caved to the political demands of Indian Affairs. They punished those they deemed "hostile" by withholding rations and even starving the community. Indian agents and churches (which were after our souls) were largely the creators of Rez corruption, spreading lies and causing suspicion and division among the politically and spiritually weakened tribes. In any concentration camp the oppressors always operate by abuse of power. It was no different in the Rez system. In the past, Indian Affairs bureaucrats made their good government paycheques off the suffering and deaths of thousands of Indian people. The "Honour of the Crown" fiduciary relationship was literally killing my people.

I have spoken on many reserves where more than 50 per cent of the Rez community still exists on welfare. I find this incredible—it's the 2020s, not the 1930s! No one lives the Canadian or American middle-class dream on welfare. No one thrives on welfare; you can only exist. No one brings their kids on holidays on welfare. No one retires on welfare. There is no pride or heritage in a welfare cheque. Where there is welfare there will never be "reconciliation." There is no "nation-to-nation" relationship in Canada when one nation's biggest budget is welfare!

The band or tribal offices did not come about until the late 1960s and early 1970s on most Canadian reserves. That very significant part of Rez history—having our own administrative offices—happened during my lifetime. Unlike most towns and cities that have had a local government office, a municipal office, for up to a hundred years or more, Natives on reserves were until recent times governed totally by white, often corrupt Indian agents who operated out of regional and district Indian Affairs offices.

Native activists and organizations pushed Indian Affairs to transfer to reserves the programs and service dollars that were being controlled in the Indian Affairs district offices. They wanted not only the programs and services but also control over the monies committed to funding. In 1975, my Okanagan people forcibly occupied the Indian Affairs office building in Vernon and shut it down, demanding those program dollars be transferred to the band offices. Chief Adam Eneas of the Penticton Indian Band organized the takeover, and many Okanagans occupied the Vernon offices for over a week. Chiefs joined together to demand that more Indian Affairs program and administration dollars be transferred to the on-Rez band offices. Today in British Columbia there is only one regional Indian Affairs office; it is located in Vancouver, with a staff of three hundred and a yearly budget of over $1 billion.

I want to thank all of those who, in the 1960s and early 1970s, first opened up band and tribal offices. Gratitude, as well, to all those who stood up to the Department of Indian Affairs' colonial control of on-reserve programs. For more than a century Indian Affairs offices across the country had been employing thousands of non-Natives and spending not millions but billions of dollars on supposedly improving the lives of Indigenous people. Thousands upon thousands of Indian Affairs bureaucrats have enjoyed a comfortable lifestyle and retired to a healthy pension while the people they were well paid to serve suffered in Third World conditions under their care. Decade after decade, Native leadership asked for those Indian Affairs dollars to be directed to the reserves because, obviously, having expensive offices and thousands of Indian Affairs staff in the cities had not worked.

Over the years since the 1970s, more program and staff dollars have been transferred to the reserves. This would never have happened had not band and tribal offices been operational on most reserves since the 1960s. Our offices need to have staff who put the client first and who gauge their own work and paycheque by how they are improving the lives of their people. To these staff members, I say: Don't just collect a grant-funded paycheque that improves your life and pays your bills while most of your people suffer under welfare programs and services. Native offices need staff who come with the "spirit to serve" stamped on their heart, who are willing to work evenings and weekends, not just the easy Monday-to-Friday bureaucratic office hours. Earn your paycheque, Rez Indians, by improving the lives of the very people on whose behalf you collect that cheque. Never forget who you work for— it is not the Queen or the federal government.

I still hear that some band offices operate with an approach of essentially "come and go as you please, show up late and carry around a coffee cup and start as many gab sessions as you can to fill in your worthless day." A Chief from back east phoned me once and asked, "How do I get band office staff to show up on time?" I told him, "Hire people with hard-working attitudes and fire the lazy asses." In the real business world, where all staff are responsible for adding or taking away from the profit, everyone has to show up on time. Band and tribal offices have to grow up and put on "business pants." We expect our daycare staff and grade school staff to show up on time. Imagine what parents would say if a teacher showed up even five minutes late for a class?

Today band and tribal offices are the heartbeat of the Rez; they are where the Chief and council work and where the much-needed cradle-to-grave social service programs are delivered. The band office, therefore, must set the standard for performance and community service. This year we added punch-in and punch-out time clocks in our offices. Most of our businesses have had time clocks for years, so now I, like Osoyoos Indian Band Development Corporation employees, have to punch in and out every day. Our attendance shows up on the clock, so there is no BS-ing your time. Being a high-performing worker is not complicated: simply earn your paycheque by showing up on time and producing good work that has measurable results—and not just talking the usual biased rhetoric about how good a worker you are.

One thing I remember doing in our band office when I became Chief was cancelling set coffee breaks. No need for office staff to gather around a table twice a day. Keep the coffee on, bring it to your desk, and keep on working. Also, I can't believe that some tribal offices shut down for two weeks at Christmas just because schools shut down. No business shuts down for two weeks and pays its employees. Too many band offices, unfortunately, have the "grant-funded disease." They deal in *funded* money, not *earned* money like in a business where everyone needs to work hard eight hours a day for the business to succeed. Band offices, just like all government operations, need to become and act more business-minded and treat funded money like real hard-earned money.

The Osoyoos Band office first opened off the reserve in nearby Oliver in the late 1960s, and our first on-Rez band office was built in 1973. Having our own Native government offices is essential in "nation building." Our tribal offices must never become mirror images of corporate or governmental institutions. That would be further assimilation and truly "selling out." As Native people, we must be careful not to colonize ourselves within our own government offices. A brown bureaucracy is no better than a white bureaucracy if it is based on the same suffocating model. Bring some of your heritage and culture into your administration.

I am a supporter of the Native media. I love reading Native newspapers and magazines and watching news on APTN (Aboriginal Peoples Television Network). Real leaders keep up with the real news (not Facebook or internet fake news). I urge all "skins" to not only read the mainstream papers but also buy and read every Native paper you can find. I subscribe to many Native newspapers on both sides of the border. Back in the 1990s I loved to get the newspaper the *First Perspective* because there was a Native writer, Ojibway journalist Gilbert Oskaboose, who wrote like all Natives should write—no pussyfooting around, no phony politics, and especially no "We-all-fly-with-the-eagles-and-beat-with-the-same-heartbeat" bullshit. He wrote about pressing Rez issues, not personal crap that no one cares about. I hate it when Native journalists take up news space and write about what they like or don't like about Christmas or their favourite food or hobbies. Gilbert Oskaboose would say, "Keep your damn mindless platitudes and sandbox beliefs to yourself." And I would add, "Who gives a shit, besides you and your family?"

My message to Native newspapers is this: Allow only real, pressing news in your paper. Don't allow mindless Facebook nonsense. Don't allow teenage/teenybopper content like photos of your plate of food, or a description of what movie you just watched, or a play-by-play of your puppy's first rollover—no one gives a damn! Write like Gilbert Oskaboose, who wrote about what was affecting his Rez and was not scared to say what had to be said. He wrote about contentious terms like "Elders"—I loved his article "White hair does not an Elder make." He wrote about "Rez vandals"—"banish the punks," he said. He wrote about how it's up to Rez people to call out the phonies and the bullies on the Rez and to step up to the plate and be part of the solution instead of part of the problem. He wrote about "Indian time," calling it "a worn out excuse" and noting, "It's 11 a.m. anywhere in Indian Country. The meeting was supposed to start two hours ago. Half the people expected haven't even bothered to show up yet."

I love Gilbert's writing. He wrote what had to be said and always threw in some good ol' Rez humour. The article below describes what is to me one of the biggest problems with the Rez culture. Every Rez has the types of band/tribal members Gilbert lists here.

"A CANOE OF FOOLS,"
by Gilbert Oskaboose

Here's a list of the idiots who can turn your special project meetings into a complete waste of time.

Idiot #1—is the fool who misses the first two or three meetings, drops by for the fourth, and has to be "brought up to speed" by dragging the entire group back over everything they've covered so far.

Idiot #2—is the little man with a little education, a lot of ego, a silly notion that the Band is about to be ripped off and the absolute conviction that he is the only one smart enough to see through the ruse and rescue the community from its own stupidity. This guy is a variation of "the little guy with an attitude over big things." He can't punch his way out of a wet paper bag but he's always in there swinging.

Idiot #3—is the sniper with a hidden agenda. He has a secret axe to grind. He's pissed off about something other than the business at hand, but is ready and willing to use it as an opportunity to vent his inner rage. He doesn't understand the difference between a vigilant "watchdog" who protects and rabid pit-bull that attacks everything in sight.

Idiot #4—is the "Indian orator." This guy fancies himself a "speaker" of extraordinary talent and clarity. He is the "voice of reason" in a roomful of madness. He's in love with the sound of his own voice and foolishly believes everybody else feels the same way. He thinks "information sessions" were created as a forum for his own incredible oral skills and the "hard, incisive questions" he clearly probes for the Truth with.

Idiot #5—is the guy who hasn't got a clue about anything— and is prepared to waste an entire meeting demonstrating it. This loony is living proof that the empty can makes the most noise. His favourite pastime is buttonholing and boring to death invited guests, prattling on endlessly about his "25 years of experience," which in reality is only one year of experience repeated 25 times.

Idiot #6—is the Band member who understands nothing but has something "funny" to say about everything. He specializes in buffoonery, trivializes everything and failing to get "a big laff" with asinine commentary, is no doubt prepared to start farting and tap dancing to amuse the gathering.

Idiot #7—is the fool who hears about a project late—after 2 years a million dollars has been invested—and stupidly wonders aloud why that can't all be scrapped in favour of his own infinitely superior "option" for accomplishing the same thing.

Idiot #8—is the brain-light and arrogant Band member who never reads information packages, never looks at notices or bulletin boards, never even asks leadership about specific projects—but is prepared to "wing it" at great length on any subject or project, regardless of its complexity. That he is unprepared to talk intelligently about anything is obvious to everybody but him.

Idiot #9—is the semi-intelligent "leader" who sees what's going on at Band meetings and allows it to happen anyway. Anarchy serves his purpose and he craftily waits for a lull in the din or the end of the meeting to step in, harrumph importantly for attention, then get in the last word and close down the meeting before anybody realizes what he's done.

Idiot #10—is a collective. He is the Silent Majority, your basic decent, docile, reasonably intelligent, long-suffering and hard-working Band member who puts up with this kind of bullshit month after month, year after year. . . .

The generic "he" is used in the above descriptions, but I'm well aware that some women can be just as disruptive and unproductive in meetings. Heaven help the community if all 10 characteristics are found in the same individual. Personally, I know of a few loonies that come dangerously close to it.

What can you do? Not a damn thing! It's human nature and, short of day-dreaming about some attitude adjustments with a baseball bat, there's little you can do. It's an interesting thought but it wouldn't work. It might seem like a good idea to get rid of all the crack-pots in Indian Country, but the truth is you'd be eliminating many of the people who make life interesting.

Although Gilbert says there isn't anything we can do about these disruptive people, I would add that the hard-working, law-abiding, respectful, and honest majority of band/tribal members have to recognize the "idiots" among us and make sure they don't get elected to council and don't get hired in any leadership position.

Another reason I so like the writing of Gilbert Oskaboose is his sense of humour. As a kid, like most youth on the Rez I didn't realize one of the real blessings of growing up on the Rez is Rez humour, and I value it now all the more!

After all the oppression and poverty and loss of language and culture, it takes a very tough people to develop a sense of humour that in my opinion is second to none. "Rez bomb," "snag," "shack up," "cuzzin deal," "Indian squeeze," "tee-pee creeping" are just some of the humorous Rez words and internal smoke signals that bind First Nations together.

We make fun of things that white people don't get. We tease and laugh at things that off the Rez would be deemed too politically sensitive. Every Rez has its characters, those whose humour fits in every facet of Rez life. The nicknames on the Rez sometimes make me shake my head (Geronimo, Red Ass, Pup), and some nicknames can only be repeated on the Rez.

Even though Rez life is intense, and sometimes bitter, I have seen Rez humour break through a heated discussion at most every Chief and council meeting. I have seen it happen throughout our businesses and even at our most serious gatherings—funerals and ceremonies. White people may not laugh and joke in church, but at every Rez ceremony I have been in, even when it gets deeply serious, sooner or later someone cracks a joke— *"Lend me twenty dollars, aye!"*

Indians know how to joke around. Often, it takes a bit of time for the white staff who work on our Rez to get the jokes. I remember one of our white construction managers always getting teased and razzed. He would tell me that when someone would take a fall on a construction site, the Rez boys wouldn't ask, "Are you okay?" They would first burst out laughing, crack a joke, and then check if the person was hurt.

I remind the "pilgrims" working for us that when the Indians begin to tease you it means they are beginning to like you. If they don't know you well enough, they won't joke around you. Sometimes our "Summa" (white) staff can't tell when we are serious or joking; it takes a while for them to understand Rez humour. But when Indians and whites hang around each other enough, the teasing starts and it should go both ways. I remember being in a hockey locker room "having a few pops," and the Indians were telling the white boys, "We missed work the other day, we phoned in sick." And one of the white boys says back, "You Indians call it sick—we call it a hangover."

No matter where I travel in Indian Country, I am always at home when I hear the Rez humour, whether it be in Navajo, Lakota, Cree, or Mohawk country. That's why one of the best Rezskin comedians, my cuzzin Don Burnstick (a Cree from Alberta) can tell the same jokes in Northern Alberta (Cree country) and in the Deep South (Apache country) and get the same Rez belly laughs.

The Rez jokes and stories are basically the same:

"You know you're a Redskin when you point with your lips."

"You know you're a Redskin when you use your parole officer as a reference."

"You know you're a Redskin when you go to an AA meeting because you ran out of coffee at home."

"You know you're a Redskin if you have blankets for curtains."

"You know you're a Redskin if you have more than five cars and only one of them works."

All tribal territories have a strong, bonding sense of humour that makes me proud. I have been at Native gatherings all over North America, and the Rez humour is a common bond between the tribes. I can buy a Native T-shirt in Arizona (*W.T.F.—where's the frybread*, or *Vegetarian—Indian word for lousy hunter*) and the jokes fit like

Redskin ballcaps on my Rez. I love the T-shirts sold at powwows like: *My Indian name is Dances with Cougars*—and I especially like the *Homeland Security* ones that show Geronimo and a few Apache warriors holding their rifles above a caption that says *Fighting Terrorism since 1492.*

Now, Rez humour is not for everyone, and that's fine—even some highly educated "urban Natives" don't get it. But I know plenty of Rezskins who will always get a belly laugh out of it. When my brother, Arnie, wrote a short story he titled "The G-spot," some of the off-the-Rez office women took offence at the title, but when the Rez women read it they burst out laughing. It was about bingo—you know, "under the G."

Every organization has a culture. Every office and company has an internal culture. Rodeo has its own culture, sports has its own culture, and so does the corporate world. The atmosphere created over time in your home or office is its culture. You can hire all the costly facilitators for strategic planning you want, but don't forget the reality: "Culture eats strategy for breakfast." Every Rez needs to improve its culture, and as Native people, we should know that culture matters. Your band/tribal office culture matters. How you treat and talk to each other is culture. How relationships are built or torn apart in your community is your community's culture. Some have asked me, "How can our community raise good leaders if the atmosphere in our offices and businesses is one of hate, greed, and distrust?" They wonder, "What chance do our kids have if they are raised in a culture of alcohol and drug abuse?"

Every Rez has the good, the bad, and the ugly. Those who live or work on the Rez are ultimately responsible for how much there is of the good—as well as the bad or the ugly. I want to be part of a community that works hard to create the good and stand up to the bad.

I (and many others) will stand up to the drug dealers and the Rez haters and punks. To all the uneducated opinion warriors on Facebook, I say, "Go smudge yourself!"

My mom doesn't like what she sees as modern "Indian laziness." Like many Elders, she grew up working hard and never had an entitlement attitude. Many years ago she gave me this advice: "The band should rent a van and load it up with all the healthy young people who don't want to get a full-time job or go to school—all the lazy asses—and fly them to Iraq and drop them off. All the ones that make it back on their own are the keepers."

We have to get back to what I call a "working culture." Every First Nation comes originally from a working culture—one based on hard work, sharing, caring, and respect. Remember: bad cultures breed bad leaders. Good hard-working Rez culture breeds good leaders.

Another very important part of Rez culture is the art and imagery of community buildings and businesses. I love art—especially Native art. I look for the art and cultural imagery when I am on a Rez or in a corporate office. Ever since grade school, when I loved looking through painting and sculpture books, I have been fascinated by the art of different countries. I am not an artist, but I am pretty good at coming up with imagery and working with artists to customize sculptures or logos and signage.

When our Nk'mip Resort (now Spirit Ridge) was being built, I wanted tourists to know they were on the Osoyoos Rez. Therefore, Okanagan sculptures had to be showpieces. I approached one of my sports buddies, Smoker Marchand, who was also one of the best local Native artists in our territory. Smoker, who is from the Colville Reservation across the border, had started doing metal sculptures.

I asked him to help me put on paper an image of a Chief sculpture that I had in my mind. After a few drafts I said, "That's it!" I told Smoker to go ahead and build it, but to let me see it at different stages, as I might want to add something. Smoker produced the first Chief sculpture, a full-size horse and rider with a headdress holding up a sacred pipe. That sculpture has since been redone many ways for many different bands, tribes, and municipalities.

Come to Osoyoos Rez and you will see our Native pride on full display in the art showcased in our businesses. It is very important to "Indian-ize" your buildings and show your culture wherever you can. A prime example is our golf course. Golfers know when they come to Nk'mip Canyon that it's owned by Natives. Now, when we took over that land lease back in the mid-1990s it already had a logo and a name that had nothing to do with the Osoyoos Indian Band Development Corporation. The white people who leased the land in 1963 gave no thought to Native imagery. When we took it over, I wanted the logo changed to a Native logo right away. I love Native logos in sports, and I had designed a men's hockey logo using our letterhead logo. Some of the white golfers were against the change and told me that if we changed the logo to a Native logo, they would cancel their membership. I have said over and over that being in business is not all about money. Sure, that is one bottom line, but there are other bottom lines too—ones that have to do with promoting and regaining our First Nations pride. The logo got changed and we lost some business. It's true the game of golf has nothing to do with anything Native, but when you come to the Osoyoos Indian Band golf course, you are going to know you are playing on a Native-owned course.

Every tribal area has awesome Native artists. Our renowned, award-winning wines from Nk'mip Cellars (the world's first Native-owned winery) have labels from Osoyoos Indian member and artist

Linda Anderson. Linda's paintings are as good as it gets. Native art can be incorporated into any business. Just get creative and showcase your Native pride every chance you get.

The bottom line is: So goes your community's Rez culture, so goes your community!

CHAPTER 3

REZ LINGO

"Courage is what it takes to stand up and speak. Courage is also what it takes to sit down and listen."

—Sir Winston Churchill

We use words on the Rez that have more meaning there than they do anywhere else.

First Nations have their own unique terms and lingo. I let consultants know that when an important notice gets sent to my membership it has to be written in what I call "Rez language." Indian Affairs documents are never written in Rez language. I remember that on an important land-lease vote a few years ago the one-page ballot had only a few sentences in legal terminology above the boxes where you could check "yes" or "no." I told Indian Affairs, "Get rid of your lawyer language crap—I want it written in simple, understandable Rez English." If the "home Rez boys and girls" who are voting can't understand it, then the document is useless.

Communication is an ongoing challenge on the Rez. Over the years I have heard certain words used a thousand times at Native meetings. And I challenge my own people on how some words are constantly being used and what their true Rez meaning is. It's important for government and corporate Canada to understand Rez lingo.

I'm constantly being asked by non-Natives, "How do we better understand First Nations—how do we better the relationship?" Any real relationship starts with communication and understanding the words each culture uses. When a word is used to denote something or someone special it is only fair and right to ask what is behind that special meaning. One of the greatest interviewers of all time, CNN's Larry King, said the greatest question to ask is "why?"

And so, I have been asking "why" for years, and asking for definitions of a few Rez words, such as "Elders," "warrior," and "grassroots." What do they mean? What purpose do those words have in Rez life? And why? If a word is considered to be important, what exactly does it mean and to what standards or code is it to be held? In hockey, there are codes of conduct—unwritten on-ice codes that let you know that if you cheap-shot anyone, for example, you'd better expect retaliation and unofficial punishment. There are also specific terms and phrases used, like "ya wanna go?" Sometimes words are unnecessary—the code is understood and all that's needed is eye contact and a nod and the gloves are off. Likewise, there are Native codes of conduct in hunting and fishing. It takes a Rez person to know them and instantly understand them.

So what about the important word "Elder"? This is, of course, an English word, and sometimes English words do not translate very well into a Native language. I hear this word all the time now, but I never heard it much in the 1970s or 1980s, and I am confused about who exactly is it supposed to apply to and what it actually means. Any important word must have a definition, a meaning, a purpose.

As I get older, I really want to believe that our people once had a definition for the role of Elder and a specific idea of who could hold that role. The word has it origins with the Mormons, who described an Elder as "a person with higher authority as a result of age and acknowledged status." But that does not fit with the Native concept. The typical English definition is more about age, but I think that's a very low bar. To me, it has to be about more than just reaching some magic age—some say sixty, some say sixty-five, some say seventy. On Osoyoos Rez there are some members over seventy who say, "I'm not an Elder yet," so who knows what this age actually is. And if the meaning of the word is just based on age, are you suddenly one day, on your birthday, an "instant" Elder? A past National Chief told me years ago that anyone who claims to be an Elder just because they've reached a certain age is a "popcorn Elder," meaning that their transformation is sudden. I don't believe anyone is an "instant Elder" in this way.

One of the very few remaining Okanagan language speakers was Archie, our school's language teacher, who was also a Chief in the 1970s. He told me the word "Elder" was not used when he was growing up. Instead, the really old people were called the "Old Ones." (In my Native language there are two words we use to describe an older person. One means basically a person who is old and the other means a person with special knowledge.) Archie went on to say the word "Elder" is now being used for political purposes by some old people to get their way and play cheap politics against the younger people. I do believe some old people can become Elders, but not all of them. I asked Tom Porter, a Mohawk friend I consider an Elder, about the word and he said, "Elders don't have to demand respect and don't blow their own horn. People know, and their knowledge and wisdom is noticed. Sometimes a very young person can be called that Mohawk word for Elder because they have special wisdom."

Similarly, a Navajo said to me, "'Elder' is a foreign word to our people. All people are treated with respect, not just the old. I am soon to be sixty-seven and in no way consider myself an Elder. I am an old woman training toward 'Elderdom.' To me, anyone can be an Elder. The one who is gifted with tenderness, kindness, empathy, love, and understanding of the world around them. Long ago, our babies, children, youth, and young adults were given great care when it came to survival. The Old Ones ate last, because it was imperative the young ate first to save the race or tribe. Nowadays they say the opposite. Elders eat first. . . . In our past, the young ones did not disrespect the old ones. They respected the old because they had lived longer and had valuable lessons to hand off before travelling on to ancestorhood."

Gilbert Oskaboose agrees with this line of thinking and has written articles with titles such as "White Hair Does Not an Elder Make," "Watch Out for Some Elders," and, my favourite, "My Elder Is Smarter Than Your Elder." Some have told me that to be an Elder you have to be respected by everyone. Now that's a very high bar. The sad fact is I don't know anyone who is respected by everyone. Everyone gets called down by someone else—it doesn't matter how old or honourable they are.

One of the Okanagan Nations language teachers told me that the English word "Elder" is misused by First Nations. Traditionally, only a few old people would ever be considered worthy of the Okanagan word *mees-choot*, meaning someone "who has special knowledge inside them that is not common to others." This word is used to describe an expert in hunting, ceremony, medicine, etc. He also said our people are not trained to be Elders anymore. Now most people just grow old and do not become highly knowledgeable in anything. Another Okanagan language speaker said her mom told her, "You don't become an Elder unless you earn it. It's a time when your heart is for everyone, not just you and your family. Plus you have knowledge and are very wise about certain things."

Over the years, other older Native people have made comments to me about the word "Elder" and the concept behind it. Here are some that have stood out:

"Elder" is a white man's word. In Nisga'a it means a bigger person, someone who has lived long enough. Even the word "Chief" should be earned—not just get elected and all of a sudden you are a Chief.

The word "Elder" is used for political purposes today. It was manufactured by unscrupulous former Chiefs and council members who needed a political word to justify their actions. Some people get asked to be an Elder for political purposes. Old people trying to get entitlements—free this or that—or maintain power in meetings.

In the sacred Indian way, not the modern political way, it's harder to see an Elder than a sasquatch.

Old people who lie and call down their own people and get involved politically and are mean with their politics are not Elders. The ones who stay away from meetings and are quiet and always nice and talk when asked upon are Elders.

There are a few genuine Elders. They know the language and teachings and make an effort to help people. And then there are bitter old people.

In Lakota it has a meaning that they have reached a status and some younger people can carry the spirit of an Elder and have the teachings and wisdom.

If a person stands up and calls themselves an Elder, then they are not an Elder. You don't acknowledge yourself as an Elder;

it's how you have lived your life in such an honourable way that people just know.

Some so-called Elders are trying to change our history. Saying things that are not true, and I know because I was there.

If the only criteria for becoming an Elder is age, then you're talking about seniors. The word has turned into something meaning to qualify for certain services and programs—like free this or that. Elders are supposed to be Knowledge Keepers.

In our First Nations today there is the idea that somehow as soon as you turn sixty you somehow have authority on everything.

An Elder in Dene culture must have respected knowledge in certain areas. Just because you are a certain age does not make you an Elder. Must have knowledge that is shared. People today have butchered the word "Elder."

If you were a fool when you were young, you will be a fool when you are old.

And, of course, when I asked one of the old-timers in Osoyoos about the word "Elder," she replied with good ol' Rez humour: "I'm only an Elder when it comes time to eat—or when there are seniors' discounts at hotels or casinos."

I have yet to hear a definition that truly captures the essence of an Elder and their important role in the community. Russell Means, the Lakota AIM activist from South Dakota, gave one of the best definitions

I heard, and a very high bar to achieve. He said, "An Elder to me has to have a very high threshold in the traditional way—it's someone who speaks their language—does not understand English—and has never been baptized."

Wow! I would love to meet one of those "real" Elders. Russell's definition made me think about how rare it is to know someone who speaks only their nation's language and practises their Indian ceremonies. To me that is something very special. I keep a Yoda figure in my office. When asked why, I say I'm still searching for a real Elder— trying to find a "real Yoda," a real Elder I can go to who is truly a master, a teacher, and a trainer of the real "Red Road."

Many years ago, a Mohawk called me an Elder. It made me feel uncomfortable. I asked, "Why would you call me an Elder?" and he replied, "You have business knowledge—you are a *business* Elder." I laughed and thought, *I do have more battle scars than most. I may have put the puck in the net a few times—but I'm no Yoda!*

Chief Sophie Pierre of the Ktunaxa First Nation in B.C. once told me, "Elders were Knowledge Holders, traditionally, it's not a matter of age. Today we have members who have master's degrees or Ph.D.s. They, too, are Knowledge Holders. Knowledge is useless if it's hidden and not shared. You become useless if you don't share it. Just sitting back and saying others are doing it wrong—then *you're* doing it wrong."

Within Rez culture, the word "Elder" does not have the particular, elevated meaning it once had. It used to apply to a very few, and now it can apparently apply to anyone of a certain age. One of my wishes is for the word "Elder" to stand for something more, for a high standard. And as with all things of a high standard, if that standard is not maintained, the title should be taken away. I am still seeking a definition that truly encompasses depth of knowledge and character, a very high standard that only a few achieve. Every Rez suffers from social and political dysfunction and needs traditional, not political or "instant" Elders.

"Warrior" is another English word that, when attached to Indians, is misused and has lost its meaning. Today, among young Natives, the word often gets thrown around when they are stoned or drunk, or when they're using their "beer muscles" on Facebook. It symbolizes aggression and toughness, a need to fight and bully and scare people— even your own people. That's not what Crazy Horse, the greatest Native warrior of all time, stood for. A few years ago I asked one of Crazy Horse's descendants about the word "warrior." Remember, the Lakota recorded some of the greatest defeats of the U.S. army while defending their lands in the 1870s. No other tribe is more associated with the word "warrior" than Crazy Horse's Oglala people. What the descendent told me was that the Lakota don't have a word that translates into "warrior"—the closest word means "defender." The warrior's purpose is to defend the land, to defend the women and children, to defend the nation's heritage and culture. To *defend*—not to go out and make war. A Lakota language teacher told me they have many related words, but the meaning of these words is closer to "police officer," someone who polices the camp.

Native traditional societies all have different interpretations of the warrior concept. But they all believed warriors had to train and do ceremony and follow a code, to provide for and protect their family and not just go out to make war. A Mohawk speaker told me, "Today our people are colonized to think like Americans and Canadians and use words that way. In Mohawk there is a word which means 'those men who carry the bones of our ancestors to protect our ceremonies and ways.' It doesn't mean to go out and fight. Fighting is not the emphasis, but they will fight if pushed to defend."

Another Mohawk speaker told me it was "hard to translate 'warrior' into our language" and said, "A better translation would be 'protector'—to protect." A Grand Chief in British Columbia told me, "In truth, warriors are peacekeepers. And yes, they are capable of protecting the community and territory. Warriors are also clean and sober and highly dedicated and trained." Today, many Native people serve in the Canadian and American military and maintain a high degree of respect and honour as modern "warriors." As was true for Native traditional warriors, today's military training is strict; there is a code of conduct to follow or you will be kicked out.

Another Elder in Saskatchewan told me, "A warrior is a mental, spiritual place as opposed to a physical place. A warrior brings people to a proper state of mind. Rarely will you see a warrior be aggressive. The spirituality of a warrior is not being taught." Look at the martial arts masters—they're the toughest of the tough, yet often the most peaceful and thoughtful people. As Bruce Lee said, in *Enter the Dragon*, fighting like a warrior is "the art of fighting without fighting."

Sadly, today the word "warrior" gets associated with being a thug or a lazy degenerate. A true warrior is not someone who goes around threatening or hurting people. A warrior is not someone who picks up a welfare cheque when they have "two hands, two feet and a heart-beat." A warrior is not someone who does not pay child support or who abandons their own kids. A warrior does not sell drugs or get drunk or stoned and then yap off on social media. An Alberta Chief told me, "a group of middle-aged men on my Rez called themselves 'warriors' and wanted bigger houses and they don't even work—and one of those so-called warriors called down my wife and I went looking for him and he hid. Some 'warrior.'"

I once asked a woman what her adult grandson was doing. She said, "Being a couch warrior." When I asked what that meant, she replied, "He's lying around on the couch all day waiting for the next roadblock, then he'll jump up and put his camo pants on." I told her if he wants to be a warrior he should get his lazy butt in a job and feed himself and help pay the electric bill that keeps the TV on all day rather than depending on his gramma to pay the bills. A real warrior gets up early and works every day and keeps the Rez clean—especially their gramma's house and yard.

A Navajo wrote this about the warrior concept, in the *Navajo Times*: "The word in Navajo translates to a kind and great heart that gets things done. A warrior is the everyday human who is struggling through life, a person who battles everyday addictions and afflictions, the caretaker of the children. The mother and father who work hard to give their children a good life and education."

The warrior spirit still exists in Indian Country. The continuing Native demonstrations prove that—the water protectors at Standing Rock, the women who started the Idle No More movement. I want to recognize and not forget one of the best examples of being a warrior: the Oka Crisis of 1990, when Mohawks reminded Canada that Native people will protect the graves of their ancestors and that unsettled land rip-offs will not be swept under the House of Commons rug. In that summer of 1990, First Nations demonstrations reached a new height in support of the warriors at The Pines in Oka, Quebec. Many of my people, including the Penticton Indian Band, set up an information roadblock on their own Rez for many months. Two members of the Osoyoos Indian Band (Arnie Louie and Ron Hall) organized an "eagle feather run" from the Okanagan to Oka to bring awareness and support to the Mohawk defenders at Oka.

There are many ways of being a warrior. The Okanagan to Oka Run for Peace was a warriors' run, and the Penticton information roadblock was also a warrior way of showing support. In my office

I display a book, *This Land Is Our Land—The Mohawk Revolt at Oka*, and a T-shirt, brought back from Oka by my brother Arnie, showing the Mohawk warrior flag and an image of a Mohawk warrior stand- ing face-to-face with a Canadian soldier. I will never forget how the Okanagan First Nation rallied behind the Mohawks at Oka. Even today First Nations are continuing to gain ground back (physically and spiritually) because of what a handful of Mohawks did back in 1990. A big shout-out (Rez *war-whoop*) and spiritual thanks to all the people who defended Mohawk territory at The Pines and upheld the true warrior spirit!

But perhaps the best definition of the word "warrior" I have heard comes from novelist N.K. Jemisin: "There is no greater warrior than a mother protecting her child."

I am also searching for the real meaning of the word "grassroots." I hear it often during times of internal Rez conflict or when someone wants to make a political statement, usually against the existing Chief and council" "The grassroots people want this or that," or "The grass- roots people think this way or that way."

Tell me, please, *who* is "grassroots"? A very experienced Grand Chief advised me recently, "'Grassroots' has turned into another political term people use when they are in the minority position and attempt to manipulate the majority. Often used by a few people to claim to represent the traditional people. And if you're elected or have a job at the band office you're the status quo and not grassroots." And a Mohawk leader told me, "Everyone should be grassroots. We all come from grassroots. It means a regular community member. Remember, the men and women leaders are chosen by the grassroots people because they are the biggest examples of grassroots. Leaders embrace what real people are. In Mohawk, clan mothers put up a leader, and in their language the word for leader means 'of the good, of the nice' and 'living an honest and compassionate life.' If the word 'grassroots' is used in other ways, it's used for political purposes."

I have reminded people that we on the Rez are *all* grassroots. Just because a few get elected or work in the administration, are they suddenly not grassroots? How is that possible? I call BS on those who claim to be more grassroots than others. Who made you judge and jury of who is grassroots and who isn't?

There are many other words that are exclusive to the Rez or used differently there. "Sellout" and "apple" (meaning red on the outside, white on the inside) are derogatory words on the Rez. You'd better have your facts and evidence and be ready to "Indian up!" and drop the gloves if you're going to use those words against someone. I was shocked a few years ago when one of the candidates running for National Chief called one of the other candidates a sellout. Maybe in the city (among urban Indians) it's okay to throw those insults around, but not on the Rez. That candidate for national Chief immediately lost not only my vote but also my respect. You can disagree with someone, you can politically oppose them, but you just don't dig so low in the mud as to call another Indian candidate a sellout!

"Sellout" is one of those words that, once said, you can't take back. These days it seems our Rez politics is becoming like white politics, where name-calling, especially on social media, is acceptable. Any time opposing views are being expressed, immature minds resort to name-calling. Just because some Chiefs and councils negotiated a pipeline deal (or any deal), that does not make them a sellout. I may disagree with the deal, but I would never call anyone that name. Rez boys angry at supposed sellouts tell me all the time, "Some of our people just need an old-fashioned ass-kicking." But when I was growing up there was a saying: "You want to talk shit, you get hit!" There was no hiding behind the cops, lawyers, or social media.

"Community" is another one of those touchy-feely words that most Natives throw around when they want to get political points— "The community feels this way"; "The community told me this or that"; "I know how the community feels." What a bunch of BS! First question I have is, "Who is 'the community'?" To me, the community is all the band or tribal members, and no one on council talks to *all* the band members (many of them are babies and kids). Okay—so those who use the word "community" must mean all those over eighteen years of age (voting age), and the fact is no one on council talks to all the community's people over eighteen. That is impossible, as members are scattered all over Canada and the United States. The obvious fact is they are only talking about their backers, or a few community members. Sometimes I tell those who say the "community" feels this or that way, "Give me five minutes, and I will find community members who oppose what you are saying."

And here's one last Rez word/phrase I think is important (though there are many others): "Indian time." I have been all over North America, and it's both sad and kinda funny that on every Rez there is still the idea of Indian time. I was asked to speak on a Rez in Saskatchewan recently. The scheduled start time was 9 or 10 a.m. and I was the first speaker, so I was arranging my flights and a ride back to the airport shortly after that. I talked to the Chief and he told me to book a later flight. When I asked why, he said, "You won't go on till near noon." I responded that the notice said the gathering started hours before noon and I was the first speaker. He said, "Well, you know how Indians are."

As soon as he said that, I knew that the issue was Indian time. Sure, Osoyoos still suffers from Indian time now and then, but I am proud to say again that 80 per cent of my people do show up on time; most are never late and most respect others' time. As usual, it's the 20 per cent that cause 80 per cent of the problem. Many of the old-timers, from Navajo country in the south to the Dene territory in the Arctic, have told me that living by "*real* Indian time" means getting there early. I had a sign made up that said *Showing up on time means you care.* You can't run a business or a school on Indian time, and neither should any band or tribal programs and services be run on Indian time! I know most white people, including my "pilgrim" buddy Roy MacGregor, got a kick out of that term when he first heard me speak. This sign I found explains Indian time perfectly:

BUSINESS HOURS

Open most days about 9 or 10. Occasionally as early as 7, and sometimes as late as 12 or 1. We close about 5:30 or 6. Occasionally about 4 or 5, and sometimes as late as midnight or later. On some days we are not here at all, but lately we've been here a lot, unless we're not here.

Words matter. How you say them, when you say them, and who can say them matters. Not long ago, Bill Maher got slammed on social media for using the N-word on his TV show, *Real Time with Bill Maher.* Maher apologized, but Ice Cube, a famous Black rapper and actor, went on the show and told Maher that that word is not for a white person to use anymore. I love Maher's show, and that he has the courage to call out political correctness, but in this case I had to agree with Ice Cube. Rez Indians understand what he was saying about the N-word—it's kinda like the word "savage." Some Rez boys actually have the word "savage" tattooed on themselves. And I love the phrase "Born-again Savage." Yeah! Words have a different meaning on the Rez or in certain communities than in middle-class Canada or America.

A few years ago two Elders on my Rez who are sisters stopped talking to each other for years. One of them later told me what happened: "She said five words to me and I said two words back to her and then we stopped talking." Yes, sometimes it only takes a few words to ruin a relationship for a very long time.

We have to learn how to communicate with each other both on and off the Rez. In this messed-up historical relationship First Nations have with Canada and the United States, we must remember, and put into action, some of the most beautiful words translated into English at the time of treaty. These words truly symbolize the unfulfilled promise and dream of our ancestors on "Turtle Island."

"For as long as the sun shines and the water flows . . . "

CHAPTER 4

NO MORE BROKEN WINDOWS

"The ultimate tragedy is not the oppression and cruelty by the
bad people but the silence over that by the good people."

—Dr. Martin Luther King Jr.

I love being on a Rez—any Rez. I have set foot on more than three hundred of them in Canada and the United States. Like most Rezskins, I seek out Indian reserves and reservations, rich or poor, on my travels. It's not a "money" feeling I'm looking for—who's got what—it's an ancestral feeling, a heritage and cultural feeling that I seem to need. Seeing Rez people young and old living and playing on their own Rez is very special to me.

But one thing that catches my eye right away, and makes my heart heavy, is broken windows on Native houses. It is really sad to see some houses with multiple broken or boarded-up windows. On one reserve in northern Alberta I saw so many houses with boarded-up windows that I mistakenly thought the houses were vacant and abandoned. I thought, *Why doesn't the leadership get rid of those eyesores and tear down those condemned houses?* The school teacher who was driving me around the Rez that day told me, "Those houses aren't empty—families live there. The way you tell if a house is empty is if the front door is boarded up."

I couldn't believe how many houses I saw that day that seemed empty but were still being lived in. How can anyone live in a house where they can't even look out the living-room or bedroom window? I took pictures of houses with every window boarded up and with graffiti—often with swear words—painted on the walls and the plywood window coverings. Families were still living in those houses! It felt like I was driving through the worst part of a rundown major city. Not all of the Rez was in bad condition, but I felt so sorry for the children who were being raised in homes like that. It is not right, anywhere in the world, for children to grow up in a house with broken or boarded-up windows. Kids and Elders should not have to walk past swear words scribbled on buildings.

To me, broken windows are unacceptable.

The big question is, Where is the leadership on that Rez? Not just where are the Chief and council members, but where are all the leaders—the department heads, social services people, those who hold the senior jobs and those who call themselves Elders? Real leaders (not politicians) stand up to obvious problems. Yet only a few blocks away from this disaster zone was a modern, fancy administration office. It was a contrast I have never forgotten. It still pisses me off.

The reason I was there was to give a keynote speech on the accomplishments of the Osoyoos Indian Band. When I travel for reasons like this, and if time permits, I always ask someone to drive me around to see two things: first, their band or tribal headquarters and other community buildings; and second, their housing and the playgrounds where children play. I have been on the poorest of the poor reserves, as well as on those that have huge economic development and are making hundreds of millions of dollars, so I want to make it clear that I'm not looking for fanciness and luxury. I wasn't raised in fanciness or luxury. What I'm looking for is Native pride of ownership. Do the people there look after what they have? Do they respect and keep clean what they have?

Most Rez Natives were raised without much material wealth. Their homes were the classic Indian Affairs matchbox two-bedroom, very modest homes. Most people, especially the old-timers, really looked after what little they had. My mom still lives in a little two-bedroom Rez house that was built back in the 1960s. I have also noticed that the best-looking yards are usually those of the old-timers. The old people suffered at the hands of the federal and provincial and state governments and had to work very hard to survive. They had to respect the home that gave them shelter and allowed them to raise their families. As Chief, I rarely get requests from the old people to fix a broken door or window.

Your yard says a lot about you. The condition of the yard is the first thing people learn about those who live inside that house. If I see a yard with garbage all over it or littered with wrecked and abandoned vehicles, I take that as a public statement by those who live there. That's why, when I'm on a Rez, I want to drive by the community buildings and houses to get a sense of community—or the lack of one. When I return home, I often get asked by my people, usually the Elders, "How are our people back East?" or "How are those Indians up north or down south?" or "How do their houses and band office look?"

You see, true Rez Indians care about the condition of other Rez Indians. The old ones might not be able to travel, but they still wonder and truly care about their relatives all over Indian Country. That's the real Rez way! The inter-tribal connection is still there. I love that deep feeling our old people have about other tribal communities. The old people know those other Native communities suffered through the same racist "Indian Problem" policies of the federal government. They know that, sadly, they're still thought of as the "Indian Problem" by most Canadians and Americans.

While I was taking pictures of those boarded-up windows and graffiti-splashed houses up north, I noticed a little kid playing in the yard of one of the worst buildings. I shook my head and vowed I would never let that deplorable, sad, heartbreaking image appear on my Rez. *Never!*

A few hours later, I was in a community hall filled with local band members—some of them likely living in those boarded-up houses. I shared my experience as a Chief and proudly spoke of the Osoyoos Indian Band's economic and social accomplishments. But I also let people know Osoyoos is not a perfect community. My Rez has dysfunctions. My Rez has some dirty yards and poorly kept homes. Some of our community buildings could use a little tender loving care. It is a mistake to think that the Osoyoos Rez, which has been called a "Miracle in the Desert," is somehow without problems. We have our share, and we, too, need a kick in the rear every once in a while to remind us to roll up our sleeves, clean up our backyard, and have "Native Pride" in what we have built.

As I finished off my talk, I wondered if I should mention how upset and disappointed I was in what I had seen in that short drive through the community. I know a politician will not tell the truth if the truth will lose him votes or put him in a bad light. But a leader says what has to be said when it has to be said, and will always stand behind their statements. I thought about bringing up the broken windows to a few council members in private afterwards, as that would have been easier and much safer.

I often ask myself, "What would Sitting Bull, Crazy Horse, or Chief Joseph do? What would Nelson Mandela do?" There is a Nelson Mandela quotation that I very much like: "History will judge us by the difference we make in the everyday lives of children."

I finished talking about the Osoyoos Indian Band and thanked the organizer for bringing me out to speak to their Rez. Then I told them that as Native people we have to look out for one another and share our stories—the good, but also the bad. And in the Indian way of teaching, some of the best lessons come from bad stories. Our Coyote (*Senklip*) stories use examples of bad situations to teach people what *not* to do. I was also taught by a Mohawk leader that "scolding" is part of our culture and that sometimes the old people must scold the younger people to get them back on track. Such scolding is a natural way of teaching. Remember, those who scold you are the ones who truly care. No one likes to scold, but sometimes it is called for, and one must be emotionally strong to do it and be willing to take it if those being scolded don't like what you're saying. It's easier not to say anything and just let the bad behaviour carry on. Easier, but not right.

Since I do care, I found I could not walk out of that hall without bringing up the very bad example—a lack of Indian pride and leadership—that I had found there. I didn't hold back. I told them how ashamed I felt to see the physical damage to property and sense the emotional damage to those who lived on the Rez. I told them no child should be growing up in a house with broken windows. A window is the view to the outside world. It is very important for kids to look out of their living room window every day and observe what is outside—to see the sky, to see the rain or snow—so that even when they are indoors they will still have that visual connection with nature.

I told them that we are all parents, grandparents, aunts and uncles. When you leave your house and your kids or grandkids are there, remember to glance backward and look at who is looking out of those windows. You want to see those little faces watching you leave, sometimes waving their little hands. And when you drive back into your yard, who is looking out of the window, waving, smiling, jumping up and down, so happy to see you back? As a grandparent myself, I always look back at my living room window to see if my little granddaughter is there watching me leave. That image always tugs at my heart. And when I pull back into my yard at the end of a work day,

I always look up at the living room window. To me, one of the best sights in the world is seeing my "little boss" jumping up and down, waving and smiling to welcome me home!

Now, I told them, imagine if my windows were boarded up. The child–parent/grandparent experience of seeing each other through a living room window would be lost. Most Canadians and Americans would never let a broken window take that experience away. I'll say it again and again: No one, especially a child or an Elder, should ever have to live in a house with boarded-up windows.

"*Indian up!*" I told them sternly.

I spoke angrily about the conditions of some of the homes I'd seen. I told the members to show some leadership and spray-paint over the swear words and graffiti. I had spoken in front of a Rez crowd hundreds of times, but this was the first time I'd felt the need to scold. I finished what I had to say and stood with the microphone in my hand. The room was deadly quiet.

Then an elderly man started to walk up to the stage. I thought he was going to tell me to mind my own business, that I wasn't from that Rez and had no right to pass judgment on the conditions there. The elderly man asked for the mic, and then spoke to both me and the silent room. I cannot recall the exact words he used, but it was very much along the lines of: "I am so ashamed that a Chief from another community had to come here and see the damage here. It is our responsibility to clean up our mess. It's about time we take a stand against the Rez punks who are giving us a bad name and hurting the childhood of our kids."

Someone else spoke up and said, "If we spray-paint over the swear words, the drug dealers will just put them back."

No one said anything, so I took back the mic and said, "Yes, the punks and the haters will probably spray-paint the houses back, but the leadership on this reserve should not give up. The big question is who is going to give up first—the good people or the punks?"

It was awesome to stand there and see other law-abiding members who cared about their reserve stand up and say, "I'll buy a can of paint."

I repeated, "No more broken windows. Get those windows fixed. And find out who is breaking them and give them a good, old-fashioned Rez-kicking."

I am very proud to say, though, that the vast majority of Rez communities I have been on still have the old Native pride of ownership. Streets and yards are clean. I have been invited to speak in James Bay Cree communities many times, and I see Native pride of ownership there. No broken windows; clean yards and nice homes. I have asked where the Rez bombs are but can find no wrecks still being driven with broken windshields and missing mufflers. Many remote reserves in northern British Columbia have very nice subdivisions. Yes, there may still be a few starving Rez dogs wandering about, but overall I give most Rez communities a thumbs-up!

The problem of broken windows goes far beyond the visual sight or, for that matter, the cost of a new window. A broken window is a reflection of the lifestyle of the family inside that house. A boarded-up window is also an indication of the broken spirit of that Rez. Some things on the Rez don't take much time or effort to fix, and sometimes the bruises reappear and have to be tended to again and again.

The bottom line is that every home on the Rez must be a safe, loving home, not just a house. Every Rez kid should be able to look out of every window in their house and see the beauty of their community.

A simple Rez rule: Keep your yard and community buildings clean! The youth are watching. So are Indians (your cuzzins) from other communities.

CHAPTER 5

PER CAPITA

"Got any per capita?"

—first question when Rezskins date

I debated writing about the "elephant in the room" on so many First Nations, or perhaps I should say the "pit bull in the room." I considered not even mentioning this very divisive and emotional topic, but it is too important to ignore—especially for the youth and future generations.

Today, many Rez people (especially on social media) talk about the youth, and about how important the future generations are. But they do this in words only. They don't do the heavy lifting of figuring out how to set money aside and create real job opportunities for those future generations. Remember: talk is cheap but positive action costs money! What most successful leaders and parents know is that it is only common sense to set aside a financial savings account for their children, all the way up to the seventh generation. This "Seventh Generation Savings Account," as I call it, must involve a portion of all band/tribal income—but most especially the monies that come from one-time land claims.

"Per capita" refers to money that goes directly into your pocket without a job being involved. It is a huge issue in Indian Country, with loud voices on both sides of the (free) coin. I have personally been involved in many arguments over the issue of how much money the

Osoyoos Indian Band should give out in per capita payments to band members. Most band/tribal community meetings are not well attended, but if you want to fill up the meeting hall just put per capita (money) on the agenda.

Money is always a main issue at election time for those bands and tribes that have developed their own source revenue. It is the same when a land claim is settled, or when a deal on a natural resource project (oil, natural gas, mining) is reached. How much of that money is going to be distributed to each member of that band or tribe in a one-time or annual per capita payment?

Now that many First Nations are creating their own source revenue to pay for their cradle-to-grave society, some communities are also paying out to members what in the business world would be called a dividend. Some reserves/reservations pay out a few hundred dollars each year, and some many thousands of dollars, to each of their members.

Obviously, this then brings up the issue of membership for those bands and tribes with money. For some phony Rez types, membership becomes *all* about the money, the per capita. How much money will each member receive yearly or as a one-time cash payment? It's sad that some now attach more value to their Rez's wealth than to their heritage and culture. What happened to being about the people, the culture, and the land? Bloodlines and ancestry should always matter more than money.

Bill C-31 was a 1985 federal bill to amend the Indian Act and bring it in line with gender equality under the Canadian Charter of Rights and Freedoms. Native women who had previously lost their status by marrying non-Indians regained their status, and their children were given status as well. However, non-Native women were no longer able to gain Indian status by marrying a registered Native man. To me, those sections of the Indian Act were ridiculous! Native women should never have lost their status by marrying white men, and white women should never have gained Indian status by marrying Indian men. I have heard many incidents of white women marrying Native men to gain "Indian rights"—especially in those communities that gave out large per capitas or came into a huge land claim settlement. Many of those white women eventually separated or divorced yet remain status Indians in Canada. Not one ounce of Native blood, but a card-carrying "plastic Indian." Ridiculous—and wrong!

When Native women were getting their status back, I got calls from women wanting to become a member of the Osoyoos Indian Band. I would tell them that if they had no bloodlines and ancestry here, the government would not assign their membership to Osoyoos. People eligible for Indian status would be placed in their ancestral lineage Rez—where they belong. Many would tell me that they had heard about Osoyoos and would rather belong to the Osoyoos Indian Band because their ancestral Rez was poor.

Even today, I get calls from Natives wanting to transfer to Osoyoos, and I am sure other First Nations with money and businesses get such calls as well. Those people want to transfer for the jobs and location. I tell them, "You don't get to decide what Rez you want to belong to. That community has to accept you as a member." Transfers are possible but difficult. We have a detailed voting policy for membership transfers. Transfer votes should not be decided by Chief and council. Nor should the vote be held at a band meeting. Accepting someone as a full-fledged member is a huge, lifelong, seven-generations decision. Therefore, membership decisions should be conducted by a fully transparent referendum in which every band member votes by private ballot.

I am not against per capita payments. In the early 1990s I was part of the council that started the yearly, ongoing Christmas per capita at

Osoyoos, based on an affordable formula. What I am against is huge per capita payments of one-time settlements. Any yearly per capita out of a community's self-generated income must be based on a solid financial rationale that can be sustained by the business and lease income. It should be no different than your personal spending, which must be based on what you can afford. It's fine to give out a dividend to all the shareholders of a company—in this case, band members—but that should be done only after the company has shown a net profit. Remember, no business can afford to give out the majority of its profit in a yearly dividend or per capita.

There are many opinions on per capita. In his book *First Nations Self-Government*, Chief Leroy Wolf Collar writes that:

> Per capita distributions take away independence and self-determination. First Nations need to invest their money on job creation, housing, education, and trust accountants for the future of their children and youth. . . . I have asked many of the unemployed people in my community who rely on the welfare system what they think about per capita distributions. . . . They say as long as Chief and Council are not creating employment and training opportunities for them, then they want an equal share of the community's settlement payouts. . . . They believe the Chief and Council and the employees of the Band are the only ones who benefit from their community wealth, while the rest of them live in poverty.

I agree a community's wealth has to be used to touch every member, either as a wage or through programs and services. As a Mohawk Chief once said, "Everything on the Rez is a priority." At Osoyoos we now have more jobs than we do band members, so people should work if

they can. I do not want the per capita system to perpetuate unemployment, poverty, and dependency. I don't want per capita to be another
form of a welfare cheque that discourages people from getting a job.

Per capita is a double-edged sword, in my opinion. There are positives and negatives to a community's leadership dipping into that
community's bank account and handing out hundreds or thousands
of dollars in a personal cheque. I am not against per capita as long as
the future generations are factored into the equation. We really do
need to think and act seven generations ahead, as our "real Elders"
have always advised. We also need to respect past generations and
their hopes and desires for their community. We need to think of our
ancestors who suffered through the lean years and who passed away
before any land claim settlement or multimillion-dollar pipeline deal.
Any money settlement received also belongs to them, does it not? Any
money made also belongs to those members who are buried. Those
members are usually the ones who started the community's businesses and land claims. The land is still their land, as they have now
gone back to the land.

Too much of Rez politics is shifting to a non-Native style of politics.
It's always "What can you do for me now?" A community's bank
account is not something to be divvied up so that everyone can go on
their happy way. But too many so-called grassroots people think only
of themselves or the current generation, giving no thought to the
ancestors or the future generations. Many members want bigger per
capitas at all costs. They want the one-time land claim settlement to
be spent only on those who are alive today, with no consideration at
all for the unborn. You have to think ahead!

A tribal member in the United States told me that, at election time,
the issue of per capita can be a huge source of conflict between on-Rez
and off-Rez members. Many First Nations communities have half or

more of their membership living off the Rez due to a lack of on-Rez jobs and housing. Come election time, some candidates will promise more and bigger per capitas. In essence, they are buying votes. In some cases, much of the per capita payment comes from timber operations on the Rez. The tribal members who have to live with the negative effects of the logging are those who live on the Rez. A member living on that particular Rez told me, "Those tribal members living in the cities don't seem to care if all the trees on the Rez get cut down. They only care about getting their per capita cheque in the mail."

You can't spend the same dollar twice. What is taken out of the community's bank account to be spent on per capita cannot be spent on that community's immediate or future needs. All programs and services cost money. And unless what is spent on per capita is somehow replaced with other income, sooner or later the Rez will suffer. A Chief in the United States told me, "When people come to me for more per capita I say look at that dental clinic . . . look at that educational scholarship program . . . look at all the youth and Elders programs and services . . . look at the new housing—that's your per capita."

When I talk to other First Nations that I know bring in a lot more money than Osoyoos, I always ask, "How much does your Rez give out in per capita payments?" When they tell me "We don't do per capita payments" I am so proud of them. I then ask, "How do you stand up to those members who keep on demanding it?" And they tell me, "Our people would rather have more programs and services, more youth and Elders programs, more housing, better roads and community buildings and higher wages—all of those things cost money." So true! Per capita payments cost millions of dollars that could be spent on other community needs now and in the future.

In Canada and the United States there are too many reserves and reservations that the local police know all too well. Big per capita payments have caused the drug dealers and gangs to move in. I have seen more than one First Nation receive a lot of money through what I call "rocking chair money"—money they never had to work for. These people never had to invest in a company or start up a company. The money came from natural resources—in this case oil and gas—and just fell into their lap. The members on this particular Rez demanded huge per capita cheques, sometimes $10,000 to $20,000 per member. And not just once a year, but sometimes multiple times a year.

In many cases, Rez members under the age of eighteen or nineteen have their per capita cheques put into a minor's trust account until they come of age and get control of the account. Some Rez youth in richer communities therefore receive hundreds of thousands of dollars when they turn eighteen or nineteen. Don't forget, an eighteen- or nineteen-year-old is still a teenager, and getting a six-figure cheque at that age is, of course, not a normal thing—anywhere in the world. No wonder there are drug dealers and gangs hanging around those communities. One community member told me, "The Rez literally had drug dealers waiting at the gates of the Rez. They knew who was turning nineteen and they were actually lending the youth money and letting them 'charge up' drugs they could pay for once they got their big per capita." This situation leads to many young people becoming addicted to drugs.

Something else many youth do when they get their per capita trust funds, as young people everywhere dream of doing, is buy a new vehicle. Car dealerships opened up around a particular Rez that was handing teenagers huge amounts of per capita money. As a result, many youth lost their lives in car accidents. You don't need research to know that if you give people who've never had money before a lot of money that they didn't need to work for, many are not going to spend it wisely.

Another First Nation in northern British Columbia got a huge multimillion-dollar settlement and gave out a few $50,000 per capitas. One of the members told me, "Before the land claim, people used to work together and talk to each other. The money caused more problems. The only ones that got rich were the lawyers and consultants. Within a few years, we went from riches to poverty. The Chief and council didn't buy any businesses and the community didn't invest the money. Some youth when they turned eighteen were getting cheques worth more than $200,000. Come to my Rez and have a look for yourself. This does not look like a place where we had lots of money—we now live in poverty."

A former Alberta Chief told me that per capita has set their band back generations in terms of much-needed housing and business opportunities. Money that was set aside for investment became an election issue, and the candidate that promised a large per capita increase got elected Chief and doled out the First Nation's savings. The community still has Great Depression unemployment rates and no housing being built. There is something terribly wrong with that picture—and a lesson to be learned.

A decade ago or so, a First Nation in western Canada received a land claim settlement of $70 million. Like many communities, they then set up a trust fund with a board of trustees to manage the money. Membership demanded that big per capitas and cheques ranging from $20,000 to $50,000 be given out over a period of a few years. A lot of negative stuff happened to many youth, and after a few years one of the community's young people volunteered to do a poll among the local youth. They were asked, simply, "What did you do with your money?" There were basically three things the youth on that Rez did with their trust money when they turned nineteen. The first was "party." The second was to give loans to parents and friends. The third was to buy a vehicle. After all their per capita money was gone, many of the youth said, "I wish I knew then what I know today. I would never have spent my money the way I did."

There was a lot of tragedy among the membership of that community, and the Chief and council decided to have a referendum to see if the membership wanted to change the trust agreement so that a youth turning nineteen would not get all their built-up trust monies in one big cheque. There would be no more six-figure cheques; instead, a youth turning nineteen would receive $20,000 per year until their trust monies ran out. Further, the youth would be required to take a course on money management. (It's important for me to add here that not all the youth in that community misspent their money. Some invested in homes, and some used it to go to college or university.)

The referendum passed, and this First Nation chose not to hand out the one-time settlement monies in per capita payments. They elected instead to think seven generations ahead and put some of the settlement funds into community building. They also used some of the funds to purchase new land. Buying land from a settlement is one of the very best things any Rez can do, as land is more important than money. And as most land claim settlements are over lost Rez land, a priority should always be to use a majority of the community's money to add land back to the Rez. I was happy to learn that that Rez still has millions of dollars left from its one-time land claim. Today, it uses only the interest earned on those millions for ongoing per capitas and community needs.

In those First Nations communities that hand out big per capitas, some adults simply stop working. The work ethic in such a community suffers. A retired Chief in Alberta and one in the United States told me the same exact thing about giving out big per capitas: "If there was one decision I could relive it would be the day our council caved in to the political pressure and decided to hand out per capita."

One of the best examples of not giving in to per capita pressure, and of excellent money management, comes from the Navajo Nation. Back in 1985, the Navajo received a settlement of $217 million in a court decision about government misuse of tribal resources. The Navajos truly made a seven-generations decision when they decided to save all the settlement money and put half of it in six trust funds:

- a local government fund;
- a college scholarship fund;
- a vocational education scholarship fund;
- a handicapped trust fund;
- an elderly citizens trust fund; and
- a Navajo academy/prep school trust fund.

Per a resolution passed by the Navajo Nation Council, the rest of the money was used to establish the Navajo Nation Permanent Trust Fund. This fund was to provide a future source of income to replace the declining revenues from the tribe's natural resources. Then-chair Peter Zah said, "These funds belong to the Navajo people. We should allow it to grow so it gets bigger. If we take care of the Trust Fund, it will last forever." Each year 12 per cent of all tribal revenues are invested in the fund. At the end of twenty years, 95 per cent of the interest earned may be used, according to a five-year strategic plan. The remaining 5 per cent must be reinvested each year. The principal may not be touched. It is intended to be a permanent source of income for the Navajo Nation.

One of the Navajo Elder trustees told me, "When a new council wants to spend the saved-up trust monies, I take out my imaginary stick and whack them on the hands." Today the trust is worth more than $3 billion, and it earns over $70 million a year, which is used for community needs. The Navajo Nation did what every Rez should do with a one-time settlement—they protected it for future generations.

The Osoyoos Indian Band experience with one-time land claim settlements is not very good. In the early 1980s, many Okanagan bands received a one-time multimillion-dollar land claim settlement for reserve lands that had been taken away around 1915. That was the first time my people ever received a per capita of a few thousand dollars each. After a few per capita payouts, the money was all gone. No land had been purchased with the settlement money—not one acre. No community buildings were built. The children born only a few years after that one-time settlement did not gain one meagre benefit, not one penny, from their ancestral right.

The second time we settled a land claim we got it half right. It was a much bigger amount, $11 million, back in 1997. We set up a trust, and nearly a dozen elected members were tasked with overseeing the fund. *First mistake!* Just as happens with big councils, the bigger the group the harder it is to make a business decision. I even called the trustees the "Seventh-Generation Trust" because I wanted them to make decisions thinking seven generations ahead. They didn't even think *one* generation ahead.

At community meetings, some of the elected trustees even started to push for breaking up the trust and giving out all the money as per capita. A band to the north of us had settled a big land claim many years earlier and had given out a few $10,000 per capita payments. Many of my people still remembered that and wanted the same for themselves. It wasn't long before there were very heated trust and community meetings and we were dipping into the one-time land settlement and, yes, giving out $10,000 per capitas. Sad.

I still get upset about how my community didn't protect the settlement money and do better for the future of our kids. This, after all, was the biggest land claim we had ever settled. Another huge mistake was that we messed up a chance to buy five thousand acres of land above the south end of the Osoyoos Rez. We missed out on that because this overly large group of band member trustees couldn't make a business decision. Many didn't want to invest in land and instead wanted to hand the money out in per capita payments. Under the watch of those trustees, our Rez lost prime hunting land that eventually turned into a housing project with hundreds of fancy homes. It's our own damned fault we didn't put our culture and heritage ahead of per capita, and that we didn't purchase and keep that valuable land. Instead, we let the majority decide and let that money slip away forever.

We eventually got rid of that trust committee and land, as many band members were telling Chief and council to take back control of the settlement funds. Once they reassumed control, the Chief and council did spend some of what was left of the trust fund money on land purchases, which has turned out to be the very best thing we could have done. Still, we should have done better and saved most of the original settlement amount for our grandkids and their grandkids.

Not long ago, a few Osoyoos members started a petition demanding the Chief and council give out another $10,000 per capita. I remember going to community meetings at that time and getting threatened by my own cuzzin for spending on the community what he and others called "their" money. I stood up and told them it wasn't just their money. That settlement belongs to all those who have passed on and those yet to be born. Many members signed that petition. I am very proud of those members who didn't sign it, and more proud of the council of the time who didn't cave under the political pressure. We had many meetings about that per capita petition, and we told our people that no Chief and council has to abide by any petition, no matter how many people sign it. Many have told us they were pressured into signing the petition, and some wanted their name removed. Others told us they were not even shown the petition, though their names were on it.

This Chief and council will not spend any more of the future generations' money. Enough is enough! What's left has to be saved or spent on land purchases, and people can express their agreement or disagreement with that in the next election for Chief and council. That's a real vote. A petition is not a vote of the people.

Another time we faced big per capita pressure was when we settled a one-time payment from BC Gas for a natural gas pipeline expansion to the existing line that runs through the north part of our Rez. It was a multimillion-dollar land right-of-way deal, and council back in 1998 decided to invest the money in two business ventures on the Rez. One was our own golf course, the other our winery. Many band members wanted the money used for per capita payments, but leadership fought against this suggestion and it was the right thing to do.

In 2005, we settled another multimillion-dollar settlement for an electrical power line and two substations built on the Osoyoos Rez. Again, we put the majority of the settlement toward community improvements—building a youth centre and paving the rest of the Rez road. There is a book by Marie Wadden, *Where the Pavement Ends: Canada's Aboriginal Recovery Movement and the Urgent Need for Reconciliation*, that is based on the sad fact that, for most First Nations reserves and reservations, the way you know you've arrived is that it's where the pavement ends.

It is very rare that I get a phone call from a band member who just wants to say thank you. In my more than thirty years as Chief, I have received only a few such heartfelt calls. But after the Rez road was paved, my uncle Paul called me. I seldom hear from Paul. Like other hard-working, fully employed members of the band, Paul gets up early and heads out to work, in his case in the leased vineyards. He never misses a day. Then, one day after the road that ran by Paul's house was paved, the band secretary tells me Paul is on the phone. I pick up the phone, kinda surprised, and wonder what Uncle Paul wants. He says, "Thank you for getting the road paved. I just called to say thank you!" I was at a loss for words, but then said, "You're welcome, and thanks for calling." It was only a ten-second phone call, but when I put the phone down I knew I and the majority of council had made the right tough decision in directing settlement funds to that project.

All financial advisors would give the same advice to an individual who had received a one-time financial settlement: "Protect the golden egg." Meaning, plan and set aside money for the future. All the First Nations I talked to said if a "leakage study" was done on where most of the per capita money went, the main beneficiaries would be car dealers, drug dealers, bars, and hotels. On the positive side, many community members do put their per capita toward home improvements, education, sports, and cultural purposes. I even know a few who have created a savings account.

Currently at Osoyoos, we give out one of the biggest yearly per capitas in the whole country. It is not based on any particular settlement but instead on a simple valuation of 15 per cent of land-lease income and 15 per cent of business profits. In 2019, the math worked out to $1,500 for every Osoyoos Indian Band member. We disburse it in December and call it the "Christmas per capita." I can defend that type of per capita because the majority of income (the golden egg) stays with the organization. It is therefore sustainable, and it's not so big that it hurts the future needs of our community and businesses. As well, it's a huge boost for families at an expensive time of the year.

How I wish we still had the majority of all those past settlements. Osoyoos would be so much wealthier now. A very wise person once said, "Invest in the future because that is where you are going to spend the rest of your life."

In the near future, many more First Nations will be receiving big land claim settlements, and the very divisive issue of per capita payments will be faced again and again by the leadership of those communities. Some members running for Chief and council will promise huge payouts and try to buy their way into office with future generations' money. My advice to all voters: Be wise—don't vote for those phony money politicians!

I hope our people don't fall for mafia-style politics. What every First Nation needs when it comes to huge money settlements is very simple: We need leadership that isn't in love with money but is in love with protecting the past, present, and future of their Rez! In his book *Leaders Eat Last*, Simon Sinek says, "Leaders would sooner sacrifice what is theirs to save what is ours. And they would never sacrifice what is ours to save what is theirs."

During my time as Chief, the council members I have served with have made our Rez a little bit better by building many modern multi-million-dollar buildings—a grade school and gymnasium, a daycare, a health centre, and a new band office. But I take the most pride in the amount of land we have added under the control of the Osoyoos Indian Band. Since I became Chief we have acquired hundreds of acres of land, both on and off the Rez. I know I keep saying that land is more important than money—but it is. *It is!*

When it comes to tough decisions, I often look to Dr. Martin Luther King Jr., one of the most effective leaders of all time. He said it best: "Cowardice asks the question, is it safe? Expediency asks the question, is it politic? Vanity asks the question, is it popular? But, conscience asks the question, is it right? And there comes a time when one must take a position that is neither safe, nor politic, nor popular, but he must take it because conscience tells him it is right."

CHAPTER 6

THE "INDIAN PROBLEM"

"America has been sick for some time. It got sick when the first Indian treaty was broken."

—Vine Deloria, Jr., Standing Rock Sioux

Canada and the United States are two of the wealthiest countries in the world, forever boasting of their sacred freedom and justice for all. Why, then, are the majority of First Nations—this land's original people—at the bottom of every socio-economic statistic, decade after decade, and now century after century?

Why?

First Nations in Canada were promised "honour of the Crown," and tribes in the United States were promised "justice, liberty and freedom." Further, during the time of European settlement and treaties, Natives were promised that the Great White Mother, the Queen, would protect and look after the First Peoples living in the part of the continent that would eventually become Canada. In the United States, Indians were told they would always have the protection of the Great White Father, George Washington, and the presidents who would follow him.

The historical fact is that Natives in North America were lied to and subject to racist laws and treatment by the founding fathers of the United States and Canada. The men governing these two countries were imperialistic liars, and their Canadian and American dreams were never meant to include the "savages" (Indigenous peoples).

President George Washington said, "There are only two things I want from Indians—the first is peace—second is their land." And when Canada's first prime minister, John A. Macdonald, pondered the suggestion that reserves should have their own schools, he dismissed it as a bad idea, given that "the child lives with its parents, who are savages, and though he may learn to read and write, his habits and training mode of thought are Indian. He is simply a savage who can read and write. It has been strongly impressed upon myself . . . that Indian children should be withdrawn as much as possible from the parental influence, and the only way to do that would be to put them in central training industrial schools where they will acquire the habits and modes of thought of white men." Hence, the greatest genocidal crime ever committed in the histories of Canada and the United States: Indian residential and Indian boarding schools!

Parliament after Parliament and Congress after Congress kept funding these residential and boarding schools, where thousands of Native children died. In Canada, we speak of reconciliation, but do we reconcile that the nation's first prime minister was also the architect of Canada's worst human rights violations? John A. Macdonald, more than anyone else, was responsible for the cultural genocide waged against the First Nations of this land—a 120-year-long attack on Indigenous children. Let us never, ever forget that this shameful episode is at the foundation of Canadian and American history.

In 1967, another B.C. Chief summed up my feelings on these issues in a speech delivered on the occasion of Canada's one-hundredth birthday. "When I fought to protect my land and my home," Chief Dan George said in his "Lament for Confederation," "I was called a savage. When I neither understood nor welcomed his way of life, I was called lazy. When I tried to rule my people, I was stripped of my authority." I can relate very well to this, as I have lived it.

It was the heartbreaking legacy of the "trail of broken treaties" in both countries that led me, at the age of nineteen, to leave the Osoyoos Indian Reserve and travel to Regina and then Lethbridge to take Native American Studies. Addressing the ongoing injustices against my people became my calling. I decided to dedicate my life to doing something about this dysfunctional relationship between federal governments and Natives—a relationship that has so often been referred by Canadian and American leaders as the "Indian Problem."

I grew up on the Osoyoos Indian Reserve and have only ever left my Rez for jobs and university. My Rez is where my heart and soul live and where my sun will one day set. Native people have an ancestral relationship with their territory that runs far deeper and is much older than the relatively young history of the colonial United States of America and even much older than the British Empire, which created Canada. Thousands upon thousands of years compared to just a few hundred.

My tribal nation, the Okanagan (Nsyilxcən-speaking) territory, is in south-central British Columbia and north-central Washington State. Like all tribal nations located near the forty-ninth parallel, the Okanagan people were split up in 1846, when the United States and the British colonial government signed the Oregon Treaty, arbitrarily creating a border between the British colony and the United States (which also used to be a British colony). Half of my people were put under the federal Indian Reserve system (eight different bands) in a country later called Canada. The other half of my traditional territory was now under the United States flag. My people on the U.S. side were placed on the Colville Indian Reservation, which was created in 1872. The name "Colville," incidentally, had nothing to do with the people who had lived on this territory for thousands of years. It came from a London governor who was once in charge of the Hudson's Bay

Company. I ask you—how insulting is that? It's like what Muhammad Ali referred to as "having a slave name."

Since that arbitrary border was created, my people have had to endure and suffer under various federal and provincial/state termination policies and programs intended to "kill the Indian in the Indian." Founding fathers of both countries spoke of getting rid of the "Indian Problem." Government policy on both sides of this arbitrary border viewed Indigenous people as "savages," beings who lacked the same human and land rights as the English and French settlers who came late to this huge continent and presumed that since they had "found" it, they now owned it.

Fast-forward to 2017—Canada's 150th birthday: most Indian reserves on both sides of the border still suffered from socio-economic conditions so bad that any caring elected provincial or state leader would have declared a state of emergency, and nothing has changed in the several years since. Yet the Indian Affairs bureaucracies in both Canada and the United States continue to spend billions of taxpayer dollars that, year after year, end up reinforcing developing world conditions on North American soil. Someone in the Canadian and American governments needs to put their hand up high and own these shameful statistics.

I have studied and worked in the trenches for four decades battling this state of affairs.

The focus of my studies, the so-called Indian Problem, has been around since 1492, and it's important to note that those colonial "castles on the hill" in Ottawa and Washington have not managed to starve or Christianize all the "hostiles" into submission. Through blatantly racist policies, generations of settlers and their governments tried to assimilate all First Nations into the Canadian and American melting pots. Thankfully, it didn't quite work out that way. First

Nations and American Indian tribes are finally, more than five hundred years after Christopher Columbus got lost and "discovered" us, First Nations are now getting off our knees and back on our economic "horse." We are challenging the historical myths of the United States of America and Canada.

As Reverend Jesse Jackson once said about the Black civil rights movement, "White folks don't want peace; they want quiet. The price you pay for peace is justice. Until there is justice, there will be no peace or quiet."

I have no intention of ever being quiet. The graves of my people are all over the Okanagan Nation territory, and I will follow the lead of the past Chiefs who could not speak English and therefore could not tell the colonists and settlers what they needed to know and should have known. I will continue their fight for economic justice, return of Rez land, and a return to the self-supporting lifestyle every First Nation once had.

Many years ago I wrote the Osoyoos Indian Band Development Corporation's motto: "In Business to Preserve Our Past by Strengthening Our Future."

It's also a motto for life.

CHAPTER 7

INDIAN RESIDENTIAL AND BOARDING SCHOOLS

"The Canadian government pursued this policy of cultural genocide because it wished to divest itself of its legal and financial obligations to Aboriginal people and gain control over their land and resources. If every Aboriginal person had been 'absorbed into the body politic,' there would be no reserves, no Treaties, and no Aboriginal rights."

—Honouring the Truth, Reconciling for the Future:
Summary of the Final Report of the Truth and
Reconciliation Commission of Canada

I cannot write about Rez culture without including something that has had perhaps the biggest ongoing negative impact on that culture: the Indian residential schools of Canada and the American Indian boarding schools in the United States. Native people's experiences in those schools are directly linked to the ongoing intergenerational dysfunction within Rez communities. You cannot speak of one without acknowledging the other.

As John S. Milloy wrote in his 2017 book *A National Crime: The Canadian Government and the Residential School System, 1879 to 1986*, "It is clear that the schools have been, arguably, the most damaging of the many elements of Canada's colonization of this land's original peoples and, as their consequences still affect the lives of Aboriginal people today, they remain so."

Nothing upsets me more than seeing pictures of little Native kids in Indian residential or boarding schools. Canada followed the United States' lead on committing cultural genocide against North America's Indigenous people by attacking the most vulnerable among them: their children. The philosophy was simple: "Kill the Indian, save the child." Some Osoyoos people younger than me were sent to residential school; I was not. I do not, therefore, have first-hand experience of the trauma caused by that failed federal government program. But I do have first-hand experience of growing up in a community that still suffers greatly from the intergenerational social and cultural trauma that has been passed on by those who did suffer such physical and mental abuse in their childhoods.

Over the last couple of decades, much national attention has been given to this important subject. In May 2006, the Indian Residential Schools Settlement Agreement was approved, which included compensation of more than $2 billion for residential school survivors and their families. I want to give a "Rez shout" to then National Chief Phil Fontaine for pushing the federal government to ante up for its crime against Indian children. This was the largest class action settlement in Canadian history. Prime Minister Stephen Harper then offered a full apology on behalf of the Government of Canada and all Canadians on June 11, 2008.

Later, the Truth and Reconciliation Commission spent many more millions of dollars examining the issue. People more knowledgeable than I am have written on the subject, often with great anguish and passion—especially those who themselves are residential school survivors. They are the ones Canada needs to listen to.

I have talked to many residential school survivors and have found that, of course, not all of their experiences were the same. Some have told me their residential school experience was not as bad as if they'd stayed at home, where there was a lot of alcoholism and kids were left hungry and cold. Some were glad to get away, and some parents were glad to be rid of their responsibilities, actually dragging their kids to the train or cattle truck that would take them away. For the vast majority, however, residential school was the worst experience of their lives.

Growing up on a Rez where a majority of the adults had suffered residential school abuse, I did not know or understand at the time where their anger, jealousy, and rage were coming from. The constant drinking, the thoughtlessness of parents leaving their kids for days, sometimes weeks, to fend for themselves. Today we look on this lack of parenting skills as the obvious result of the residential school experience: these people could not possibly have picked up such skills, as they were taken from the parents who might have passed them on. The post-traumatic stress is undeniable. Parents today would be arrested if they treated their kids with the kind of neglect that was happening on the reserves in the 1950s, '60s, and '70s.

You have to ask what kind of countries have elected leaders who perpetuate a systematic attack on the children of a targeted race. We must never forget that the Canadian and American flags were proudly flown over every federal government-funded, church-run residential school and boarding school for more than a century.

Over the years, I have read many books and articles on how the Canadian and American political leadership at the highest levels enforced their solutions to the "Indian Problem." Imperialistic, racist federal policies were designed to destroy Native tribalism by physically, mentally, emotionally, and spiritually attacking what is the most vulnerable and defenseless segment of any society—its children. In Canada, the so-called honour of the Crown was carried out by elected politicians who held before their name titles such as Honourable Member of Parliament, Right Honourable Prime Minister, and Honourable Minister. Other than the systematic attacks on Native villages by government armies and cavalry, the residential schools and boarding schools were the cruelest and most heartless federal government programs ever conceived by the Americans and Canadians—and all in the name of justice and under the convenient cover of Christianity. The churches did the devil's work. The priests and the nuns who abused innocent Native children should all rot in hell.

In the past couple of years, there has been much debate about Canada's first prime minister, John A. Macdonald. While he has been praised as Canada's founding father, he has simultaneously been condemned as a racist, and his statues have been vandalized and destroyed in the streets. No matter how one sees him, though, there is no denying Macdonald's role in the creation of the residential schools. Macdonald had his hired gun in Duncan Campbell Scott, remembered by some Canadians as a gentle poet but remembered by Native Canadians as the architect of the hideous residential school system. As the first superintendent of this system, Scott wrote, "It is readily acknowledged that Indian children lose their natural resistance to illness by habituating so closely in the residential schools, and that they die at a much higher rate than in their villages. But this alone does not justify a change in the policy of this department which is geared toward a *final solution of our Indian Problem*" (italics mine).

But although the Canadian and American governments were responsible for the cultural genocide, a question that is seldom asked is, Why didn't Native leadership or the parents do more to prevent their kids from being taken away? Mohawk journalist and residential school survivor Doug George-Kanentiio addressed this issue following the completion of the Truth and Reconciliation Commission's report. The Commission, he wrote, failed in this important area "because it left out the active participation of the Band councils in removing the children from their homes." He continued:

> No Native person, then in authority, has ever been questioned about why they went along with these removals or why they never, to my knowledge, asked what was being done to the children in those schools. In all those bitter months as an inmate at the Mohawk Institute (located on Six Nations land in Brantford, Ontario) no Native official of any kind bothered to investigate our situation. The Cree and Mohawk boys and girls would sit near the windows looking down that manicured driveway for some adult to come to our aide yet no one did. The last we saw of the Band councils was their hiring of someone to place us on those trains and expect us, as ten-year-olds, to find our way 350 miles from home to the Institute. We wanted to know why the Commission did not hold Native officials culpable . . . it was disturbing to us that the Mohawk people, the chiefs and others, did nothing to stand in defence of their children, that which is most sacred to any community.

When I asked my gramma what she remembered about kids being sent to residential school, she said, "I would see some parents dragging their kids crying to the train or bus and pushing their kids away." I asked, why would parents do that to their kids? My gramma replied, "So they could go drinking." I know some parents were threatened with jail if they didn't send their kids to residential school in the early years, but in the later years that was not the case. I know most of my people were poor and had trouble putting food on the table. Some parents wrongly thought their kids would eat better and get a better education in residential/boarding schools.

In Canada, the last of these genocidal institutions did not close, remarkably, until 1996. In 1879, the Canadian federal government's Davin Report recommended Indian residential schools be based on the American model. Davin reported the boarding school approach was the best answer because it "took the Aboriginal child from the reserve and kept him in the constant circle of civilization, assured attendance, removed from the retarding influence of his parents."

How could citizens from "the land of the free and the home of the brave" and "the true North strong and free" possibly allow president after president, prime minister after prime minister (and don't forget the pope), to oversee the perpetration of this systematic cultural genocide on thousands of innocent Native kids? It was a national crime, a human rights violation, and government cover-up at the highest level. In Canada from the late 1800s to the 1990s, some 150,000 children were taken from their families and sent off to residential schools. The Truth and Reconciliation Commission estimates that over four thousand of them died while at these schools, but the exact number will never be known because no one (government or church) was really keeping count—no one cared. Many of the children were buried in unmarked graves, as the church and the federal government had no shame in not providing a proper burial for the thousands of Native children under their care. To me there is no forgiveness or "reconciliation" for that.

Wake up, citizens of Canada and the United States! We are not talking about ancient history! On the Osoyoos reserve, many of my people were sent to either the Kamloops or St. Eugene Indian residential schools near Cranbrook, on the Kamloops or St. Mary's Indian reserves. Some people even younger than me were still being sent to Kamloops Indian Residential School in the 1970s. I take a very personal interest in how the Canadian and American governments

legalized the tormenting, abuse, and killing of Native children. This
legislation caused intergenerational grief, alcoholism, hatred, mistrust, and community and family breakdown in Native communities
across the continent, which persist to this day. I have learned first-
hand that much of the negativism and political civil strife on the Rez
comes from the experiences our people had at residential school. And
I have listened to some of my people's own first-hand experience as
kids in those government- and church-run human laboratories.

One of my people, Ted, is a residential school survivor of the 1960s
who was sent to St. Mary's Residential School in Cranbrook. When he
was in grade school, he got strapped many times, once for asking a
simple question about love. Ted remembered the priest preaching about
the importance of love—the need to love thy neighbour, love thine
enemy, love everything. Recalling all those beatings and strappings,
Ted put up his hand and asked, "Why don't you love us?" The priest's
face got very red, and within a few minutes he called Ted into his office.
Ted knew what was going to happen. Out came the long rubber strap.
"I covered up," Ted told me, "and I didn't want to say 'Stop!' because
I knew he wouldn't—and I didn't want him to see me cry." That's the
kind of "love" thousands of little Native kids learned from these institutions supported by the Canadian and American governments.

Ted ran away many times, even though he was nearly five hundred
kilometres from Osoyoos and had to travel over mountains and through
territory filled with danger. Many children attempted such dangerous
escapes. A few years back, Tragically Hip frontman Gord Downie produced a much-praised album and film that paid tribute to one such
brave boy, Chanie Wenjack, an Anishinaabe from Northern Ontario
who died trying to return home after escaping residential school. Ted
ran away in winter, despite the threat of freezing, and he was lucky to
survive. Many kids froze to death trying to get back home. The food at

the residential school was very bad, he told me, and many kids resorted to stealing to stop the hunger pangs. Yet the priests and nuns always had hot cooked food that many of the kids could see and smell every day.

Imagine a school where the adults eat well and the kids are malnourished. Imagine a school in Canada where kids live in fear, with bruises and cuts on their face, where parents are not allowed to see their child for ten months of each year. In those schools, boys and girls were kept apart, so if you had a sibling of the opposite sex, you couldn't talk to or eat with them. And there was no Christmas dinner or birthday cakes or presents. Can you imagine your kids not having birthdays or presents throughout their childhood? The deprivation of things as simple and fundamental as the yearly family celebration of children's birthdays had a devastating socio-psychological impact on Native communities. Now that Osoyoos has its own gym, the facility often gets used for kids' birthday parties. I love seeing and hearing the sounds of kids in our gym having a birthday party.

Ted says he can still remember the crying of other kids and the ugly sound of an adult fist hitting a little kid's face. Hearing and watching other kids being abused made him feel totally helpless. Lloyd, another Osoyoos Indian Band member, came back from Cranbrook physically handicapped for life. He had been pushed down the stairs by one of the "brothers" and had badly broken his leg. The authorities at the school accused him of faking an injury and didn't bring him to the hospital for weeks. When he couldn't get up and stand, the brother made him crawl to his bed—all the while strapping and kicking him as he crawled along the floor. I get so pissed off when I hear and read of the suffering many of my people endured as kids!

It is a farce to me that priests and nuns could be so mean to defenceless Native children. Most every day Native kids would get strapped and ridiculed for doing what every kid has done—wetting the bed. As punishment, boys were often forced to wear a dress for the whole day. My American Indian friend, Smoker, told me that in boarding school (in Washington State) they slept on bunk beds and one of his friends was always getting strapped for bedwetting, and that "the priests were always humiliating the kids." Those who wet the bed faced cruel punishment, such as being thrown in a cold shower while other kids were forced to watch. "A boy about nine years old slept on the bottom bunk," Smoker said. "I slept on the top bunk. I tried to help hide his bedwetting. One day I woke up and he had hung himself with a towel tied to our bunk bed. He was just in grade four and couldn't take the humiliation by the priests anymore. Many kids tried to run away and put themselves in real danger by travelling through the mountains, so they would not get caught and sent back. While I was there one child who ran away died falling off a cliff."

How's that for a childhood memory?

Many Native kids committed suicide in residential and boarding schools all over North America. And those who returned home brought the violence back to the Rez. "The abuse was so fucking terrible," Ted told me. "We bottled up our own anger. I wouldn't let them see me cry. Every day we could see the pain and the hurt in the other kids. When we got home we took the anger out on our own people. They damaged us so much. I blamed the residential school for everything."

It should never have been this way. As St. Francis de Sales, the patron saint of writers, once wrote, "You learn to speak by speaking, to study by studying, to run by running, to work by working; in just the same way, you learn to love by loving." It's really pretty simple. Ted should have been loved, and been shown how to love, from that very first day, and every day that followed.

On the Rez, many Native kids have witnessed domestic violence on a level that is heart-wrenching. So many of my peers have told me that, as little kids, they saw their mom being punched and saw adults being drunk on a regular basis. No children should have those memories as part of their childhood. And with high rates of alcoholism and drug abuse comes sexual abuse. Yes, there was sexual abuse committed by the priests and nuns against defenceless Native kids in residential schools and boarding schools. Many of those rape victims came back to the Rez with a broken spirit and fell into a cycle of addiction and abuse. Today sexual abuse continues because of prevalent alcoholism and meth, coke, and crack cocaine use. Many women on my Rez, and on most other reserves, have been sexually abused, as have many men.

As a child, I myself experienced far too much alcoholism and drunken violence: Kids looking after kids because the parents are gone for days drinking. Kids having to feed themselves and build a fire to stay warm because no adults are around. Kids getting woken up by drunken adults fighting in their house. Kids left on Main Street in a car for most of the day and night while their parents are in a bar. This last situation has improved because today the police would not allow little kids to sit waiting outside a bar all day, but back in the 1960s and '70s that was common—so hard to believe!

Because of all this, many Rez kids were adopted out. In Canada, the "Sixties Scoop" caused terrible multi-generational trauma. Through these policies, which were enacted beginning in the 1960s, some twenty thousand Native children—no one knows the exact number— were taken away from their parents and adopted by white Canadian families. This would have been bad enough, but many children were shuffled around the messed-up foster care system and never permanently adopted.

Add this long history of cultural genocide to the underfunded on-Rez programs provided by Indian Affairs and you have all the ingredients for a Rez dependency/unemployment culture—designed by the Canadian and American governments and carried out by well-paid Indian Affairs employees.

I give a shout-out to those few Natives who have come forward and written about their personal experience—like Bev Sellars, whose book *They Called Me Number One* gave me insight into why some of my people still feel jealousy and bitterness when someone on the Rez gets a common necessity such as a vehicle or new shoes. Describing her own experience as a child, Bev said that when kids got new shoes they would go and scuff them up and get them dirty to avoid being teased or bullied. She recalled,

> Kids can be mean at the best of times, but, when you are in a situation where negativity surrounds you 95 per cent of the time, kids can be downright cruel to satisfy their own negative feelings. We really had to be careful we didn't violate anyone's turf or offend someone by appearing better than anyone else, like what happened when someone would get new shoes. . . . This should have been a joyous occasion, but *no one* wanted to get the new shoes. With new shoes came the burden of trying not to *look* at your new shoes. The other kids saw this as "showing off," and that could easily earn you a punch or two from someone.
>
> The message of "don't try to be better than anyone else" had an effect on me for years. . . . Don't strive to be the best, strive to be the least! And it was seen as okay to be the least. We had a saying at the Mission if we did anything stupid. We excused ourselves with the line, "Oh well, I'm just an Indian" . . .

Bev concludes by saying, "What a messed-up world in which to raise whole Nations of impressionable Aboriginal children." Now I understand where the continuing jealousy and backstabbing on the Rez comes from.

I experienced this when I was speaking on a Rez in northern Alberta a few years ago and the Chief gave me a ride back to the airport in a rough-looking car. He told me, "I always buy my wife a beat-up used car so my people won't say bad stuff about her. She does not want a new car or people will spread bad rumours about me." I thought, *What a bunch of "Rez BS." A hard-working man can't even buy his wife a decent car without ignorant Rez politics raising its ugly head.* That residential school jealousy and hatred is still around today!

Most elected white politicians—federal, provincial, and municipal—haven't grown up around drug and alcohol abuse and poverty and violence. But like most Chiefs, I run out of fingers when I count my family members and close relatives who became alcoholics, committed suicide, or have done serious jail time. Much of the family and community dysfunction I grew up with and witnessed is a legacy of the physical and mental abuse perpetrated by the residential school system.

What kind of people, what kind of country, could allow this? What kind of elected leaders would permit this? Who the hell elected those federal governments every four years or so to sanction cultural genocide and sexual abuse of defenceless Native kids? The fact is, it was the Canadian and American people who elected those "honourable members" of Parliament and Congress who did nothing for more than a century to protect the countries' most vulnerable citizens. I have asked many white fathers what they would do if someone came to take their kids away, and their answer is usually, "I would kill anyone who tried to take my kids."

Not so long ago in the Okanagan, there was an elected B.C. official who asked, "When are Natives going to get over residential schools? Why can't we just look forward and quit bringing up the past?" When

I think about my people struggling with addictions, struggling to stay out of jail, struggling to ensure their children aren't taken from them, all I see are those cursed government- and church-run schools. The federal governments allowed pedophiles, church priests and nuns, to use the cover of the cross to physically and sexually abuse thousands of Native kids for generations. Rez-elected leaders today are burdened with a colonial cancer—a residential and boarding school disease whose symptoms continue to plague our communities. It's difficult to truly comprehend the physiological toll on generations of children being raised in such an inhumane way for more than one hundred years in two countries that claim to be the world's best examples of freedom and justice.

I want to take a knee and raise a fist every time I hear the words of the Canadian and American national anthems. All citizens of Canada and the United States from the 1870s to 1996 have to bear the responsibility for the ongoing socio-economic costs of rebuilding Native communities.

Many white people have told me that they didn't know Canada or the United States was carrying out a genocide on Native children. Okay, maybe you didn't know, but *now* you know. No more hiding it. No more denying it. It's time for Canada and the United States to acknowledge their historic war crimes against the First Nations people within their own borders. Apologies are a good baby step, and so is compensation, but in Canada, a country that prides itself on being bilingual and multicultural, we need to focus on the First Nations languages and cultures that this same country spent millions of dollars to destroy in its schools. The government must now provide millions of dollars to help save and revive those same First Nations languages and cultures it tried to destroy.

Native people are filling up prisons and treatment centres because of the legacy of residential and boarding schools. When I was at the

University of Lethbridge I heard Tom Porter, a Mohawk leader, speak about this issue. He said something like:

> It was because of how we were treated in these schools as defenceless little kids that Natives have the highest alcoholism rates, the highest suicide rates, the highest welfare rates. That Native parents don't know how to be parents, that Native fathers punch their wives in front of their kids. To middle-class Canada, to middle-class America, what would happen to you if China took over these lands and said to all the white people from this day forward, no more Christianity—burn all the Bibles. From this day forward no more English or French. And if we hear one more English or French word out of you—you're gonna get whacked on the head!

That's how Native kids went to school in Canada and the United States for more than a hundred years. I didn't go to residential school, but I grew up surrounded by its after-effects. I have witnessed the broken lives of some of my people, the violence, the lack of respect at some of our meetings. I have seen the jealousy and hatred. I want to see the bar raised in Indian Country. I want our people to work hard and earn an honest living and own nice things. I don't want to see my people driving Rez bombs or living in "standard/modest" housing. Those who get an education, those who work hard, those who earn a promotion, those who earn a higher wage—these deserving people should all be able to buy better vehicles, have a bigger house, and go on nicer vacations without being ridiculed or called down by those who want to disparage achievers. How did our people devolve from having a hard-working traditional culture rooted in supporting and respecting one another to suffering from the "Indian crab syndrome," where we are jealous and hate seeing our people owning nice houses and vehicles? It's clear to me that this is a direct legacy of the residential/boarding school system.

That's residential school dysfunctional thinking. Come on Rez people, time to put on "grown-up pants" and act like hard-working, respectful skins. We should be proud to see our people who work hard for their paycheque driving nice rides, living in great-looking houses, and having nice yards. The Rez has to rid itself of that destructive thinking that gets passed down to our kids.

As Chief, I carry a lot of the anger and sadness of what residential and boarding schools have done to my people. Every week I deal with the community dysfunction. I have given hundreds of speeches at conferences all over North America, and only once have I become so emotional that I broke down on stage. After a speech in Vancouver there was a Q-and-A session. Most of the questions were about First Nations economic development. But then I got a question about residential schools. At first I answered it like I would a normal question, but then my feelings flared up with so much anger and sadness that I teared up and cursed at the same time.

After that, I couldn't talk and couldn't take any more questions.

In May of 2021, the skeletal remains of 215 children were discovered at the site of the Kamloops Indian Residential School. Canada lowered its flags and all levels of government offered prayers and sympathy. I have had enough of nice gestures for the day or the week—I want a full criminal investigation. Those unmarked graves should be declared a crime scene. What would Canada and the RCMP do if the remains of even two white children were found? The children that were by Canadian law sent to residential schools were not lost, they were stolen. It is well documented in the final report of the Truth and Reconciliation Commission that over four thousand Native children died at residential schools across Canada. It is also well documented that many of the priests and nuns who administered those schools sexually and physically abused children. There were many pedophiles among the priests and nuns. Anyone who would rape children and break their bones should also be suspected of outright first- degree murder. Therefore a murder investigation is what is required for not only the remains recently found on the Kamloops Rez but for all the other recently found unmarked graves at other residential schools. Let's not forget that all these Native children died while under the care of the priests and nuns! How many of those priests and nuns have been charged with murder—zero! How many murder investigations have been done at residential schools—zero! Why do the churches up to now refuse to release their records? How many church records have suspiciously disappeared over the years? Canada and the churches involved must be held legally liable for the thousands of deaths at Indian residential schools!

Many First Nations leaders are asking for an apology from the Pope. To me a forced apology is not a sincere apology. In politics and business I have heard many phony apologies—especially after someone gets caught doing something illegal. I have no trust or respect for anyone who gives a forced apology. Now some Chiefs want the Pope to make a forced apology—"please, pretty please will you apologize for the genocide your organization inflicted on Indian children?" Phony apologies and lowering flags are not action! Honoring the missing children means getting to the whole truth of why thousands of Indian children are buried in unmarked graves. Now the world is watching, there should be nowhere left for Canada and the churches to hide. There is a time for sadness and ceremony, and then there is a time for criminal justice, a time to get mad and uncover the whole truth, "nothing but the truth, so help me God!"

The Canadian public should realize that it was their tax dollars that funded every government residential school for over 100 years. The

Canadian government handed over millions each year to the churches. Don't forget the Roman Catholic Church is a multi-billion-dollar organization. The priests and nuns who worked there got a regular paycheque and probably a good pension to torment and rape Native kids.

On June 5, 2021, I attended a motorcycle ride organized by a group of East Indian (Sikh) who offered support and prayers following the discovery at Kamloops Indian Residential School. It is good to see that the ordinary Canadian has been emotionally moved by the discovery of a mass grave of Native children. And so many are willing to do more than just bow their heads for a minute, then move on. I was amazed at how many people (Native and non-Native) were gathered in front of the school to welcome the riders. After the Sikh bikers did their prayers, the Native drummers took over and I witnessed a moment in time I will never forget. I saw above the front entrance carved in stone: Kamloops Indian Residential School A.D. 1923. And below that archway were hundreds of Indians from many different Tribes with hand drums out, speaking their Native language and singing a warrior song. I sat on my "iron horse" (my Harley) thinking about what brought me to this moment. I looked at the dark school windows above the crowd where in the past thousands of defenceless Native children had stared out so homesick every day for 100 years. I felt so many sad and mad feelings at the same time. Looking at those empty windows above the hard drumming sound and feeling the heartbeat of countless Native drums, I thought, those priests and nuns didn't complete their evil plan. We are still singing our songs. Some are still speaking their Native language. We are still holding our eagle staffs. We are gathered here today in front of a red brick building built by Canada and administered by the churches to destroy us and we are still standing as First Nations people. To hell with your genocidal schemes. Many residential school survivors were in the crowd hitting the drum hard and war whooping and letting the spirits of the children know "They did not kill the Indian in the Indian!" As I and the others started our motorcycles, the drumming got louder and as we drove by lines of brown raised fists I thought once again, "Damn, I'm lucky to be an Indian." It was a very special moment. The irony is that one of the most proud moments of my life occurred outside of a Canadian government building built to get rid of the "Indian problem."

On June 21, 2021, National Indigenous Peoples Day in Canada, over 100 members of the Osoyoos Indian Band made a special memorial caravan to Kamloops Indian Residential School. Many who went were survivors of that school. I was so proud of my Rez—from the very young to the very old—who made that very emotional trip. As we were leaving the Rez, I noticed something in plain sight I had never seen before—how the local non-Natives have also been woken up by the 215 at Kamloops. As we got on the public road that borders our Rez, hundreds of white people (most wearing orange shirts), kids, teachers, parents and grandparents, and people we didn't even know were lined up on both sides of the road waving at us. Some held up signs about the tragedy of residential schools. As we drove miles away from the reserve, I was so surprised to see there were yet more non-Natives wearing orange shirts standing on the side of the road displaying real support. I thought, "How did they know we were heading up to Kamloops?" Social media sometimes can work wonders when used right. As I waved at all the non-Native support in our local small town, that scene proved to me that most Canadians want something done about the ongoing Indian residential school cover-up. And now most Canadians, and especially the politicians and corporate elite, have been forced to wake up to Native issues. Now will the Canadian elected leadership go beyond nice words into action?

As I stood with my people in front of the Kamloops Indian Residential School and listened to Sherry Stelkia speak our Native language and watch our kids pick up their hand drums and proudly sing the "Okanagan Song," I couldn't help but once again look up at all the dark windows on that three-story building. I thought of the hundreds of little Native kids who would have looked out of those windows so home-sick for their parents and grandparents, beaten, hungry, and scared. I stared once again at those dark empty windows for many minutes with such anger and sadness. Then once I turned to look back at our Native school drummers, Native pride—Rez pride—took over. After all the genocidal crimes against my people, I thought to myself: "we are still standing—we are still speaking our language and singing our songs outside a Canadian institution that tried its best for over 100 years to 'Kill the Indian in the Indian.'" The 215 buried only a few metres away brought us here and have woken us up. The Indian inside of us is still standing loud and proud!

I have seen the Native pride in the First Nations people of Australia, New Zealand, and in those all over North America. I have heard the personal stories of the deep wounds and scars inflicted by the racist government policies toward Native kids all over the world—the "stolen generations." The historical fact is, Native people everywhere are survivors. I feel that deeply when I watch and hear the Osoyoos Indian kids playing in our playgrounds and in our gym, bringing out the drum and singing our songs.

That's where most of my hope lies.

CHAPTER 8

NATIVE SPORTS LOGOS
AND REZ LIFE

"Get high on sports not drugs."

—motto, Inchelium Native youth camp

Just before Christmas 2020, the Cleveland Indians baseball team announced they would drop the Native Indian head logo and begin the process of coming up with new branding. Earlier in the year, the Washington Redskins had announced they would, for the time being, be called just the Washington Football Team, with no reference to the Native name and logo that players and fans once embraced with passion.

When I hear that some Natives are against professional sports teams using Native logos or names, that they feel such use is disrespectful and offensive, I disagree with a passion—and I have lots of evidence to back this up.

Few have been on more Indian reserves and reservations than I have. Being a dedicated sports fan, I pay attention to the Native sports culture. I have been to hundreds of Native sports tournaments and games, and I notice when someone is wearing a sports logo. I especially notice when someone is wearing a Native sports logo or has one in their home or office.

A person competitive in sports is usually also competitive in life.

Patrick Murphy, the Alabama Crimson Tide softball coach, says, "Un-coachable kids become unemployable adults. Let your kid get used to someone being tough on them. It's life—get over it." Most of my lifelong inner circle of close friends come from my experiences in sports. Nothing matches the camaraderie and heartfelt highs and lows that sports competition leaves etched in the hearts and minds of players, coaches, and fans. And sports logos are a very important part of those memories.

It's the same for Natives who live and breathe the Native rodeo culture. They always notice when someone is wearing cowboy boots or a cowboy hat. And they can quickly pick out the phony "urban cowboys." As a one-time bull rider myself, I always pay extra attention to those wearing a cowboy hat. A cowboy hat is a very important symbol to those in the rodeo culture—something most people wouldn't understand. Likewise, a leather motorcycle vest is not just another leather vest. A motorcycle vest and the patches that riders attach to their vests are a very important part of the biker culture— and I'm not talking about motorcycle gangs. I'm talking about thousands of passionate individual riders like myself. People who are serious motorcycle riders will know exactly what I mean.

Those who are obsessed with political correctness won't get this, but I continue to see Rez kids and adults wearing caps with the Cleveland Indians logo. They don't wear the logo because they are Cleveland Indians fans, or even because they are baseball fans. They wear it because it's a *Native* logo, and they like it!

The first question I have for Natives who are upset about the use of Native names and images in sports is, Are you even a real sports fan? If you were a real sports fans, you would realize a sports logo is a very serious emblem and is one of the highest honours in sports. It symbolizes your team and is the face and image of your team. In sports, your team logo and name becomes part of your *family*, which is something non-sports fans would not understand. Your team and that jersey and name is of utmost importance, respect, and a source of pride.

I wonder how many of those Natives who oppose the use of names such as Cleveland Indians, Chicago Blackhawks, and Washington Redskins spend significant time on their Rez and take notice of how many of their people wear those logos? Are they urban Indian academics caught up in campus or Facebook political correctness? I notice Redskins, Blackhawks, and Indians ball caps on reserves and reservations all over Indian Country. I even see some of these logos at powwows, where Native craft vendors will often sell beaded "Redskins" logos.

Obviously, Natives (like every race of people) don't all agree on every issue. As with every race, Natives have a variety of positions on most every aspect of life. The public and team owners should realize that, yes, there are some Natives against the use of Native logos and names, but also that the media loves to play up conflict. The fact is, there are a lot of Natives who proudly wear and support those logos every day.

Some Natives say the Washington Redskins name is offensive, but most Rezskins are not thin-skinned and don't take offence. On the Rez we have far more pressing economic, social, and cultural issues to deal with than this, and we don't have time to listen to those who make the issue of Native sports logos and names an ongoing priority. On my visits to more than three hundred Indian reserves and reservations, not once has a Rez Indian brought up the so-called serious issue of Native sports names and logos.

I side with the skins and have ever since I was a kid. I will continue to support and wear the Blackhawks, Redskins, and Cleveland Indians logos. The first hockey jersey I bought, back in 1976 when as a sixteen-year-old I started playing hockey, was a Chicago Blackhawks practice jersey, with the proud-looking Indian head on the front and my personal sports number, #13, on the back. That jersey is still one of my prized sports jerseys. I am not even a Blackhawks fan—Habs all the way!—but I see that Indian head as one of the very best logos in all of professional sports. To me and to many First Nations people, that logo is a sign of RESPECT. For Natives, how can it be anything other than something in which to take pride? No way is it degrading or embarrassing!

The Canadian Broadcasting Corporation (CBC), an organization that, like many reserves, lives off of government funding, recently sent out a notice: "CBC Sports will stop the use of Indigenous names in reference to teams and symbols." What a worthless gesture. Come on, CBC! If you want to help First Nations people, try reporting every day on the ongoing injustices of land claims, water quality, and treaty issues. Why not call out the churches and the Pope for more than a century of physical and sexual abuse in Indian residential and boarding schools? Or is that subject too close to the Canadian and American heartbeat?

I recently received an email from a senior men's hockey team a few hours east of Osoyoos. The players were getting beat up on social media for using the name "Warriors" and wearing the Blackhawks logo. I told them, "You are in my traditional Okanagan/Syilx territory, and as far as I am concerned, keep on wearing that proud Native logo. Tell those overly sensitive pilgrims to find a more important cause to protest. Tell them, 'Why not change the imperial/colonial/settler "white names" of all the mountains, rivers, and creeks back to Native names?'" Especially those on Rezes named after racist Indian agents and forts. Fort names and settler names should be changed.

In 2020 the Black Lives Matter demonstrations happened all over the United States and Canada—which was long overdue. It was great to see players taking a knee during the playing of the national anthems.

Taking a knee does not mean you disrespect the flag or are not patri-
otic. Some people purposely misinterpret things for their own political
purposes—just like the idea that wearing and using Native sports logos
and names is being racist or insensitive to Native people.

The Edmonton Eskimos of the Canadian Football League also
recently bowed to the pressure of political correctness and decided to
drop the familiar "Eskimo" from their name, as this term is no longer
used to describe the Inuit of the Canadian Arctic. Jordin Tootoo, the
first Inuk to make it to the NHL, responded to this decision brilliantly:

> . . . My father's generation connects [with] this term to describe
> who they are. He would refer to himself as an Eskimo. My gen-
> eration refers to itself as Inuk. What is important to me is that
> people understand this. . . . So, this makes me ask the question,
> does the term Eskimo for the Edmonton franchise bring back
> feelings of oppression for the Inuk people? For me, it does not.
> That is not a reason to keep the name. There could be others for
> whom it does create those feelings. I encourage the franchise to
> explain why they chose the name Eskimos in the first place. Was
> it racially charged, or, was it because of admiration for the abil-
> ity of the Eskimos to thrive in cold climates, for their mental
> and physical toughness and for their resilience? My point is that
> context really does matter. . . .

As a Native person, and especially a Native sports fan, would you rather
see our people wearing team logos and names that have no connection
at all to Native culture and history? Not likely. One wise Elder from the
States asked me, "Will the general public remember us Native people
more if Native sports logos go away?" He shook his head and said,
"Images—art—remind people."

Think about the Indian Motorcycle name and logo. Are they racist or degrading? Heck, no! I have seen Native Vietnam combat vets and Elders trade in their beloved Harleys for an Indian motorcycle. Why would a Native biker who has ridden a Harley for twenty years or more switch to an Indian-brand motorcycle? I know why. It's so simple. It's because of the name and logo! I have even seen many First Nations bikers who have the Indian Motorcycle name and logo tattooed on their arm.

Native sports logos bring together people who would otherwise never talk. There is a brotherhood around sports and motorcycle logos. I have many times gone up and talked to strangers I see wearing Blackhawks or Redskins jerseys or caps. The sports name and logo connection goes a long way. If I see a person with a Habs jersey or one with a Native logo stuck on the side of the road, I'm stopping to help out my fellow sports fan (though maybe not if they're wearing a Leafs jersey—aye!).

I love that one of my council member's daughters, who is now going to hockey school, wears her Chicago Blackhawks cap proudly every day to the rink. It makes me think about one social media petition to get rid of the Blackhawks logo that quoted the American Psychological Association's call in 2005 for the "immediate retirement of all American Indian mascots, symbols, images and personalities by schools, colleges, universities, athletic teams and organizations" because of the "harmful effects of racial stereotyping and inaccurate racial portrayals, including the particularly harmful effects of American Indian sports mascots on the social identity development and self-esteem of American Indian young people." It seems to me that sometimes the more education you have, the further removed you are from the people who are the real-life Rez grassroots. The Rez kids I see wearing Native sports logos are not lacking in self-esteem.

I recently spoke with a representative from the Chicago Blackhawks, and that team has this statement on the logo controversy:

> The Chicago Blackhawks name and logo symbolizes an important and historic person, Black Hawk of Illinois' Sac & Fox Nation, whose leadership and life has inspired generations of Native Americans, veterans and the public. . . . We recognize there is a fine line between respect and disrespect, and we commend other teams for their willingness to engage in that conversation.
>
> Moving forward, we are committed to raising the bar even higher to expand awareness of Black Hawk and the important contributions of all Native American people . . .

I support the Chicago Blackhawks organization. They are on the right track toward real reconciliation and understanding because, as research has proven, following or playing a sport breaks down racism. I also agree with what the organization says about the spinoff economic, educational, and social benefits of Native sports logos: "The continued use of Native logos should be leveraged to create opportunity, create avenues of commerce and business, pathways for education and additionally create awareness of Native issues and concerns."

In my office, I proudly display a Washington Redskins helmet signed by Joe Theismann. On my Harley, I proudly have a Redskins logo. Yeah, I am a Redskin! Nothing racist or shameful about it.

The issue of Native names and Native logos being used in sports came up again in early 2020 when the Kansas City Chiefs won the Super Bowl. I love that team's name and logo. I love the chanting and the "tomahawk chop" that the fans do to encourage their team. Yes, some things are over the line, like wearing war paint or Chiefs' sacred feathered bonnets. I support those things being banned. At its highest level, football is about bravery and competition. There's no rougher, tougher team sport than football. Yeah, I wear a Chiefs cap. Why not? *I am a Chief!*

I cannot stress strongly enough the importance of sports to Native culture. One of my big regrets in life is that I didn't get a chance to play minor league hockey. My single mom was raising several kids on her own and couldn't afford to have us in hockey. We never got any good hockey equipment, only yard-sale tube skates that nobody else wanted. Sometimes we had to wear many socks to make the skates fit better. But we didn't complain. I was happy just to "lace 'em up."

I learned to skate on the local creeks and river. In the Okanagan, the outdoor frozen pond season is short. I would find a small frozen pond and stay out there by myself or with my two brothers until dark. We were isolated from just about everyone else. Our nearest reserve neighbours would be more than a kilometre away. The Okanagan River doesn't often freeze over, so there was no opportunity to learn the game of hockey the way most other young people do in Canada. I didn't get to skate in an arena until I was sixteen.

We played a lot of street hockey, though there were no paved streets, only our dirt backyard. We would make our own sticks by getting broken ones, hammering on a blade, and then bending the nails back so we wouldn't cut each other with accidental (or not-so-accidental) slashes. We'd make our own goalie nets out of scrap lumber, and we'd play until dark, when we'd have to quit because we couldn't see anymore. No street lights in those days.

I remember my mom often saying, "Go outside and play." She would kick us out of the house. For us, there was no sitting around watching TV for hours. We had the best playground in the world—the mountains and the river. We would run around in the mountains or play at the river all day, often racing home at night when the coyotes would howl and scare us.

Back then, people in Osoyoos had only a black-and-white TV with two channels to watch. On weekends, after a full day of playing out-side, we would watch football and hockey, and I became a real sports fan. I still religiously watch the Habs, Redskins, and Blue Jays play. As I mentioned before, sports are where I and many others started our leadership journey. Sports have been, and will always be, a big part of who I am.

I pitched in little league baseball and played most positions. My mom signed me up for it and I would pedal my bike to Oliver for the practices and games. I was also the leadoff hitter for whatever team I was on because I could always get on base—in part because I was a little guy with a small strike zone, and in part because I was a pretty good hitter.

Little league baseball was very competitive back then, and in those days very few Native kids played little league. I was the only Indian on my team and I became lifelong friends with many white kids. Again, sports breaks down race barriers. Later on, we played fastball and I pitched. We had two Native men's fastball teams on the Rez and one women's softball team. Osoyoos was the only Rez in the Okanagan territory to have two nice fastball diamonds side by side. The white teams in the area loved to play fastball on the Rez diamonds. I am grateful for the facilities previous Chiefs and councils and adminis-trations built with the money that came from a few land leases. Back then, we had a small population, but sports were a big part of our Rez culture. There were also two men's hockey teams.

A lot of that, unfortunately, has been lost now. Most of the Rez youth are not as active in sports as the older guys once were, mainly because of their obsession with electronic devices—like young people everywhere. There is no more men's hockey league in Oliver. In the 1980s there was a men's rec league and it was very competitive. In the 1990s, however, the league needed to attract new players as the old guard retired, so the organizers banned slapshots and watered down the league to the point that the competitiveness soon went downhill. Making things less competitive lowers the bar. Not keeping score and "playing just for fun" isn't actually fun for those with the competitive juices in their veins. There is an old Chinese saying: "In a system where no one fails, no one succeeds."

I disagree with anyone who says that, traditionally, Native people were not competitive. I don't know where that myth came from (again, not from any Natives who play sports), but I have heard some Natives use it as an excuse for why our people tend to be shy. History shows, however, that our people were highly competitive before the English and French showed up lost and hungry. No one can tell me horse- and canoe races weren't competitive. No one can tell me lacrosse wasn't competitive. And go to a stick game, bone game, or hand game and you'll see that the competitive emotions run very high. It was broken treaties, reserve land rip-offs, the residential/boarding schools, and corrupt Indian agents and churches that forced Natives to their knees and damaged our competitive spirit for many generations. Some of us are now getting our competitive spirit back again.

By the late 1990s there were virtually no Rez hockey or fastball teams on Osoyoos. No more fastball leagues, only slo-pitch, a game in which the catcher—such a key player in baseball and fastball—serves as little more than a janitor, picking up missed balls and sending them back to the pitcher. Still, it's good to see the ball diamonds being used at all by younger people. My mom's "Get outside and play" should be a rule everywhere. There is no doubt that on Osoyoos, like virtually everywhere else, sports are suffering as youth spend too much time indoors and too much time twiddling their thumbs and fingers on video games or cellphones. Electronic addictions are getting really bad among many youth today.

Another important part of Native sports back in my day was the lifelong friendships it created between competitive teams from different Rezes. Every month in the 1970s and '80s, there was a Native hockey, softball, or basketball tournament close by. Most Native youth on every Rez in our territory knew each other, either from playing or attending the Rez Hall dance that followed the tournaments. I made lifelong friends on every Rez in the Okanagan territory on both sides of the border through sports. Today most OIB youth can't name even one person their age on the other reservations/reserves. There are very few Native sports tournaments these days in the Okanagan Nation territory, and that's very sad. I give a big warrior shout-out to all those organizers of Rez sports who, against the odds, keep Native hockey, basketball, softball, or any other sport going.

Today I see too many youth walking or sitting around with their heads down, holding onto the "black rock"—their cellphone. They are, as one of my Elders put it, "the head-down generation." And I hear youth are bored or that something on Facebook has upset them and they've got nothing to do, and so they get high or drunk. Remember, there are many things to get high on—it doesn't have to be drugs or booze.

Years ago, I saw a few Rez kids on the Colville Indian Reservation in Washington State wearing T-shirts that said *Get high on sports not drugs*. That's one of the best quotes I have ever seen. Get high on sports! Go to the gym or go running and get a "runner's high." I love seeing my people jogging. Yeah! Get high on exercise. Get high on your language and culture (Indian up!). Get high on hanging around animals. Get high on reading. Get high on personal growth and life-long learning. Get high on working hard and buying nice things. Get high on owning a nice "iron horse" (car, truck, or motorcycle). Get high on hanging around hard-working, successful people. Get high on being around your family—especially the little ones. Get high on bringing your grandkids to the playground and watching their smiling faces. Get high on hanging around the old-timers and listening to their stories. Go get a "Harley high."

A "Harley high" is one of the best boosts out there. After work, or on weekends when the weather is nice, my "good medicine" and therapy is to start up one of my "iron horses" and get out on the road, crank up the tunes, and go for a motorcycle ride. Get some wind and look at the land. I've got plenty to keep me high, every day of every week of every year.

If my vehicle ever breaks down and I am stuck on the side of the road, I hope I have a Blackhawks, Redskins, Seminoles, Braves, Chiefs, or Warriors jersey to put on. Because I know that there are thousands of real sports fans out there who, once they spot a Native jersey, will not hesitate to pull over and help out a fellow sports fan.

Long live Native team names and logos!

CHAPTER 9

IT'S THE ECONOMIC HORSE THAT PULLS THE SOCIAL CART

"Native people will never rise out of poverty through dependence on government. We must re-build Tribal governments; develop a professional Tribal administrative structure with professional practices and procedures, clean lines of authority, responsibilities and reporting. Rigorous controls over Tribal finances were adopted. Definite personal policies and performance requirements were mandated."

—**Chief Phillip Martin, in Peter J. Ferrara's** *The Choctaw Revolution*

As a Chief, when it comes to the quality of life on your Rez, you only have two basic options: You can either become a Chief who is an administrator of poverty and underfunded government welfare programs, or you can become a Chief who creates revenue-generating jobs that make money for your First Nation. It's either a dependent (someone else feeds you) model or an independent (feed yourself) model. A "nation-to-nation" relationship with Canada or the United States based on poverty and dependency is a shameful model. I choose to get off my knees and back on my ancestral economic horse to create jobs and make money for my Rez!

My people have heard me say many times, "Life is as simple or as complicated as you make it." As a single, physically healthy adult you have three basic options: One, stay in school. Two, get a job. Now, if this is your situation and you're not in school or in a job, then obviously your life is messed up. The third option is to get some counselling. Maybe it's addictions counselling you need? If so, go get it. But I also believe employment counselling is some of the most important help a person can get.

A big *war-whoop* to past National Chief Ovide Mercredi, a Cree from Manitoba, who said, "It's the economic horse that pulls the social cart." History shows that, pre-contact, every tribal society was self-sufficient and had an economy based on the land and water and on inter-tribal trade. Our businesses were more dependent on currents than currency, as we used the rivers to provide food and travel and commerce. The first entrepreneurs in North America were the First Nations. Archeological evidence proves beyond any doubt that tribes did trade with one another, and often over great distances. Natives had existing trade routes thousands of years old.

Clearly, the First Nations were business people and had business networks well established long before the French and English invaded our lands. A few years ago in Osoyoos, a provincial park backhoe dug up one of my people's ancestral graves. The grave was more than fifteen hundred years old and in it were items that came from a place now called Oregon. More proof that my people had trade and commerce long before the Canadians and Americans planted their flags in Okanagan territory.

The original business relationship with the English and French, who were based in territories to the east, was built on the fur trade. The Hudson's Bay Company capitalized on the existing trade routes that had been well established by the various tribes. The company also hired many Native people to guide them over these routes. Many Iroquois came west with the Hudson's Bay Company, working as guides and labourers. My great-grandfather Manuel Louie had a picture of his dad, who he said came from back east and was an Iroquois. So I have eastern tribal roots, too.

The federal colonial government continued the business relationship through many pre- and post-Confederation treaties. The original treaty relationship, therefore, was a *business* relationship—not a *dependency* relationship, which is what such relationships would become. British common law and French civil law both say that treaties are made between nations. Perhaps that was the original concept behind the treaties signed in North America, but as the settler population grew and spread across the continent, the Native business relationship became less important and the takeover of Indian lands became the main quest of the governments. Imperialism ruled the day. The colonization formula was applied in North America, Australia, New Zealand, Africa, and India—in most of the world, for that matter. First a business/trade relationship with the Indigenous people, then a dependency relationship, then assimilation or termination—all rationalized by the Christianization of whatever Native people happened to be there when the Europeans arrived.

White religion, Catholicism and Protestantism, was used as an oppressive force against Indigenous people. In order to control and break down any Indigenous people, the colonizer must first take away the ability of those people to support themselves. You can't colonize a people who are economically independent. Killing off the buffalo was economic and cultural warfare. Natives were kicked off their economic horse, and I am telling all Indigenous people that we must get back on. We must support ourselves, not forever be "hang-around-the-fort Indians"!

The Canadian and U.S. federal governments imposed a sense of Native dependency in an attempt to solve their "Indian Problem."

This led to a cycle of poverty and welfare that still exists on most reserves/reservations and to a mentality of dependency that is firmly imbedded in the psyche of many Natives. A Chief from many years ago told me, "The worst thing Indian Affairs ever brought to our community was welfare." In Alberta a few years ago, at an Indian Affairs social service conference, I heard the term "Freedom 18" for the first time. I asked an Indian Affairs social development worker what that was, and he told me that today's youth on the reserves are using that term. It means that when they turn eighteen they are entitled, under government policy, to get a welfare cheque of their own.

I couldn't believe it.

The concept of "Freedom 18" shows just how desperate and un-ashamed some Native youth have become. I got pissed at Indian Affairs for allowing this to happen, but also at the Native leadership for not standing up against such a discouraging welfare-dependent mentality. Many Elders have told me it was once considered shameful to have to resort to welfare. I have heard older people say, "You got two hands, two feet and a heartbeat." In other words, *Get your ass to work!* Yes, welfare is important and helpful for single mothers or for those who need financial help after being laid off from their job, but only as a bridge to getting back to another job. Welfare should never, ever be a goal in itself!

The federal, provincial, and state governments caused our degraded state of poverty. But now it's up to us to get back on our economic horse. Leadership must focus on rebuilding our economies. Independence, through economic development, is real leadership work. Staying dependent is for phony politicians and hang-around-the-fort Indians. True independence, true sovereignty will only happen if our First Nations begin to make their own money and create good-paying jobs on the Rez that will attract and keep the community's hardest workers and brightest people.

I have met many Natives who have told me they only came back to their Rez when there were job opportunities. A sad Rez statistic is that, in most communities, half the membership now lives off the reserve. I realize that some of our people grew up elsewhere, and that some are off-Rez because of the Sixties Scoop or because of housing shortages on the Rez, but the main reason so many live off-Rez is the lack of on-Rez jobs. Hard-working, educated people always go to where the good-paying jobs are. Educated people—those with degrees or trades—will not stand in a welfare line with their hand held out.

James Bay Cree Grand Chief Billy Diamond, one of my great heroes, once wrote, "Economic development is the key to extending Native rights. Eighty per cent of revenues leave the community. Our aim is to keep the money in the villages, to build an economic base. You can have all the constitutional conferences about self-government that you want, but unless you have economic self-sufficiency it doesn't matter." I was so proud to see that the James Bay Cree have established their own airline, Air Creebec. In some cases the Indian economic horse can actually fly!

Everyone on the Rez says our future leaders are the youth. Everyone says our number-one asset is our people. Everyone says education is a priority. Nice words—but without economic development there will be no jobs for your educated people. Without land leases and profitable businesses, who's going to pay the tuition and living expenses for your youth as they seek that higher education or training? Education is not free. It's a myth that Natives get a free education.

At Osoyoos, we contribute hundreds of thousands of dollars of land-lease revenue toward education. I wish those on the Rez who vote against land leasing and business development had the backbone to sit in front of our future leaders, the youth who will need this funding to go to college and university, and tell them No! It is a Rez's Chief and council who have to make tough decisions on where the money is going to come from to pay for all the community's priorities. When Elders need a walk-in shower, or a ramp built because their legs are giving out, where is the money going to come from? Good words are like wooden nickels. They don't pay for education or immediate health needs.

I remind First Nations that if you claim to support education, then you'd better also support economic development. Teachers' wages and student costs are not paid by bingos. Fundraising at your community hall has its good points—brings people together for a worthy cause—and it's good to see people dig into their own wallets to ante up. But a responsible First Nation government does what non-Native governments do, and that is to create a sustainable economy that will fund essential services like schools, infrastructure, and education.

Even the preservation of language and culture costs money. Our salmon ceremony feast at Osoyoos costs $25,000 to put on each year. Those Native groups that put on winter dance ceremonies and summer powwows must raise thousands of dollars in food and gifts. Sweat houses cost thousands of dollars to maintain each year. That money must come from somewhere. Our communities should not be solely dependent on grants and fundraising for their needs.

In today's world, if you want to call yourself sovereign, you had better be economically and financially strong. And you'd better have the bank account savings to prove it. Operating from year to year on grants is *not* being sovereign or independent. Tribes have been hanging around the funding trough for far too long. I was taught by the hard-working old-timers that there is no such thing as a free lunch. Indians gotta stop looking for that free lunch!

One of the Osoyoos Elders told me years ago that the most important word in our language is "scalow," which means money. Yes, even culture and religion cost money. In church, they still pass around the collection plate. You can always pray for money to somehow fall out of the sky, but it takes real earned bucks to build and maintain those churches. Native religion and spirituality also cost money— even if we don't go around building cathedrals. Even if it's traditional food—moose meat and fish—someone behind the scenes will have paid for that food. Bullets, rifles, fishing gear, gas, pickups . . . they all cost someone money. Language programs are important, but they also aren't free. Language teachers need to be paid properly.

It has only been within my lifetime that some First Nations have invested time, money, and effort into starting their own band or tribal businesses. Osoyoos Indian Band's first company was a vineyard back in 1968. Not very many bands had their own companies back in the 1960s. The Osoyoos Bands first land lease, for the golf course, was signed back in 1963. Today, on a per capita basis, Osoyoos ranks at the very top of First Nations with band-owned companies. Our biggest source of revenue comes from band-owned land leases, but this is far from our only source of income, as this list shows:

OIB Leases

- Arterra winery (Jackson-Triggs), Canada's biggest western winery lease—since 1980. Our most important business partnership
- residential (trailer park/single-family housing units)
- 1,100 acres of premium wine vineyards
- Area 27 (one-of-a-kind high-end racetrack)
- provincial prison
- Sonora Dunes Golf Course
- Spirit Ridge (four-star resort, 230 rooms)
- Tim Hortons/gas station
- District Wine village

OIB Businesses:

- 300-acre vineyard
- two gas stations/convenience stores
- Nk'mip Cellars winery (joint venture—Arterra Wines)
- cement/sand/gravel
- golf course
- campground R.V. park
- cultural centre
- utilities (sewage/water)
- forestry
- day care
- cannabis stores (two—joint venture)

I also want to give a shout-out to some other bands/tribes in Indian Country that are getting back on their economic horse. I am so damn proud of my Rezskin relatives who are competing in the real business world. They are raising the bar higher and higher. Today not only are First Nations doing multimillion-dollar projects, but some are doing *billion*-dollar deals! I love it when I hear the Vancouver-area First Nations are doing important development deals with big-time sports owners like Aquilini Development (the owners of the Vancouver Canucks). Or when I'm watching a ballgame and I see the Pequot Tribal Nation's "Foxwoods Casino" sign behind home plate at Boston's Fenway Park. To me, that's a big "wow"! I was watching a Phoenix Coyotes hockey game last year and I happily noted that their home rink is now called Gila River Arena, after the Gila River Indian Community. That's a first. Being able to afford an advertising sign in a pro-sports venue is for top-notch companies, but to be able to afford the naming rights to a whole arena, you gotta be doing really big business!

Yeah, some of our communities are climbing the corporate ladder and "running with the big dogs." Some of what we have accomplished in Osoyoos was inspired by the awesome business deals that other First Nations (on both sides of the border) have pulled off. I heard about their achievements and we followed their path. Membertou is a Mi'kmaq community near Sydney, Nova Scotia, that has one of the best trade and convention centres and best hockey rinks on any Rez. Whitecap Dakota is a Rez near Saskatoon, Saskatchewan, and has one of the best-ranked golf courses in Canada. Kamloops Indian Band, near Kamloops, B.C., has the biggest industrial park on any Rez, with more than four hundred leases so far. Westbank First Nation, near Kelowna, B.C., has every business chain one can think of, and also over four hundred leases. Over ten thousand non-Natives lease residential land on Westbank and have built thousands of houses. The Seminole Tribe of Florida is a billion-dollar tribe that owns the Hard Rock Café restaurant chain. Enoch Cree Nation Rez borders the city of Edmonton, Alberta, and has one of the best hotel/casinos in Canada. Tsuut'ina Nation, near Calgary, Alberta, has one of the best golf courses and housing developments (Redwood Meadows), plus a hotel and casino, and they recently attracted Costco to build on their Rez. Squamish Nation Rez, which borders Vancouver, has many leases, including Park Royal Mall, and recently announced a billion-dollar housing development. Tsleil-Waututh Nation, also located near Vancouver, has a joint-venture $200 million condo project. Tsawwassen First Nation, near Vancouver, settled a modern-day treaty a decade ago and has a billion-dollar mall development happening. As well, their treaty lands have attracted Amazon to build a distribution centre, which alone created seven hundred jobs. And the Colville Tribe in Washington State, part of my tribal nation, has economic development in everything from forestry to gaming, doing an annual business in excess of US$200 million.

In every province or state there are a handful of reserves or reservations whose leadership is pro-business and who share my guiding philosophy: "the future is now." They are creating hundreds of jobs and making millions of dollars and becoming part of the economy of their traditional territory. No more "hanging around the fort" waiting for government rations. No more waiting on the fiduciary (federal government) to fulfill one hundred years of broken promises. No more believing in the Queen (Mother) or the Great White Father. Today it's Indian leadership's responsibility to "Indian up!"

In 2003, I was chosen, along with a few others, by the U.S. State Department to go on a two-week tour of American Indian tribes. On that tour we stopped by some of the bigger tribal-owned casinos in Indian Country, including Foxwoods, owned by the Mashantucket Pequot Tribal Nation, whose lands lie between Boston and New York. We also visited some of the tribes near Phoenix, Arizona. On that tour I heard the Rez phrases "BC" and "AC." Now, I know that, back then, state governments were having issues with tribes exercising their rights to open up casinos on reservation lands. At the time, most states had laws prohibiting casinos. But in Canada and the United States, the Rez is under *federal*, not provincial or state, jurisdiction. Many U.S. tribes saw a business opportunity, which they seized, and today Indian gaming is big business in the United States. Tribal leaders told me "BC" means "before casino" and "AC" means "after casino." Before casino we were very poor, and now, after casino, we who have those establishments can fund all our programs and services properly, and we can pave our roads and have modern community buildings and send our students to the best colleges and universities.

All successful bands and tribes have one thing in common: None of them let Indian Affairs run the Rez. Casinos have contributed a lot to the ability of tribes and bands to push back in this way. Casino jobs and revenue have made many tribes self-sufficient. To me, BC and AC is like "before Columbus" and "after Columbus," but in reverse! Before Columbus, tribes were self-sufficient and had their own economy. After Columbus and colonization, tribes were economically and socially enslaved. Many tribes, through casino developments, have been able to get back on their economic horse, and many states and cities close to Indian gaming sites have also felt the economic spinoff benefits of Indian casinos. In Canada, many First Nations have followed the gaming path of the U.S. tribes.

I need to mention the most important "Rez lesson" I learned from that trip. No matter how wealthy bands and tribes become, they must not behave like corporate Canada or corporate America. It's good to see monetary wealth in our communities, yes, but it's not good to see spoiled, nose-up-in-the-air, privileged "high-society Indians." Sadly, on our tour, the rich tribes we visited had layers of staff around their council, and seldom did their Chief (or president, or chairperson, or even an elected leader) make time for us.

We were hosted "just okay" by those rich tribes. Tribal hired staff took my group to their fancy hotels, and the food was okay. I never care much about the hotel or food (remember, I'm an Indian biker and a Rez boy at heart), but I wanted to meet and talk to Rez leadership, not staff who weren't even from that Rez, people with no blood connection to the land or the people. On our visits to poor tribes, I noticed right away they still practised "Rez hospitality." Those poor tribes gave us the best they had and, most important, their leadership gave us a bit of their time. That's the Rez way—you give some of your time and you host "visit'ers" (guests) properly. The poor Indian communities made sure their Chief and council (or chairperson or president) were there to greet us and eat with us. The very best meal I remember having was in an old, rundown building, while sitting on torn chairs. We ate on paper plates, and for drinks they passed out pop cans. The leadership, not staff, sat at the table with us and hosted us to the best lunch—nothing fancy. I don't look for fancy. I look for good ol' Rez First Nation hospitality— the old way! I was disappointed in some of those rich tribes, as they had gotten too fat-cat corporate America.

I returned from that experience and vowed that the Osoyoos Indian Band Development Corporation would never become too "corporate Canada." We will never forget Rez hospitality and we will always make time to meet and share our stories with our Rez relatives who come to visit the Osoyoos Rez!

Once the governments took away the economic ability for tribes to support themselves, the funded-mentality disease began. In the early reserve/reservation era, all tribal organizations had to depend on government funding to survive. They survived by hanging on to the Great White Mother's apron. There is a huge difference in discipline between getting a paycheque as a government employee and getting a paycheque from the sale of your product or service in the real business world. A former Chief from the Yukon told me that when he worked for his band, and later for Tribal Council, no one he worked with cared where their pay was coming from. They all knew it was grant money. People could show up late for work, leave early, and take long breaks because grant money was treated like play money—there was no accountability for how this money was being spent. Then the funding got cut back. The man who told me this story left Native politics and started his own restaurant, and he gained a new respect for money. "I picked dimes and quarters off the floor because I paid attention to all revenue and expenses," he told me. "When I worked in tribal government, we only paid attention to who would write the next grant application and BS the yearly government report."

I constantly remind Natives that we have to move from *spending* grant money to *making* our own money. That's a mindset shift! We need more business minds in Indian Country—not more grant-dependent bureaucrats. We need more staff on the business side of the scale, not more social services staff. Look at the dependency model: most staff are collecting a paycheque from federal or provincial grants. Look at tribes that are becoming independent: most of their staff paycheques come from the real business world. Those First Nations that are poverty stricken will have more staff on the social service side (spending money) than on the business side (making money). Bands need to keep a simple scorecard detailing where most of the tribe's income and jobs come from.

It's true that it's the economic horse that pulls the social cart. I'm not saying those social service jobs aren't important. I'm not saying those federal transfer dollars are not owed to us. Yes, education, health care, drug addiction programs, all those band and tribal office jobs, are an important part of every Rez, but they should not make up the majority of the jobs on the Rez. Not everyone can or should be working for the band's or tribe's government arm. The other arm— the economic development arm—should be the stronger arm, not the weaker. Off the Rez, in every stable town or city, the strongest arm is a healthy economic arm. Therefore, the economic/business part of the Rez should be the main provider of the income and infrastructure that supports the social service side.

In the book *Descendants of Warriors* by Kamao Cappo, there is a section I very much agree with, which reads:

There has been talk about our people first needing nurturing and healing before we can properly address our economic

development issues . . . one would need to imagine 200 years
ago and a young man with a family sitting in the teepee and
he refuses to go out and hunt buffalo with the other men
because he feels he needs nurturing or healing first. The point
is self-explanatory, in that the men would have to fulfill their
function of going out and providing for the family and only
later in their free time would they seek out an Elder for guidance or they would attend a ceremony to assist themselves.

If someone can't hold a job because they need "healing and wellness,"
then they should quit lazing around doing nothing but drinking,
playing video games, drugging, and sleeping until noon and go get
some healing and wellness. The treatment centres and professional
counsellors are waiting for them! And those who seek treatment
should know that a job opportunity will be waiting for them. Even for
those in jail, a top priority of their release plan should be for them to
get a job. There is no shame in going to a treatment centre or going to
a counsellor. Whether it's for substance abuse or depression or whatever else might be holding you back from getting and keeping a job. I
have seen many of my people get their lives back on the working road
after treatment or counselling.

Many years ago, I read an excellent article by Don Marks in a Native
newspaper, where he wrote, "Social work serves a good purpose, so
does counseling, crises intervention workshops, adult up-grading,
anti-alcohol and drug abuse programs and cultural programs. We are
surrounded by these programs in Aboriginal country—so they must
be good. My question is why is there so much emphasis placed on
social development? Necessary as it all might be, where is the economic development? Business development that would create wealth
and employment without any government funding?"

This is so clear to me. Anyone who focuses on healing must also focus on employment and on creating jobs. A good-paying job is one of the best healing programs. Those hard workers need opportunities now that can bring the Rez much-needed jobs and income. It's misguided to take the dependency approach and say "no economic development until the minority are ready for it." This is chicken-and-egg thinking. What comes first—a real job or healing? The fact is that a good-paying job *is* healing. A job is a big part of a healthy person's lifestyle. Take your paycheque away for even a month or a few weeks and see how healthy and well you are mentally, emotionally, physically, and even spiritually. Yeah, most people would be praying hard to get their paycheque back!

It sometimes takes years to get a lease or business off the drawing board. And once it's up and running, it takes more years to get that enterprise into a profitable situation. It's just wrong-headed thinking to say that First Nations have to wait until we have worked through all our social problems before we can achieve economic success. Sometimes a business opportunity comes around only once, and if you fail to seize the opportunity, it's lost forever. Often a developer who approaches a Rez will go somewhere else if the Chief and council are not business ready. We need to change our thinking and be ready! As Noel Pearson (an Australian Aboriginal leader) wrote in *Our Right to Take Responsibility*, "If we are to survive as a people we have to get passive welfare out of Aboriginal governance. We must get rid of the path of welfare mentality that has taken over our people. We have a right to build a real economy. We have a right to demand of government that we have access to resources from a real economy."

I'm a big believer in youth summer jobs. Rez leadership must provide summer student jobs with opportunities for real-life learning. Leadership should reflect on when and where they first learned to hold a job. When and where did they get their first paycheque? A wise prairie Chief once said, "The first cheque our youth receive should be a paycheque, not a welfare cheque!" Most of my people got their first job around age twelve or thirteen. Every OIB youth was expected to be in a summer job. For youth, summertime should be get-a-job time. Student summer jobs develop real leaders, and it surely follows that youth unemployment does real harm to the development of a work ethic. Summer jobs are where our future leaders learn to earn paycheques, learn customer service skills, learn to respect authority, learn to show up on time, and learn business manners.

Kelly Lindsey, a Métis who is president and chief executive officer of the Canadian non-governmental organization Indigenous Works, believes, "Every Aboriginal person should have a dream job." In Osoyoos, we hope that's true for our youth. In some of our companies, there are dress codes and youth must learn to dress for business, whether they are working summers on the golf course, at the hotel, or in a store. Dressing for success means no hoodies or baggy pants or T-shirts with dumb shit written across the chest. We try to encourage them to have pride in whatever job they might be doing.

If your Rez doesn't have businesses or leases, where will your youth learn to earn a paycheque and have pride in holding down a real job? There must be more opportunity for our young people than working in the band office or mowing grass or picking up garbage. I love seeing our youth work in tourism operations or in businesses where they learn at a young age to work hard and interact with customers from all over the world. As youth back in the 1970s, we had to work hard, show up on time, and listen to our bosses. It is said that a summer job experience can last a career, and we believe in that profoundly. First jobs often create the person.

There are some good government-funded employment programs in

Canada. I admire the Okanagan Training and Development Council, which gets funding from Employment and Social Development Canada and sets aside a component for Native employment and training in the millions of dollars. The Indigenous Skills and Employment Training Program is one of the best government funding programs for Natives, because it focuses on one of the most important facets of life—jobs!

But I also want to give a shout-out to all the Native organizations in every province and state that help Indigenous entrepreneurs develop and grow. Native economic development organizations have only been around since the 1980s, as Native North Americans were left out of the continent's economy for centuries. I'm so proud of all of these organizations and will list just a few essential Canadians ones here:

- Aboriginal Financial Institutions (AFIs), which provide loans and business financing to First Nations, Métis, and Inuit entrepreneurs. There are fifty-nine AFIs across Canada. All Nations Trust, founded in 1981, serves my region, and Native business leaders such as Dawn Madahbee Leach and Ruth Williams have championed Native business start-ups.
- CANDO (Council for the Advancement of Native Development Officers), founded in 1990 to provide much-needed programs and services to community economic development officers.
- AFOA Canada, founded in 1999 to help Native people better manage and govern their communities with a focus on financial management.
- Indian Taxation Advisory Board, founded in 1989 to regulate and make recommendations to the federal government regarding the approval of on-reserve tax bylaws under section 83 of the Indian Act. Chief Manny Jules of Kamloops

has been the leader of this initiative that has brought millions
of dollars into many First Nations communities.

- Indigenous Tourism BC, formed in 1998 to advocate and grow
  tourism opportunities for Native people in British Columbia.
  Brenda Baptiste, a member of the Osoyoos Band, has led this
  important organization for the past sixteen years.

I also have to give Indigenous Services Canada (ISC) and Crown-Indigenous Relations and Northern Affairs Canada (CIRNAC) credit where it is due. All Canadian Chiefs have a love-hate relationship with the federal branch of government that deals with Rez land—it's like a bad marriage we can't get out of. But every now and then some of those billions of dollars that the federal department receives each year to improve the lives of its clients on the reserves actually do hit the Rez level and leave a positive impact. I have been telling countless ministers over the years that only more investment in economic development programs can change the hundred-year "F" report card that the department continues to get from us year after year after year.

At Osoyoos, most of our economic development businesses and projects would not have been possible without the much-needed seed money from the few—I'm tempted to say "rare"—Indigenous Services Canada and CIRNA economic development programs. Our Spirit Ridge resort—which is one of the biggest and most diverse resorts in Canada and includes a campground, RV park, golf course, cultural centre, the Spirit Ridge hotel and conference centre, and the award-winning Nk'mip Cellars winery—would not have been built without the millions of dollars in federal government economic infrastructure funding our Rez received. Then-Minister of Indian Affairs Robert Nault and Senator Ross Fitzpatrick joined me for the official sod-turning in 2002. Further, our business park, *Senkulmen*

(Okanagan for "a place to work and play")—a forty-five-hectare industrial/commercial site—was likewise dependent on Indian Affairs economic development funding. I want to thank former senator Gerry St. Germain for helping us secure the necessary economic funding for that development. Those two projects in which Indian Affairs and Indigenous and Northern Affairs (INAC) invested on the Osoyoos reserve have produced more than $200 million in capital value and created more than five hundred jobs.

The Osoyoos story is but one example of how an investment in economic development can not only provide a greater financial return to all levels of government but also reduce the social ills of poverty on the Rez, setting the foundation for real economic recon- ciliation and a more equal and fair nation-to-nation relationship. Hundreds of non-Natives come to work on the Osoyoos reserve every day. Some have bought homes on leased OIB property and are raising their kids on the reserve. They even send their children to our daycare and grade school.

I tease some of the non-Natives I grew up with who now work on Osoyoos Rez: "I bet you never thought you would be earning a living, getting a paycheque, feeding yourself and family from a job on the Osoyoos Rez!" They always smile and shake their head. No, they never imagined such a thing—but it happened and it's happening. Natives and non-Natives working side by side in full-time, well-pay- ing jobs. To me, that's the true nation-to-nation relationship! That's the original treaty relationship. No dependency. No unemployment. No welfare. Our unemployment rates are your unemployment rates and vice versa. Our standard of living is your standard of living. Our housing looks like your housing. Our community facilities look just as good as your community facilities. That is my vision for a nation- to-nation relationship.

Sometimes, living and working side by side, we can get on each other's nerves. There's no denying that. If someone says some dumb shit in a business relationship, you can usually work through it, but there are those times when you can't help but say, as Six Nations former NHLer Stan Jonathan used to, "*Ya wanna go?*"—and it nearly ends up outside. But then it blows over and we all get back to work and get the job done. Work hard and play hard! That's a true nation-to-nation relationship. That's what the old treaties represented.

Getting back on our economic horse also means reclaiming governing jurisdiction within our Rez lands, and kicking the province and state out. In Canada, the province used to tax Indian reserve leased land. Every time we did a business lease the greedy province would send a tax assessor onto our Rez and would tax the non-Native business and yet provide no services—even though Rez land is deemed federal land. I want to give a big shout-out to Chief Manny Jules of the Kamloops Indian Band, who, when elected Chief back in 1985, led the very first Native amendment to the federal Indian Act, which was later called the "Kamloops Amendment." This important amendment put an end to the provincial taxation of reserve leased land. Finally!

Taxation income is very important for legitimate governments all over the world because governance costs a lot of money. Yet among some Rez Indians the word "taxation" is taken as a call to arms. We had a big internal fight at Osoyoos in 1994 when we passed our taxation bylaw, which had nothing to do with taxing band members or their land. Some of the "Rez liars" tried to stir up fear by saying a taxation bylaw included taxing members, which it did not. It only had to do with collecting taxes for non-Native use of Rez lands.

Since 1991, those First Nations with taxation bylaws (110 communities and counting) have collected from non-Native use of Rez land over $1 billion in taxes. At Osoyoos, because of our land leases and gas and power line right of ways, such taxation is our second-largest source of income, and it pays for essential resources like playgrounds, roads, and community buildings. The Kamloops Amendment proves that one change to jurisdiction can have a huge financial impact. It did not take ninety-four "calls to action"—which is what the Truth and Reconciliation Commission has called for. All it took was one business-minded Chief and some common sense. The Osoyoos Indian Band, and all the other First Nations now collecting taxes off their Rez leases, should be forever grateful to Chief Manny Jules!

I have been saying the same things for years:

- People can't protect their culture when they're on welfare.
- The band does not owe its membership dependency. It owes them opportunity and a chance to become independent.
- Real warriors hold a job.
- Visioning, dreaming, and ideas are free, but reality costs money.
- Native people have always worked for a living.
- I have been on the poorest Native communities and the wealthiest, and though I have seen Native pride in poverty, I choose Native pride and profit.

The bottom line is, I want us to get back on our Indian "economic horse"—to create jobs, real career-oriented jobs, and make our own money instead of waiting around for the next grant. In this way, we can afford to pay for everything we say we care about and pull our own social cart (*mic drop*)!

CHAPTER 10

"IT'S THE ECONOMY, STUPID"

"As long as we do not control our own purse strings, those that
do will control our destiny—in the final analysis the only real
solution is the economy, stupid."

—Calvin Helin, *Dances with Dependency*

A few years ago on CNN, a reporter asked a U.S. leader, "What's the
biggest problem facing every inner city in the United States?" The
answer he gave was, "Young unemployed Black men." Right away I
thought, *That is so true,* but in relation to my own people. The biggest problem Canada as a nation must own up to is unemployed
Native youth—which is also Canada's youngest and fastest-growing
population.

The federal government has concentrated resources (more than
$8 billion a year) and energies toward providing social programs to
rebuild First Nations. But the fact is that without an economic base
from which to operate, First Nations will never be in control of their
future. Most First Nations have cash-flow problems, and one in five
are in financial difficulty, mainly due to their leadership's inability to
manage community cash. That's reality.

Most Native organizations have become dependent on government programs and grants. Many are satisfied to live with the illusion
that a "grant economy" will sustain their community and their future
generations. Such foolish thinking! First Nations leadership needs

business and financial training. They need an understanding of professional bankable business plans, budgets, cost analysis, break-even analysis, debt-equity ratios, cash-flow projections, rate of return on investment, etc.

Cash-flow statements are an excellent tool to help you stay in control of the day-to-day and longer-term finances of your operations. All band/business operations need to establish indicators and targets. Know your numbers and watch them, as that is where most of the truth is. There is a saying in business: "What gets measured gets done." But how many of our Chiefs and council members and Native managers know how to carry out any of these necessary business practices? Spending money and making money are two totally different things, with two totally different skill sets.

How much money a company spends and where it is spent is very important. The sad fact is some council members and managers do not want their business numbers (which serve as the company's report card) shared with the community members. That's wrong, as it is the community members who are the real shareholders and who have a right to know exactly how their company is doing every year.

I once heard an Okanagan Chief say, "Economic development is easy—it's the easy road." What a bunch of BS. If it's so easy, then why don't communities with high unemployment and a high welfare load just create businesses and jobs and income for their people? There is a big skills difference between, on the one hand, waiting for government grants to come in, and on the other hand, getting a bank business loan, producing a product or bringing a service to the market place, and competing against other companies in the real business world. Real business hours are not the easy Monday-to-Friday grade-school work hours. Real business does not take just forty hours per week. It involves working evenings and weekends and doing extra shifts. For jobs in tourism, like many on the Rez, there is no such thing as summer holidays, as summers are when tourism businesses make their money.

It's the Rez leadership that either establishes a safe, secure business climate that attracts business or allows civil wars to rule the Rez. These petty little wars provide an unsafe, highly dysfunctional and politically unstable Rez environment that scares away investment and projects. As Russell Means wrote in his book *Where White Men Fear to Tread*, "Few things are less attractive to investors than political instability . . . business disasters happen all the time on Indian reservations because there is little political continuity. Council members generally care about nothing but keeping their jobs, collecting a paycheque, and spending government funds."

There is a hard-and-fast business rule that says, "Money and business will only go where it is safe." Leadership must always act mature, especially when guests are around. But a mob mentality, thug attitude, and threatening tones can still be experienced around most Rez council tables and community meetings. Come on! The sixties and seventies are over! It's time for us to grow up and conduct ourselves in a professional manner at all times.

In 2005, I was invited to Ottawa to appear before the Standing Senate Committee on Aboriginal Peoples, where I presented a document titled "The Solution to Aboriginal Poverty," which underlined certain basic facts of First Nations in Canada at the time. We had:

- the highest unemployment rates,
- the highest dropout rates,
- the highest incarceration rates,
- the highest child welfare rates,
- the highest drug-alcoholism rates,

- the worst health problems, and
- the highest levels of substandard housing due to poverty.

I told the committee, "The federal government's past one hundred years of neglect on Aboriginal economic development is the biggest problem when it comes to 'Aboriginal poverty.'"

Why is Indian Affairs still practising the old beads-and-blankets trick? Welfare is still Indian Affairs' biggest budget. This is racist and oppressive, and whenever governments fall back on such phrases as "wards of the state" when talking about programs and services for First Nations, it suggests total colonial dependency.

People, please . . . it's 2021!

The more-than-a-century-old welfare/dependency formula is still being used against our people. In 2017, welfare spending on Canadian First Nations reserves increased by over $100 million, yet spending on Indigenous economic development programs has stayed the same over the last three years. In Canada, federal spending on Indigenous programs has reached $8.5 billion, yet economic development funding makes up less than 5 per cent of the budget.

Do the kindergarten math—that's the *wrong formula*, people.

Further stupidity is that economic development funding is called "discretionary" spending by Indian Affairs, whereas the welfare budget is called "non-discretionary" spending. Does that mean that, according to the federal government policies, Indians are entitled to welfare but not to an economy? The federal government continues to provide funding for every First Nation to hire a full-time social worker and a drug and alcohol counsellor but not a full-time economic development officer. What kind of "nation-to-nation" thinking is that? Obviously, it's colonial "independent-to-dependent nation" thinking. What G8 nation calls its economy "discretionary"?

What kind of independent nation has welfare as the biggest part of its budget?

Middle-class Canada and America should try living on a welfare cheque and providing for their families. It's easy to connect the dots. The higher your community's level of unemployment, the higher its rate of diabetes is going to be. Unemployment, which equates to poverty, negatively affects your health and the health and education of your kids. Many years ago a health report published by Canadian nurses concluded, "The #1 indicator of good health is personal income." Go figure! Is it really true that the more personal income you have, the better food you can afford? The more personal income you have, the better housing you can afford? The higher paycheque you have, the better lifestyle and educational opportunities you can provide for your kids? Of course!

Next to my Rez, there are two small towns, Oliver and Osoyoos, with a combined population of around ten thousand. Over the last decade, both towns have faced a possible shutdown of their elementary schools. Of course, there was a public uproar over this possibility and the councils petitioned the provincial government not to close down the schools. Education costs money. Public schools are one of the biggest costs for any government. When school enrolment drops, what is the major reason? It should be obvious. Working families move to where the jobs are. If a town or city loses a major employer, if factories shut down, then schools and hospitals are affected. Eventually, you have a ghost town.

All the bleeding hearts come out when there is talk of closing down an elementary or high school, yet few people connect the dots. If you want your schools and hospitals to continue to provide the same level of service, then that community needs more jobs and more economic development to bring in families and maintain or increase the population tax base.

That's why at election time I often say, "It's the economy, stupid."

Non-Natives won't stand for double-digit unemployment. If the unemployment rate is in the double digits, then that prime minister, president, premier, governor, senator, member of Parliament, mayor, or councillor is voted out. White people at election time won't put up with leaders who don't focus on the economy and create jobs. The same "jobs and economy" election scorecard should also be applied all across Indian Country. In Canada, who is it that sits next to the prime minister or premier and holds the second-highest position among the cabinet? It's the minister of finance, because in any modern government, "It's the economy, stupid." That's any independent nation's main concern: the economy! It's the money from the economy that pays for public health, schools, police, military, infrastructure, and everything else.

Today on most reserves and reservations, unemployment exceeds that of the Great Depression. At the height of that global economic crisis, in 1933, the unemployment rate in the United States peaked at 24.9 per cent. In Canada that same year, up to 30 per cent of the labour force could find no work. I have been on many reserves and reservations where the unemployment rate in recent years has exceeded 60 per cent. For most First Nations, then, it is fair to say that they have been under a Great Depression for more than a hundred years. Yet Indian Affairs sticks with the same old welfare-mentality funding formula that has caused an endless cycle of unemployment and welfare. Anyone with common sense would know that's "ass-backwards." Robert Nault, a former Indian Affairs minister, said that all of Canada needs to understand that "there can be no social justice without economic justice." I couldn't agree more.

The late Jim Prentice—an insightful minister of Indian Affairs when he served in the federal cabinet of Prime Minister Stephen

Harper—said back in 2007, "We need to make a clear commitment to economic development as the key to ending poverty and ending dependency. We have to shift focus away from social programming to economic development. When you travel around this country to First Nation communities that are totally dependent on government transfers, you find poverty." Jim Prentice recognized that "It's the economy, stupid." He knew that the obvious way forward is to shift away from social programming to economic development. There has to be an end to the vicious cycle of First Nations poverty. To me, Jim Prentice's statement stands as one of the smartest observations a high-ranking Indian Affairs cabinet minister ever made. Smart words that, sadly, have not been acted upon.

All past National Chiefs have stated that economic development must be a priority. Chief George Manuel believed, "Without an economic base our communities will never be able to be in control of our future." Chief Mathew Coon Come vowed, "Economic development will be my first priority." Chief Phil Fontaine said, "Government and resource companies should pay royalties into an Aboriginal Economic Development fund." Unfortunately, Indian Affairs has yet to make economic independence for First Nations a priority.

For First Nations, negotiating impact benefit agreements with mining, oil and gas, forestry, or pipeline development companies is extremely important. Often First Nations have only one chance at it. For some communities, it is their only chance to bring in much-needed jobs and revenue. Of course, there are times when a natural resource development should be opposed for environmental or cultural reasons. Buying into such agreements or turning down such agreements requires a great deal of thought and decision-making.

The Harvard Project on American Indian Economic Development has done some of the very best research on why some tribes are successful and others are not. They found that it's those tribes and bands that are generating their own source revenue and creating an economic climate on the Rez that are breaking away from federal government dependency. Native leadership at the national, provincial, and state level needs to have an inter-tribal business focus. What comes first—economic or political power? Ask those tribal leaders who now have some political capital. They will tell you that once you have some economic muscle, political leverage always follows. I love reading in Native newspapers that more and more tribal people, especially the youth, are demanding that their leadership provide a Rez economy that creates good-paying jobs and independent governance.

One recent letter to the editor of the *Navajo Times* put it perfectly. Writing about his people, the Dine', Wally Brown argued that "Getting Dine' out of poverty is a cause. Dine' leadership should be willing to accept that cause as their personal cause for justice. Pure and simple. The solutions to the poverty of our Dine' is economic development. Any leader not comprehending that should willingly resign for the greater good. Petty behaviour in leadership has no place when 87 per cent of Dine' are doomed to poverty."

Child welfare is a significant part of that same issue. According to recent estimates, forty thousand Native kids are in the child welfare system in Canada. That is more than half the total number of kids in care in this country—yet Indigenous children make up only 7 per cent of Canada's child population. Where is the "honourable," trusted leadership on this embarrassing and deplorable situation? People everywhere now agree that the most shameful government program was the Indian residential/boarding school system. But despite this new awareness, today in Canada there are more Native kids in foster care than there ever were at the height of the genocidal residential school era. Is that not a crisis? Why not put "reconciliation feelings" toward overhauling the First Nations child welfare system?

Think about that, people!

What does that say about nation-to-nation promises? What does it say about "truth and reconciliation" promises? Where is the Canadian or American dream today when the policy of "kill the Indian in the child" is still being carried out, only now in camouflaged, white-instituted foster care programs and services that are apprehending Native kids at record rates? On Canada's widely celebrated 150th birthday in 2017, how could it possibly be that record numbers of Native kids were in foster care? Excuse us if we don't feel like partying with the rest of the country.

One of the main reasons for this crisis is, obviously, the continuing "Great Depression" in Indian Country. The idleness bred by unemployment is like a cancer. A welfare-dependent existence is not a life in which to raise healthy children, and achieving "Freedom 18" is no proper ambition for a Native youth. Again, it all goes back to "It's the economy, stupid."

I want to give a Rez shout-out to Cindy Blackstock of Gitxsan First Nation, who has been a long-standing advocate for Native child protection. Cindy has been fighting the Canadian and provincial governments' failed child welfare system for many years. She brought a landmark discrimination case to the Canadian Human Rights Tribunal to challenge the federal government's chronic underfunding of children's services on First Nation reserves. As Cindy says, "Words don't change children's lives. Real action by the government and equality would."

In 2019 the federal government signed into law Bill C-92 to reduce the number of Native youth in care and allow First Nations to create their own child welfare systems. But there was no funding tied to the law. Cindy Blackstock argued, "That's why the funding element is so critical to really making this bill a real game-changer for kids." The federal government has always had the money to deal with issues it deems a crisis, as shown only a year later with the billions of dollars it quickly spent on COVID-19 relief. Sadly, the government only deems Native issues a crisis when roadblocks are put up to remind them.

Economic development and good jobs on the Rez are also connected directly to Rez housing, which itself is obviously connected to family well-being. Currently, the vast majority of First Nations have a huge housing shortage, which hurts families. Overcrowding conditions exist on every Rez, and many Rez houses should be condemned. It is sad when television news shows much on-reserve housing looking like it's in a developing nation. Many tribal members can't move home because of housing shortages. Our people end up in urban Native slums like the east side of Vancouver or "the hood" in Regina.

There is a common notion that Indians get free housing. This is not true! On Osoyoos, as on most reserves/reservations, my people pay rent. On Osoyoos, most people have full-time jobs, and many have invested their own hard-earned money into home improvements. I have seen the good and the bad in Indian Country when it comes to housing. Simply put, those communities with economic development and more job opportunities have better housing. Where unemployment is high, there is more of a housing problem. Better jobs equal better housing, and better housing means a stronger family structure. Building houses where people have no jobs is a formula for sustaining the cycle of poverty.

Many years ago, I sat in on a Chiefs' meeting where some Native family-child agency was asking for political support for more funding. I had a question for the Native woman who was a front-line worker for that organization. "I bet," I asked, "that in the vast majority of cases you have seen, when you're called in to a troubled home and the kids are at risk of being apprehended, there is not an adult in that home with a full-time job—correct?" The child care worker answered just as I expected: "Yes, most of the time there is not a working adult in the home." The reality is a "better job = better life." Economic development and the foster care crisis have a direct connection.

I reminded all the Chiefs present at that meeting that this is exactly why my focus is economic development. Wise people have been saying for years, "The very best social program is a job." It's not a 100 per cent cure, but it's the most effective means of keeping Native kids out of foster care. Native kids need to be raised in households where at least one adult has a full-time, decent-paying job. Any social worker will tell you, "Role-modelling is important." One of the very best role-modelling options for Native kids is for them to grow up in a household where at least one parent is getting up early, fully employed, and going off to a job they love. As Chief Darcy Bear of Whitecap Dakota has said, "There is no better role-modelling than seeing mom and dad go to work."

In late 2017 I came across an article in the *Globe and Mail* entitled "For Foster Kids to Succeed, They Need More than Just Care." It was written by Jane Kovarikova, herself a survivor of the foster care system. The article talked about the outdated system and made a lot of common sense. Kovarikova noted,

Our system has stagnated in the "activity trap" by focusing on activities and outputs rather than outcomes or impact measurements on youth who have gone through the protection system. In Ontario, and most Canadian jurisdictions, youth outcomes after care have never been tracked. If you don't check what happens after care, how can you know if anything you did before worked? We don't allow a drug for a headache to hit the market before rigorous clinical trials measure its impact, but we trust the lives of some of the most vulnerable children in our country to a system with absolutely no impact measurements. . . .

We need a government that does more than just care about its children. We need a government that checks its own parenting to ensure policies and programs are improving life outcomes. . . . The solution to an effective and progressive child-welfare system is simple: a commitment to evidence-based and outcomes-focused policy-making.

Come on Indian Affairs and all other government programs—especially provincial child welfare agencies: produce a scorecard that really tells the truth about your programs and services. The overrepresentation of Native kids in care should be a wakeup call for everyone.

No nation is free if it's depending on foreign aid. Do we want Canada and the United States to one day have to depend on foreign aid? Every First Nation needs a Rez land base that is economically strong and capable of creating the jobs needed in order to free its members from government welfare. No more promises, studies, or apologies. As I have been saying for decades, communities making their own money and creating their own jobs is what gets rid of First Nations poverty.

I think it is absurd that most Native conferences do not talk about the importance of jobs and business development. It's sad that only within the last twenty years or so have Native conferences on wealth creation and economic development been taking place. There are conferences in Indian Country every week on how to spend underfunded grant program dollars in health, education, child welfare, housing, healing and wellness, etc. I once was part of an Indian Affairs economic development conference planning group back in the 1990s. For the first time we were going to have a Chiefs conference in B.C. on economic development. I remember that when the discussion came to who would be the keynote speaker at the gala and the names were coming up of past National Chiefs, I said, "Come on, man—really? None of those Chiefs have ever run a business in their life. This conference is about business, not politics. I want the Chiefs to listen to a successful businessperson. I want the Chiefs to listen to a millionaire—or better yet, a *billionaire*. Someone who knows what it takes to make their own money and not depend on grants or subsidies." I took the lead on finding a keynote speaker. It was a memorable night when B.C.'s most famous businessman, Jimmy Pattison, was the keynote speaker at our Chiefs Business Summit.

I want Rez leadership to go to school on business success, to have more Native business conferences and develop a network of business contacts. As a very wise Lil'wat Elder from Mount Currie once said, "We need a new kind of hunter today. Native teens need to also be hunters for jobs, education, hunters for business."

In my Rez travels I always seek out Native businesses, as I want to be a customer and support Native enterprise. But some Natives and Native-owned and -operated companies are conducting stupid, embarrassing business. I still show pictures of a Native-operated gas station and store that I once came upon in Alberta. There was graffiti all over the side of the building that faced the highway. I couldn't believe it! What really pissed me off was that crude swear words were on full display for potential customers and their kids to see. Who would want to stop at such a place?

I could have done what most people do—ignore it. But remember: what you walk by, you accept! When I got back to my Rez I phoned the Rez that owns that gas station. I asked to speak to the Chief and left my number. I received no phone call back so I phoned again and left a voice mail saying something like, "Get those swear words off your gas station/store—that's an embarrassment for all First Nations who are doing good respectable business."

I tell First Nations that if you are going to go into business, do it right or don't do it at all. Stay, if you prefer, with underfunded programs from Indian Affairs. Because once you open up a Native business, you are representing *all* Native communities. If you open up a Rez gas station, that gas station belongs to the family of Native gas stations. If you open up a Rez hotel, that hotel automatically belongs to the family of First Nations-owned hotels. As Native communities, we get painted with the same brush by the general public. If a customer gets treated badly in your Rez business, they are going to think that is how all Rez businesses are. If your hotel is dirty, people are going to think the hotel on the Osoyoos Rez is dirty. It is very true that the success of one is the success of many.

When I stay at the Enoch Cree hotel near Edmonton, I get a real sense of Native pride, and I am not even from that Rez. But that's just how it is in Indian Country. Hundreds of Native people have told me how proud they are of the Osoyoos Indian Band's businesses. As Native people we are interconnected because of the Rez culture and what our communities have gone through, and we truly want to be customers at Native businesses and have a special customer experience. We have to hold each other's businesses accountable and, when something is not right, say so. We have to hold each other's Rez companies to the highest possible standards—standards that would make our ancestors proud!

I was honoured to share the speaking stage with one of my Rez heroes a few years ago, Chief Phillip Martin, a Mississippi Choctaw who is featured in Peter J. Ferrara's excellent book *The Choctaw Revolution*. The book tells how a Chief who focused on business development eventually freed his people from poverty.

Chief Phillip Martin says it all when he states, "Economic Development is my freedom program."

CHAPTER 11

KINGS, QUEENS, PRIME MINISTERS, PRESIDENTS . . . AND OTHER GREAT WHITE SUPERIOR MYTHS

"When Jesus Christ came upon the earth, you killed him, the son of your own God, you nailed him up! . . . And only after you thought you killed him did you worship him, and start killing those who would not worship him. What kind of a people is this for us to trust?"

—Tecumseh, Shawnee chief and warrior

Christopher Columbus did not "discover" America. *We* found *him*—staring dumbfounded at land he ridiculously mistook for some other place halfway around the world. It has been good to see some historical reconciliation going on recently. In 2020 a statue of Christopher Columbus was torn down by protestors in Baltimore's Little Italy neighbourhood and thrown into the harbour. This was because of increasing anger about Columbus's association with the genocide of Native Americans.

There was an article not long ago in the *Globe and Mail* that said Alexander Mackenzie "discovered" the Mackenzie River that runs through the Northwest Territories to the Arctic Ocean. He was in fact guided on that river by Natives who had been paddling it for many centuries. Donald Trump did not invent the idea of fake news. Canadian and American historians and reporters have been writing it since 1492. Anyone with any historical sense would know no white man discovered any land or river in North America. Alexander Mackenzie did not discover the river that bears his name. Truth be told, he was terrified of the "monsters" the Dene people he encountered told him awaited him downstream. I can imagine them holding their sides and howling with laughter as he turned back. He called it the "River of Disappointment." The Dene called it "*Deh Cho*," which in their language means "Mighty River." Maps should go back to displaying the proper name for that river.

Canada and the United States like to think of themselves as leaders of the "free world." But it was "free" only in that they paid nothing for lands they stole from Indians whose culture they then tried to destroy. The founding fathers of the United States wrote the Declaration of Independence in 1776, a document that is to this day held up by American leaders as the country's "Ten Commandments." One of the Declaration's so-called truths is that "all men are created equal." This disregards the fact that tribe after tribe had been declared "hostile" and forced onto federal-government-controlled reservations. This "truth" is simply laughable and shameful to anyone who doesn't have the "right" colour of skin or who cannot trace their heritage back to Europe.

The American people still proudly uphold and get teary-eyed over the Declaration of Independence, and every July 4 they hold a national birthday party based on that founding document. Don't Americans realize the Declaration actually contains blatantly racist language about First Nations people?:

. . . He [the King of Great Britain] has excited domestic Insurrections amongst us, and has endeavoured to bring on the Inhabitants of our Frontiers, the merciless Indian Savages, whose known Rule of Warfare is an undistinguished Destruction of all Ages, Sexes, and Conditions.

Yes, the founding fathers of the United States called Indigenous people "merciless Indian Savages" in one of their founding documents. A Navajo woman recently wrote in the *Navajo Times*, "When the U.S. founding fathers in 1776 wrote the Declaration of Independence they systematically took our freedom away." The reality is, Native people, just like Black people, were not included in the ideals proclaimed in the Declaration of Independence. George Washington is viewed today as a hero, and his face is on the U.S. dollar bill, even though, like several other presidents of the United States, Washington was a slave owner and an "Indian fighter." When the first American president found that Indians were reluctant to sell their lands, with some fully refusing to do so, his response was that the United States should "extirpate" them, meaning destroy or wipe them out.

In the United States and Canada, president after president and prime minister after prime minister sought to carry out cultural genocide against Native people—even after tribe after tribe was either wiped out or forced onto reserves or reservations. The racist abuse of power against all Native people was at the core of addressing the "Indian Problem" in both of these countries. In Canada, Confederation was based on the federal lie that First Nations title and jurisdiction didn't exist.

It is "truth and *some* reconciliation" that real history is finally catching up with Canada's first prime minister, John A. Macdonald, who starved Indians on the prairies during the treaty era and conceived of the genocidal residential school program. Statues of

Sir John A. Macdonald have been vandalized or torn down in Charlottetown, Kingston, and Montreal, as well as removed from the steps of the city hall in Victoria.

The British and the French settled on tribal lands and later gave that tribal territory such colonial names as New England and New France. The second great European myth came from the imperial minds of English and French kings and queens, who spouted the nonsense that they were "ordained by God." The "Doctrine of Discovery" was issued by Pope Alexander VI in 1493, the year after Christopher Columbus got lost and the currents pushed him onto our shores. The Doctrine dictated that lands not occupied by Christians could be claimed in the name of the explorers, who were, of course, agents of the European sovereigns. Indigenous people were consistently referred to as "savages" by all the European empires—an undeniably racist term coined by thieving minds to justify, in both religious and legal terms, the theft of Indian lands.

The Doctrine upheld the notion that, because Indigenous people were non-Christians, they were inferior, uncivilized, and not human—and therefore their land was empty or "*terra nullius.*" In 2012 the United Nations Permanent Forum on Indigenous Issues concluded that the Doctrine of Discovery was "shameful" and that it was the root of all the discrimination and marginalization that Indigenous people face today.

In 2015 Canada's Truth and Reconciliation Commission released its ninety-four "calls to action," in which it twice repudiated the concept of the Doctrine of Discovery. All First Nations should call upon federal, provincial, territorial, and municipal governments to look closely at concepts that uphold European sovereignty over Indigenous peoples and lands, such as the Doctrine of Discovery and *terra nullius*, and then to reform those laws, government policies, and litigation strategies that continue to rely on such concepts. I and many other Chiefs often hear, "Why don't we just look forward?" "Why don't Indians just forget about those old treaties and old injustices?" But the old founding myths do matter. It's time for the U.N.'s Permanent Forum on Indigenous Issues and Canada's Truth and Reconciliation Commission to state that it is necessary for the U.S. and Canadian federal governments to officially repudiate this more than five-hundred-year-old doctrine that perpetuates the North American founding myths that are still oppressing Native people.

At Osoyoos, the joint federal-provincial McKenna-McBride Royal Commission, under pressure from white settlers, continued the racist "Honour of the Crown" theft of First Nations' lands. In 1913, First Nations reserve land in British Columbia was taken away and given to white people. At Osoyoos, we had our most important ten-thousand-year-old fishing grounds, located at OK Falls (Osoyoos Indian reserve #2), taken away by the stroke of a government pen.

In 1885, Prime Minister John A. Macdonald voiced how Canada regarded its relationship with those who were here first: "Indians are simply living on the benevolence and charity of the Canadian Parliament, and . . . beggars should not be choosers." If you know the genocidal history of kings and queens toward First Nations, then you have to be disgusted to know that today we are still hearing in throne speech after throne speech talk of the "Honour of the Crown," "nation-to-nation," and now "Truth and Reconciliation."

The "Honour of the Crown" will only be upheld when all the First Nations on both sides of the border get our old reserves and reservations back and all the original treaties are observed! And where there are no treaties, land reconciliation *must* happen. It is the responsibility of today's non-Native politicians to reconcile the Indian land thefts of the past.

—

Once the English and French had erected settlements on First Nation territories, the "Manifest Destiny" myth began to be preached in 1845. Manifest Destiny held that the United States was destined, by God himself, to expand its domains. The United States was brutal in its mistreatment of Native Americans. Relocation and termination of tribes was official U.S. policy for most of two centuries. In 1838, President Andrew Jackson ignored the Supreme Court decisions that ruled the Cherokee were a sovereign Nation (*Worcester v. Georgia*, 1832) and ordered the U.S. Army to forcibly remove Cherokees—men, women, and children—to walk more than a thousand miles to Indian Territory in Oklahoma. More than four thousand died on the "Trail of Tears." A government soldier who was there wrote: "I fought through the war between the States [Civil War] and I have seen many men shot, but the Cherokee Removal was the cruelest work I ever knew."

It's time to peel away the racist history of both countries. The old historical lies and colonial propaganda are being challenged daily. In some states, there is talk of changing "Columbus Day" to "Indigenous Day." In 2017, the Elementary Teachers' Federation of Ontario asked that all schools and buildings in the province named after John A. Macdonald be renamed because of his outright racist treatment of First Nations. The first prime minister was not only the architect of the genocide against Indigenous people, he was also the prime minister who hanged Métis leader Louis Riel, the true founder of the province of Manitoba, for high treason.

Macdonald felt no guilt in starving First Nations people to make way for settlement and a railroad. As he told the House of Commons in 1882, "I have reason to believe that the agents as a whole . . . are doing all they can, by refusing food until the Indians are on the verge of starvation, to reduce the expense." There are historical reports of white travellers coming across hundreds of Natives so starved they had trouble walking. The Canadian Pacific Railway was built on the suffering of Native people. A Liberal member of Parliament at the time called it "a policy of submission shaped by a policy of starvation." No wonder Victoria City Council voted for the removal of that statue.

Macdonald was hardly alone. There were other colonial heroes in Canada such as Edward Cornwallis, the founder of Halifax, who called for the outright killing of Native people by offering a bounty to anyone who scalped a Mi'kmaq. In Halifax, in 1930, they erected a statue in his memory. The Mi'kmaq Chiefs called for his statue to be removed, and in 2018 it was finally dismantled. Other government sculptures of such racists are coming down slowly. In May 2017, in New Orleans, a statue of Confederate general Robert E. Lee was removed. In 2020, the governor of Virginia declared that the statue of Lee in the state capital would be removed.

Those statues have their supporters, of course, but such symbols are an affront to today's standards of morality and justice. Both countries can no longer ignore and misrepresent their shameful and racist "Indian Treaty" pasts. In British Columbia, the British Columbia Treaty Commission was formed in 1992 in an attempt to reach fair modern-day treaties. The 1982 Canadian Constitution formally recognized Aboriginal rights, and since then First Nations have been dissecting the "Honour of the Crown" in high-level court cases throughout the country. The Supreme Court of Canada is being forced to listen to the pounding of First Nations drums calling for justice— and the Maple Leaf is shaking!

On Canada's shameful Rez scorecard there are hundreds of unsettled Indian reserve land thefts. Natives were removed from their ancestral village sites, their "homes" for a thousand years or more, to make way for white settlers who would then take over the best land and, as a result, prosper. In British Columbia, the Williams Lake

Indian Band were removed from their original reserve in the late
1800s. Today, the city of Williams Lake occupies original reserve land.
A 2018 Supreme Court of Canada decision ruled the Williams Lake
Indian Band is due financial compensation for the historical theft of
its land as far back as 1860. Based on historical evidence, the highest
court in this country has ruled that Canada can be held legally responsible for pre-Confederation wrongs.

Yet, just like Osoyoos, the Williams Lake Indian Band would rather
have their original reserve land back. This is the land that our ancestors lived on and believed would be there for future generations. But
it is all now in private ownership, and in many cases a town or a city
has been built on it. How do you reconcile that?

To appreciate the true history of this country as well as the
unmatched oratory of First Nations people, I return again and again
to that speech delivered by Chief Dan George on Canada's centennial.
He called it "A Lament for Confederation":

How long have I known you, Oh Canada? A hundred years? Yes,
a hundred years. And many, many seelanum more. And today,
when you celebrate your hundred years, Oh Canada, I am sad
for all the Indian people throughout the land.

For I have known you when your forests were mine; when
they gave me my meat and my clothing. I have known you in
your streams and rivers where your fish flashed and danced in
the sun, where the waters said 'come, come and eat of my abun-
dance.' I have known you in the freedom of the winds. And my
spirit, like the winds, once roamed your good lands.

But in the long hundred years since the white man came,
I have seen my freedom disappear like the salmon going mysteriously out to sea. The white man's strange customs, which I

could not understand, pressed down upon me until I could no longer breathe.

When I fought to protect my land and my home, I was called a savage. When I neither understood nor welcomed his way of life, I was called lazy. When I tried to rule my people, I was stripped of my authority.

My nation was ignored in your history textbooks _ they were little more important in the history of Canada than the buffalo that ranged the plains. I was ridiculed in your plays and motion pictures, and when I drank your fire-water, I got drunk _ very, very drunk. And I forgot.

Oh Canada, how can I celebrate with you this centenary, this hundred years? Shall I thank you for the reserves that are left to me of my beautiful forests? For the canned fish of my rivers? For the loss of my pride and authority, even among my own people? For the lack of my will to fight back? No! I must forget what's past and gone.

Oh God in heaven! Give me back the courage of the olden chiefs. Let me wrestle with my surroundings. Let me again, as in the days of old, dominate my environment. Let me humbly accept this new culture and through it rise up and go on.

Oh God! Like the thunderbird of old I shall rise again out of the sea; I shall grab the instruments of the white man's success _ his education, his skills, and with these new tools I shall build my race into the proudest segment of your society. Before I follow the great chiefs who have gone before us, Oh Canada, I shall see these things come to pass.

I shall see our young braves and our chiefs sitting in the houses of law and government, ruling and being ruled by the knowledge and freedoms of our great land. So shall we shatter the barriers of our isolation. So shall the next hundred years be the greatest in the proud history of our tribes and nations.

The Truth and Reconciliation Commission of Canada was launched in 2008 as part of the Indian Residential Schools Settlement Agreement. The Commission tabled its report in 2015, after hundreds of meetings with Native groups across the country. Remember, as I keep repeating, everything costs money, and it cost over $60 million to come up with those ninety-four "calls to action" I mentioned earlier.

The thing is, I don't need ninety-four calls to action—only a few. It takes only a few common sense changes to not only right the injustices of the past but also to give First Nations a chance at taking control of their own destiny. Reconciliation must start with the huge elephant in the room—Indian land rights! All other reconciliation and "calls to action" would be looked after if only Canada and the United States first addressed the broken treaties, reserve land thefts, mismanagement of Indian trusts, and the shortcomings of modern treaties.

To me, former prime minister Paul Martin has proven he is a leader and not a phony politician. After retiring from politics, he continued to spend his own time and money on improving the lives of Native people by creating, in 2008, the Aboriginal Youth Entrepreneurship Program. The *Honourable* Paul Martin (yes, I am using that word "honourable" in reference to Paul Martin because he has earned it), both while he was prime minister and especially outside of politics, has said: "It's a matter of economics. If you invest in young Aboriginal children today, they will make major contributions in the future. If you don't, they will be a major draw on the economy."

Why can't the federal government and the provinces do the grade-school math? The youngest and fastest-growing population in Canada is Aboriginal peoples. As former Prime Minister Martin has said many times, "I believe the well-being of Indigenous peoples is currently the greatest economic, social and moral issue facing Canada." The Martin family's Aboriginal Youth Entrepreneurship Program is for grade eleven and twelve students and is offered in more than fifty schools across Canada. The curriculum is based on provincial business courses, supplemented with Indigenous content. Native youth learning about entrepreneurship, becoming independent, and reclaiming their inherent right to be part of the economy in our traditional territories—that's how socio-economic gaps are closed!

I want to give a special shout-out to Paul Martin, the only top-ranked elected leader in Canada (federal or provincial) who truly put their words into action when it came to developing a real "nation-to-nation relationship" with First Nations. Back in 2005, he was the one who carefully orchestrated the first-ever agreement between the Government of Canada and the majority of Native national organizations, the provinces, and the territories when all parties signed onto the historic Kelowna Accord.

Back then, Prime Minister Martin said, "My goal was quite simply to redress the history of centuries of broken promises. It was clear to me that no comprehensive approach was going to succeed without the full support of Native people themselves and their leaders." Talk about "herding cats" or "too many Chiefs and not enough Indians"—this was a colossal undertaking. It took more than eighteen months and hundreds of meetings across the country before all the parties could finally gather in Kelowna, B.C, and reach a $5 billion agreement officially called "First Ministers and National Aboriginal Leaders: Strengthening Relationships and Closing the Gap"—but better known as "The Kelowna Accord."

The goal was to close the gap in the standard of living between Indigenous and non-Indigenous people. The Kelowna Accord was based on Native organizations setting the priorities, not the government. Prime Minister Martin told then National Chief Phil Fontaine, "*You* set the agenda." Working groups were to be set up that would allow for ongoing future consultation. The Kelowna Accord was not just another feel-good statement. Its first purpose was to establish ongoing cross-country working tables to develop a real nation-to-nation relationship and commitment to goals that included committing:

- $1.3 billion to reduce infant mortality, youth suicide, childhood obesity, and diabetes by 25 per cent in five years and by 50 per cent in ten years;
- $1.8 billion for education in order to increase the high-school graduation rate to levels equal to the graduation rate of the non-Indigenous population;
- $200 million to develop economic opportunities (employment, etc.) for the Indigenous population;
- $1.6 billion for housing and infrastructure; and
- $170 million for "relationship and accountability"—supporting Aboriginal organizations in developing accountability practices and working with governments, particularly on land claims and self-government policies.

Former Conservative prime minister Brian Mulroney told me: "Prime Minister Paul Martin's greatest achievement was the Kelowna Accord." It was to be the biggest investment toward addressing Native poverty ever in Canada. Sadly, within months of the historic signing of the Kelowna Accord, a federal election was called, the Martin government was defeated, and the Conservative government under the newly elected prime minister Stephen Harper squashed the Accord. It is a national tragedy that, more than fifteen years later, the federal,

provincial, and territorial governments are still talking about "closing the gaps." The usual equation of good words with little financial
backing equalling no results.

Real leaders push on, however, and in 2008 the Right Honourable
Paul Martin presented a private member's bill to the Standing Senate
Committee on Aboriginal Peoples—Bill C-292, "An Act to implement
the Kelowna Accord." Unfortunately, it did not pass. "Any reckoning
of Canada's history and any analysis of our progress as a nation will
show that Canada's Indigenous people have been, quite simply, shut
out of Canada's success," the former prime minister said at the time.
"The plight of Aboriginal society is our national shame and therein
lies our challenge. We know the history and we know that must not
be our future."

In 2005, thanks to Paul Martin's Kelowna Accord, the vast majority of Native leadership saw Canada actually putting its money where
its mouth had been for the first time since Native organizations came
together during the 1980–82 Constitutional talks and forced Canada
to include section 35 in the Canadian Constitution: "The existing
aboriginal and treaty rights of the aboriginal peoples in Canada are
hereby recognized and affirmed . . . " The good words "nation to
nation" have not, unfortunately, been allocated the funds required
to put them into action!

Still, I want to thank the Native leadership that came together in
the early 1980s to oppose being left out of Prime Minister Pierre
Trudeau's initial proposal to patriate Canada's Constitution.

Today I look back on the Kelowna Accord and recall that Gordon
Campbell, then premier of British Columbia, played a big supporting
role in attempting to improve First Nations relations. What a huge

missed opportunity. The government of B.C. has a long history of being a key blocker of a true "nation-to-nation" relationship. I find it appalling that the province with the most First Nations (more than two hundred) and the most Indian reserves (more than fifteen hundred)—the province with the most to gain or lose when it comes to First Nation poverty or wealth—has among the worst records when it comes to past injustices toward Native rights. More Native Supreme Court cases come out of British Columbia than any other province.

How great this country could one day be if only it would truly honour the rights of Indigenous people and section 35 of its Constitution. Real truth and reconciliation may one day happen. It has to, for the sake of us all. Canada and the provinces need to set party politics aside when it comes to genuine truth and reconciliation. First Nations are at the doorsteps of every courtroom. The injustices of the past—injustices that built this country—will be put to the "truth and reconciliation" test.

In Paul Martin's 2008 autobiography, *Hell or High Water*, he leaves this important message:

> That the Conservatives reneged on Kelowna, and in so doing condemned another generation to the same compromised lives to which their parents were condemned, is my deepest regret at losing the election of 2006 . . . . This government may have walked away from the Kelowna Accord, but sooner or later the Kelowna approach will be the law of the land. Sooner or later a future government will have to come back to the Kelowna principles: the goals we set for Canada must be no less than the educational, health, economic, civil and social equality of Aboriginal peoples with their fellow citizens; and all of this can only be done with the consensus and collaboration of Canada's Aboriginal people.

It needs to happen in both Canada and the United States. There are small signs that it can and will happen. In 2019, Albuquerque, New Mexico, became the first American city to recognize tribal sovereignty by establishing government-to-government relations with the surrounding tribes. We need more of that.

There is an old saying: "what goes around comes around." My Indian name—my ancestral name—is "*K'il law na*" (Kelowna) in Okanagan, which means "Grizzly Bear." Grizzlies have strength and determination. Maybe the time is near for the Kelowna Accord to come back around.

I was so proud of the Four Host First Nations at the 2010 Winter Olympics in Vancouver—the Squamish, Musqueam, Tsawwassen, and Tsleil-Waututh—who reminded British Columbia and the whole country that the Winter Olympics were not going to happen in their traditional territory unless they played a major role. The government was not just going to allow them to sing or dance or recognize whose tribal territory the Olympics were on (the usual cheap, in-the-spirit-of-reconciliation tokenism talk). The Four Host First Nations Chiefs and councils pushed "nation-to-nation" words to a meaningful new level, to the point of not only being involved in planning but also having authority in several areas. And, of course, money and resources had to be committed to the Indigenous side of the 2010 Games. The proudest moment for me was to see the Four Host First Nations Chiefs sitting in the president's box at the opening and closing ceremonies with the premier and prime minister, and being formally recognized as "Heads of State."

Such recognition stands in sharp contrast to the lazy-drunken-Indian myth. Still today, as I travel throughout Canada and the United States, I hear that Indians are lazy, are drunks, that they get a free education, free health care, free housing, and that the government looks after them. *Really? Canada and the United States looks after their Indigenous people—like the slave owners looked after their slaves— like kings and queens looked after the peasants? Like the South African British looked after the Black people in South Africa?*

I have a personal experiment that I do to take the pulse of Canada and the United States. Often, after I get off a plane and into a taxi, I will ask the cab driver, "How are the Native people in this city doing?" At first they don't want to be honest. So I tell them, "Nothing you say will upset me or make me ashamed to be an Indian, and the more honest you are the better I will tip you!" Most cab drivers then get into the "Lazy Drunken Indian Myth." I have noticed most cab drivers have an accent and are people of colour, so I ask, "Where did you come from?" Usually it's some poor overseas country. Many have only been in the country for a few years, and yet these newcomers have somehow internalized the image of the "Lazy Drunken Indian who gets everything free from the government." How can this be?

The country they were raised in did not embed this myth in their mind. So where do so many recently arrived cab drivers learn this? The fact is, there is too much racism in every Canadian and American city. The fact is, too many Canadians and Americans don't know the real truth of their county's origins and history. Most people's knowledge about Indigenous people comes from John Wayne movies or the news—for example, when Natives get pushed to the limit and put up a roadblock to protest. I correct the cab drivers' views of Native people. We do not get a free education. We do not get free housing. The government does not pay Indians not to work (that was a new one to me!). And yes, many Natives have drinking problems, but so would the white people in England and France if the Nazis had been successful in invading and stealing those lands, and, along the way, took their children, condemned their religion, and forced them to live in poverty generation after generation.

It's not the cab drivers' fault they have such a low image of Indians—it's the country's fault! It's the fault of leadership in government and the fault of corporate Canada and corporate America. After 150 years, First Nations in Canada are still waiting for the "Honour of the Crown" and the chance to participate in the Canadian and American dream. During these conversations with cab drivers, it doesn't take long for the talk to shift. Most cab drivers are people of colour, and they quickly understand what I am telling them about white systemic oppression. Many of them and their relatives in their old countries went through the same historical oppression, often also under British and French rule.

My short history lessons with cab drivers remind me that it doesn't take long to get a basic education regarding the true history of Native and white relations in Canada or the United States. Sometimes all it takes is one cab ride!

In 2020, Minneapolis police used excessive force on a Black man, George Floyd, that was caught on video. There are hundreds more police murders that are not caught on camera. In the wake of the horrific event and the sometime violent protests that followed, an emotional and often difficult national conversation on race relations began. As challenging as the days immediately following Floyd's murder were, it was good to see American racism front and centre. The events surrounding Floyd's death have led some Americans to consider the country's systemic racism and to do some work toward reconciliation: Confederate flags being banned at NASCAR events; old statues of racist leaders being toppled; a call for name changes of army bases. I want to see more of statues of racist heroes being pushed over, in Canada and the United States. I want to see more of our mountains and lakes renamed to take back the Native language names that stood for thousands of years—and to get rid of names that are nothing more than colonial racist propaganda. First Nation sacred sites need to be managed by First Nations and named by First Nations.

Like First Nation people, Black people have experienced Canada's and America's "racist" dream for hundreds of years. For Native people, systemic racism started in 1492. Beginning in 1619, Black people were brutally brought to North America as slaves. At the time, First Nations peoples were already enslaved in their own homeland.

Real "Truth and Reconciliation" must be specific and not done with more "beads and blankets." I hate general statements like "We want justice." If you want the cops locked up, say it! But you must also say for how long. Don't just say "we want justice." Come out and be specific—"Lock up murdering cops for twenty or thirty years!"—whatever length of time people of colour get for committing such a crime. If you want cops not to use excessive force, be specific. Fighting for laws that prohibit choke holds, for example, is specific and makes sense.

Elected leadership must be forced to make legislative changes. After a police shooting or use of excessive force against people of colour (a.k.a. a crime), I don't want your thoughts and prayers. I want someone punished. I want a ban on machine guns and hand guns. I want over-hunting and over-fishing to stop. I want steeper fines for billionaire companies that cut corners and damage the environment. I want the upper middle class who commit white-collar crime to be locked up just like poor people who commit low-cash crimes. Rich people and rich lawyers are still getting away with crimes that would land poor people in prison.

Social dominance by white America and Canada over people of colour is as American and Canadian as apple pie and maple syrup.

Canada and the United States need to reconcile their shameful history toward First Nations and Black people. It's shockingly shameful that more than a half-century after President Lyndon B. Johnson signed the Civil Rights Act into law in 1964—which banned segregation in public places and employment discrimination—North America is still facing up to systemic racism. There have been hundreds of Black Lives Matter protests in all major cities. This proves—as First Nations have known ever since the first Indian treaty was signed and broken more than two hundred years ago—that neither Canada or the United States honours its written agreements, let alone its political promises.

In an interview in June 2020 with the *Globe and Mail*, former prime minister Brian Mulroney said the federal government needs to study and implement the recommendations put forth in the 1996 Report of the Royal Commission on Aboriginal Peoples—which released 440 recommendations. "The Aboriginal leaders themselves viewed this [report] as the Bible," the former prime minister said. "In other words, they were saying if we can get this implemented, we can become full Canadian citizens and [a] much more productive part of society."

He added that "Canadians need fresh new thinking."

"I consider the Aboriginal situation, the Indigenous situation in Canada to be the single greatest blight on citizenship," said Mulroney. "We can't move ahead with a new agenda for Canada if we don't deal with the Indigenous people and systemic racism."

Systemic racism in Canada and the United States is a reality. It's not just a few racist cops or healthcare workers, or a few mayors and council members, as some would have you believe.

The message to Canadians and Americans is simple: the civil rights movement did not end in the 1960s. It is still a necessary movement.

As Martin Luther King Jr. so perfectly put it, "Injustice anywhere is a threat to justice everywhere."

CHAPTER 12

RECONCILIATION: TIME FOR CANADA AND THE UNITED STATES TO TELL THE TRUTH

"No historian would accept accounts of Nazi officials as to what happened in Nazi Germany because these accounts were written to justify that regime. Yet American historians are still subjective about their own history. Genocide is colonial policy, not accident."

—Roxanne Dunbar-Ortiz, Cheyenne, and a professor of Native American history

There is a legal principle that says "Ignorance is no defence."

We're a long way from real reconciliation in North America. There is a lack of truth-telling and an unwillingness to really address long-standing injustices (on several levels). Until governments on both sides of the forty-ninth parallel show themselves willing to be honest about the past and the ways in which its wrongs should be righted, there will be no such thing as truth and reconciliation.

Reconciliation starts with telling the truth—"the whole truth, and nothing but the truth, so help you God." Christianity is based in truth. The ninth commandment is, "Thou shalt not bear false witness against thy neighbour." It is a sin to lie, Christians believe. Do the Christians who created and still control Canada and the United States really believe their own commandments? Do they put them into action?

Is it just a sin to lie to other Christians? Are Natives included in that commandment? The elected leaders of Canada and the United States have been lying to First Nations since the British made the first "claim" on our land and promised "Honour of the Crown." In the United States, a piece of paper that all Americans swear allegiance to serves as their Constitution, yet the act of writing something down does not guarantee that what is written will be implemented justly. Both the American and Canadian governments were blatantly racist toward all Native religions. The First Amendment in the U.S. Constitution—the one that guarantees "freedom of religion"—obviously didn't apply to Indians. Some "freedom," when colonists were so quick to outlaw the Sundance, Potlatch, and sweat houses. Instead, they arrested Native people for attempting to practise their religious rights.

Politicians on and off the Rez need to start at the foundation of the problem and quit trying to pacify their guilt by obsessing over the symptoms produced by the problem. The conflict between Natives and Canada and the United States has always been and continues to be over land and unfulfilled treaty rights. Only a few years ago all of Canada heard Prime Minister Justin Trudeau, soon after being elected, say, "No relationship is more important to Canada than the relationship with Indigenous people—building a nation-to-nation relationship." It was a powerful statement to make and a welcome one to hear.

One of the Trudeau government's first commitments was to address the appalling situation concerning potable water in First Nations communities. Between the fall of 2015 and Christmas of 2020, ninety-eight long-term drinking water advisories were lifted. This is to be welcomed. At the same time, fifty-eight such advisories remain in effect. It is urgent that the situation be fully addressed, as the federal government has promised.

Before they talk of "reconciliation," the leadership of the federal and provincial governments needs to look the word up. It means more than "the restoration of friendly relations or making one view or belief compatible with another." It also means *let's get down to the financial bottom line*—"the action of making financial accounting consistent." To me, "reconciliation" in the nation-to-nation relationship starts with a reconciliation of land and money. In accounting, "reconciliation" means that two sets of records are in agreement. In Native and white relations, that means making sure the balances match at the end of particular accounting periods. In essence, the Native balance sheet matches the Canadian balance sheet.

Most Canadians and Americans need a simple history lesson on the foundation of their "dream" countries. The Canadian and American dreams are only a few hundred years old, and they started as a nightmare for all First Nations. I find it amazing how long my people have been forcing Canada and the United States to uphold Native rights by taking their cases all the way up to their Supreme Courts. Native land rights are part of the Canadian and American foundation—as they should be. Yet most Canadians and Americans have a racist, biased view of history when it comes to the foundation of their country. They conveniently leave out the "First Peoples'—the Indians.

To understand modern land claims and conflicts over jurisdiction one needs to go back to a few very important Supreme Court cases on both sides of the border.

In *Worcester v. Georgia* (1832), the U.S. Supreme Court ruled the Cherokee Nation was sovereign and that the state of Georgia had no right to enforce state laws on the Cherokee. As often happened when Natives won in the highest court, the ruling was ignored. President

Andrew Jackson ordered the relocation of fifteen thousand Cherokees from their homelands in Tennessee, North Carolina, Georgia, and Alabama, leading to the infamous "Trail of Tears" mentioned earlier.

In Canada, Native title claims did not get to the Supreme Court until the Calder (Nisga'a) Case in 1973. The Crown used to argue that Canada, then a colony under the British Crown, *gave* Native people Aboriginal rights. In the Calder case, the Supreme Court of Canada ruled that First Nations rights are "inherent rights" that exist because First Nations were occupying their lands before the Europeans came. The Crown didn't *give* these rights to First Nations; the rights exist independently of any Crown actions.

After the Supreme Court ruled on the Calder (Nisga'a) case, Prime Minister Pierre Elliott Trudeau said: "You Indians have more rights than I thought you had." Trudeau recognized the legal realities of Native title in Canada and, in 1974, opened up the Office of Native Claims. In 1982, when Trudeau patriated Canada's Constitution, section 35 was added to provide constitutional protection to the Indigenous and treaty rights of Indigenous peoples in Canada:

> 35. (1) The existing aboriginal and treaty rights of the aboriginal peoples of Canada are hereby recognized and affirmed.

> (2) In this Act, "aboriginal peoples of Canada" includes the Indian, Inuit and Métis peoples of Canada.

Now, I get the importance of symbolism when it comes to treaties. The treaties pre- and post- Confederation are the foundation upon which Canada was built. So let's start with a very simple and easy step the federal government could take in terms of *real* financial reconciliation—a common sense, no-brainer reconciliation that would cement this "nation-to-nation relationship." Adjust the 150-year-old treaty annuities to today's value.

Who brings a suitcase full of cash to Indian reserves in Canada every summer? The mafia, drug dealers, maybe slick pipeline negotiators? Nope—none of those. It is Indigenous Services Canada, representing the Canadian government and accompanied by none other than the Royal Canadian Mounted Police in full regalia! It's Treaty Day on those Indian reserves occupied by Natives whose ancestors signed Treaties 1 through 11 between 1871 and 1921.

The Indian Affairs agents (I wonder if they wear trench coats and dark sunglasses) call for a drum roll; then they carefully place that suitcase full of cash on a table and open it. Behold—as the sun shines and an eagle flies overhead whilst a tape of "God Save the Queen" plays—Canada's important "nation-to-nation" relationship is happening in living colour as hundreds of Indians line up to receive a newly minted Canadian five-dollar bill from the Mountie dressed in that world-famous Red Serge. Oh! And the Chief gets twenty-five dollars and a box of bullets. After making billions off of First Nations land for hundreds of years, Canada and the provinces and all of their citizens have no shame in continuing to hand out "beads and blankets" in the new millennium. Disgraceful!

It's now 2021—150 years after Treaty 1 was signed. Anyone who respects the long-standing treaty doctrine "as long as the sun shines and the waters flow" knows there is absolutely no way Canada should be bringing a suitcase full of five-dollar bills to modern Treaty Days. To pay First Nations people five dollars each in the 2020s makes a farce out of a real "nation-to-nation relationship" and does not show respect for the "spirit and intent" of those treaties.

When I first heard of this ongoing Treaty Day payment scenario I couldn't believe it. I had to call up some of my prairie cuzzins to confirm. A Cree Council woman from Treaty 8, in Alberta, told me, "Yeah, we still get a lousy five bucks! I'm not going to stand in line for five dollars. I wait every four years and let mine build up. I'll stand in line for twenty bucks!" A Chief from Treaty 4 in Manitoba told me he gets twenty-five dollars and two flags (the Union Jack and the Canadian flag) and a box of .22 shells. What can you shoot to eat with .22 shells? A squirrel? A fact for the Canadian government: none of my people hunt squirrels. I told the Manitoba Chief: "Tell the cheap Canadian government next year to reallocate one cabinet minister's "free lunch" and tell them you at least want a box of real bullets—.60 calibre!"

I have heard every prime minister and premier in my lifetime say "Canadians are fair and honourable people and respect the very important relationship with all First Nations." If so, then why is the Canadian government against reconciling the simple accounting of treaty annuities? Handing out a five-dollar bill in 1871 is obviously not the same as handing out a five-dollar bill in 2021. I'm sure that's one thing the Liberals and Conservatives could agree on without spending millions on forming a time-wasting and costly audit committee. Remember, millions of acres of First Nation land was involved in those treaties. You can look it up—the maps are public documents. Today, those lands send the federal and provincial government revenue in the billions.

It's so easy to reconcile the five-dollar bill in 1871 and what the minimum payment per Treaty Indian should be today. Canada should be ashamed to send its middle-class-income Indigenous Services staff and decently paid RCMP to Indian reserves to hand out five-dollar bills to those who often barely exist on government welfare. Inflation alone argues that Canada should now be paying every Treaty Indian $105 on Treaty Day, to honour that very important historical commitment. Is that really too much to ask? And even at an adjusted rate, standing in line to get your annual treaty payment is demeaning and insulting.

In all business relationships, if the sides can't resolve the small stuff, the big issues will never get settled. Come on, Canada! Come on, provinces! Put your money where your mouth is—in "true" reconciliation. Show historical respect for the "spirit and intent" of the original treaties. Buck up or shut up!

Now we come to the words "Truth and Reconciliation," the latest political term used both on and off the Rez. I first heard it in connection with the federal government's $60,000,000 Truth and Reconciliation Commission, which came out of the 2008 official residential school apology and settlement agreement. But what, exactly, in a First Nations context, does true reconciliation mean? How does reconciliation look when it comes to Natives and the federal and provincial governments? A Mohawk language speaker told me, "To fix past wrongs." But there are so many questions that need answering: *What needs fixing? Who broke it? What's the plan to fix it? What do both parties want fixed?*

I hate it when I hear white government, business or school officials say, "We gather here today in the spirt of reconciliation . . . " and then allow Indians to drum a song or do a prayer or fly a flag at municipal hall. Those are nice gestures, but they are baby steps, and cheap ones at that. After one hundred years of abuse and injustices at the worst human level, it's time, Canada, for "adult steps." Time to grow up and put on adult pants and do some real reconciliation!

One of Canada's media icons, Peter Mansbridge, once asked me an important question: "How do you feel when you hear a speaker say, 'We want to recognize that we are gathered on your First Nations unceded traditional territory?'" I told him it bothers me if it turns into a casual throwaway gesture, something that's no better than a quick "How are you?" Saying those words does nothing to correct past injustices. And saying them while standing on stolen Indian reserve land is a huge contradiction as well as an insult. Unceded is a fancy word for "stolen." It's like taking over someone's house, kicking them out into the yard, and then forcing them to live in a tent while those now living a middle-class lifestyle in the house give thanks and recognition before dinner to the tent-dwellers. That recognition is a small historical gesture that needs to be followed up with land claim settlement action!

"Truth and Reconciliation" means reconciling past wrongs! It does *not* mean taking a few seconds to mention whose traditional unceded land your meeting is being held on.

To me, economic justice and true reconciliation have to start with the land. I am waiting for the provincial and federal governments to say, "In the spirit of reconciliation and to repair one of the biggest injustices between our people, we sign the original Indian reserves back to your First Nations." Natives need land from which to rebuild their nations, not more fluff words.

Thousands of Indian reserve and reservation land rip-offs happened all over Canada and the United States. In Canada, these injustices are called "Specific Claims." Natives just don't make up land thefts. Now that we can hire lawyers and researchers we can prove that. Law-abiding Canadians and Americans should be ashamed of how their governments stole Native peoples' Rez lands. The history is there for the reading, and the storyline tends to be the same across the country. As more settlers came into a region where a Rez was established, the settlers would petition their local government, which would then demand that the federal government take Indian reserve or reservation land away from the Indians. The plea from settlers was always the same: "Those Indians are not doing anything with the land and we need it to make a living. So we elect you to take the land away and give it to us." Most Canadians and Americans don't realize that hundreds of towns and cities are built on land that was originally set aside as an Indian reserve/reservation for the nearest First Nation. In Canada, there is huge backlog of Specific Claims that need to be "reconciled."

Land claims are not the only important unfinished business between Indigenous peoples and various levels of government. Many of the injustices of the past go beyond land. In 2019, the Blood Tribe in Southern Alberta reached a $150 million settlement over the federal government's mismanagement of their cattle in the early twentieth century. In the late 1800s, the Blood Tribe had developed a successful cattle herd that numbered well into the thousands. Local white ranchers complained to Indian Affairs that the Natives had unfair advantages. Indian agents took over management of the herd and eventually destroyed the tribe's cattle business. The mismanagement of tribal resources at the hands of Indian Affairs has happened hundreds of times, and the federal governments in both Canada and the United States continue to be sued by tribes and bands who want back what originally belonged to them.

It is disgusting how Indian Affairs has discharged its fiduciary obligation toward all First Nations. Thousands of white bureaucrats have made a good living and enjoy good pensions while their clients—the Indians on the reserves and reservations—live and die in poverty. Indian Affairs in North America is a multi-billion-dollar industry that has been built on the pain and suffering of Native people. I have told many Indian Affairs staff that, "My people want what you get every two weeks—a good paycheque and a good pension. But we won't get paid to sleep softly while Indians suffer."

Back in the mid-1800s, the Department of Indian Affairs in Ottawa created a cross-country bureaucracy of regional and district Indian

Affairs offices. Their purpose was to control and assimilate Canada's Indigenous people and to stop the provinces and settlers from taking advantage of Indian reserve land. The district office in my Okanagan territory was in Vernon, two hours straight north of Osoyoos. The regional office was located, and remains, in Vancouver. Indian agents were appointed to every reserve. These federal government officials would regularly come to every Okanagan reserve to deal with reserve land and Indian Act administration matters. They came whenever the federal government, the province, or private companies wanted to encroach on reserve land for highways, gas or transmission lines, irrigation ditches, and other public infrastructure. It happened regularly. The provincial government attitude was, *Heck, just put public infrastructure through Indian reserves. Those Indians don't care if their land is expropriated, and it's cheaper and easier than dealing with white landowners in the region.*

This racist Indian agent era lasted more than a century. No wonder that in the 1960s and 1970s, North American Natives, just like Black people in the United States, had had enough of such oppressive treatment and staged marches and road blocks. The media paid far more attention to the Black civil rights movement in the United States, for sure, but in both Canada and the U.S. there began, finally, an Indian civil rights movement.

In the late 1800s and early 1900s, most of our people could not read or write, so the Indian agent would set up meetings and push the federal, provincial, and municipal agenda when it came to expropriating Indian reserve land. Even after reserves were created and our best lands had already been set aside for white people, this continued to happen. In Osoyoos's case, even before the ink was dry on the original reserve boundaries, forty-two hundred acres of Osoyoos Indian Reserve #1 was ripped away by a provincial magistrate. My ancestors' best agricultural land and river access was taken from them right in front of their very eyes.

The Osoyoos Indian Reserve was created in 1877 and has suffered through several major federal and provincial land thefts. Today, much of our reserve boundary follows the hills and rocks, no longer the Okanagan River with its good and fertile lands along the shoreline. Hundreds of white families have made a very good living off of our original Indian reserve land. The provincial and state governments have made billions of dollars in taxes off of original Osoyoos Indian Rez land. Our land.

As if that 1877 injustice to the Osoyoos people wasn't enough, roughly three decades later, and under pressure from British Columbia citizens, the "Honour of the Crown" was evident once again, in all of its racist glory. In 1912, the joint federal-provincial McKenna-McBride Royal Commission was established to resolve the province's Indian reserve "question," paving the way for the elected and so-called honourable leaders of Parliament and the legislative assembly to orchestrate yet another "on behalf of Her Majesty" legal land theft from Natives.

Four years later, the commission predictably recommended the removal of nearly fifty thousand acres from fifty-four reserves. Perhaps it's worth reminding readers that the Indian Act, an act of the Canadian Parliament, states that "An Indian reserve means a tract of land the legal title to which is vested in Her Majesty, that has been set apart by Her Majesty for the use and benefit of a band . . ." Who, then, does the land belong to? The Indians? Or the Queen? I know none of my ancestors ever signed our Okanagan territory over to any Queen.

The historical fact is both the United States and Canada were built on broken Indian treaties and outright theft of Indian reserve and reservation land. With the simple swipe of an official pen, governments were able to steal original Indian reserve land. It stands to reason, then, that it can today, with the simple swipe of an official pen, return all the original Indian reserve land now under provincial control. That's where mature adult reconciliation has to start.

Rez land thefts not only occurred all across Canada but also all over the United States. My people on the U.S. side of my traditional territory were also forcibly removed from their traditional village sites and later had over two million acres stolen from their original Colville Indian Reservation.

On April 9, 1872, President Ulysses S. Grant issued an executive order to create the Colville Indian Reservation consisting of 2.8 million acres. As settler demands grew over the following twenty years, the government took away the north half of the reservation right up to the Canadian border, just south of Osoyoos. The U.S. government deemed over one million acres of my people's Rez lands "excess land" and opened it up for (white) settlement.

In its racist tradition, the sacred Black Hills in South Dakota were also unjustly taken from the Lakota under pressure from settlers. In 1876, Sioux Chief Standing Elk told the U.S. Commissioners who were threatening to cut off rations if a proposed treaty was not signed that: "Your words are like a man knocking me in the head with a stick. What you have spoken has put great fear upon us. Whatever we do, wherever we go, we are expected to say, 'yes, yes, yes'—and when we don't agree at once to what you ask of us in council you always say, 'You won't get anything to eat! You won't get anything to eat!'" Deliberate starvation was a Canadian and U.S. government policy that was used against First Nations in order to take over their lands. What kind of people, what kind of governments have starvation of families as part of official government policy?

The United States sees itself as the land of "liberty and freedom" where "all men are created equal"—which is a bunch of BS. Military force was used again and again to outright massacre First Nation peoples, take away their freedom, and force those who weren't killed onto reservations. In Colorado in 1864, more than one hundred Cheyenne and Arapaho (mostly women and children) were killed by the U.S. Army at what became known as the Sand Creek Massacre. The attitude of the United States Army and the government toward the First Nations at the time was clearly stated by Colonel John Chivington, who was also, believe it or not, a Methodist pastor: "Damn any man who sympathizes with the Indians . . . I have come here to kill Indians, and believe it is right and honorable to use any means under God's heaven to kill Indians . . . Kill and scalp all, big and little . . ." Historian Ari Kelman wrote, "We remember the Civil War as a war of liberation that freed four million slaves, but it also became a war of conquest to destroy and dispossess Native Americans."

Like most First Nations people, I get upset when our place in Canadian and American history doesn't get mentioned. Every time I hear on the news after a mass shooting that "this is the worst mass shooting in American history," I think, *Don't Native people count as human beings? And when does American history on mass shootings start? What about the Wounded Knee Massacre?*

In South Dakota the last registered massacre of Indians occurred at Wounded Knee in 1890 where, as I mentioned earlier, more than 250 Lakota, mostly women and children, were gunned down by the United States Army. There is a saying in Indian Country: "Remember Wounded Knee." I now know what that means. Being at the Wounded Knee mass gravesite reminds me of the "real truth" of how Canada and America were founded. My people buried in that mass grave were not attacking white people. They were leaving one reservation to go to another reservation, and they were starving and freezing. They loved their language and culture and wanted to remain Indian (Lakota). Instead, they had to suffer the racism of the Indian agents and white ranchers who harassed them until they had to leave their homes. The United States Army chased them through the cold South Dakota winter and surrounded them. They called it a "battle." It was no such thing. It was a massacre.

Just a few weeks before Wounded Knee, General Nelson A. Miles sent a telegram from South Dakota to Washington, D.C., saying, "The difficult Indian problem cannot be solved permanently at this end of the line. It requires the fulfilment of Congress of the treaty obligations that the Indians were entreated and coerced into signing. They signed away a valuable portion of their reservation, and it is now occupied by white people, for which they have received nothing."

Nothing was done. Miles's telegram went unanswered. On December 29, 1890, the United States Army surrounded the Lakota encampment and perpetrated one of the biggest mass murders on American soil. "There was a woman with an infant in her arms who was killed as she almost touched the flag of truce," recounted one eyewitness. ". . . A mother was shot down with her infant; the child not knowing that its mother was dead was still nursing . . . The women as they were fleeing with their babies were killed together, shot right through . . ."

In its racist tradition, the U.S. Army awarded the 7th Cavalry Regiment twenty Medals of Honor—its highest commendation for "bravery"—for shooting down fleeing Indian women and children. In 2001, the National Congress of American Indians passed two resolutions condemning the military awards at the Wounded Knee massacre and called on the U.S. government to rescind them. No U.S. soldier should ever be remembered for receiving a medal for the massacre of Indian women and children. As for those on social media calling for the removal of Native sports names and logos, why are they silent when it comes to advocating for the removal of those twenty Medals of Honor?

In the renowned book *Bury My Heart at Wounded Knee*, author Dee Brown writes: "It was the fourth day after Christmas in the year of our Lord 1890. When the first torn and bleeding bodies were carried into the candlelit church, those who were conscious could see Christmas greenery hanging from the open rafters. Across the chancel front above the pulpit was strung a crudely lettered banner: PEACE ON EARTH, GOOD WILL TO MEN."

Every First Nation child and parent, every Canadian and American who truly believes in "truth and reconciliation" needs to "Remember Wounded Knee" and go to the mass grave. Go there, and think about it.

Millions of tourists go into the Black Hills of South Dakota every year to view a United States shrine: Mount Rushmore National Memorial. But few visitors know their own history. Few know that long before there was a Mount Rushmore, the Fort Laramie Treaty of 1851 set aside the Black Hills as part of the Great Sioux Reservation. The government of the United States knew it; it stole that land and in the 1980s America's "conscience" drove it to reconcile this past injustice. The U.S. government set aside more than $1 billion as a reparation payment to the Sioux Tribes for their loss of the Black Hills. The tribes of the Fort Laramie Treaty have for decades turned down the money. As Chief Sitting Bull and Chief Crazy Horse said more than one hundred years ago, "The Black Hills are not for sale!"

The U.S. government broke that treaty, reduced the Sioux reservation by more than seven million acres, and built Mount Rushmore on stolen Lakota land as a "Shrine of Democracy." The irony has not been lost on Native Americans. I've seen—and love—an Indian poster from the 1970s that shows half of Chief Sitting Bull's face creeping up behind the carved heads of the four presidents. Below it, in big letters, the caption reads: "The Shrine of Hypocrisy!"

There are unsettled land claims all over North America. The more than hundred-year struggle for justice and the return of stolen reserve and reservation lands continues to test the core character of Canada and the United States. Our old Chiefs were deemed illiterate by Canadians and Americans back in the late 1800s, but there is more to intelligence than the ability to read and write. I beg you to read their speeches; you will immediately know their concerns and their grasp of reality. The oratory of our leadership back then was second to none. Remember, all First Nations were oral societies; your word was your bond, and history and law were passed on through the spoken word. All teachings—social, political, spiritual/religious—were learned through talk. Native languages had to be precise and all encompassing.

The original languages of North America were very descriptive and beautiful. I love listening to Native languages, the original languages of this land. Those sounds and words are thousands of years old and are spoken nowhere else in the world. First Nations languages are the historic poetry of North America. "Illiterate" is a word used to describe someone who cannot read or write. It does not mean some-one who cannot think or communicate.

Early historians marvelled at the oratory of Indigenous leadership in Canada and the United States. When the reserves and reservations were being created, federal reserve commissioners would often incorporate Native words and ways of explaining things into treaties. The line "As long as the sun shines, grass grows, and the river flows . . ." is an example of how languages can paint a picture through words. Tribal Nations all over North America were put through the same Federal government "forked tongue" scam. They wrote one thing in their treaties, using our own words to do it, but then did the exact opposite.

One of my heroes, Chief Joseph of the Nez Perce, said:

> In the treaty councils the commissioners have claimed that our country had been sold to the Government. Suppose a white man should come to me and say, "Joseph, I like your horses, and I want to buy them." I say to him, "No, my horses suit me, I will not sell them." Then he goes to my neighbour, and says to him, "Joseph has some good horses. I want to buy them, but he refuses to sell. My neighbour answers, "Pay me the money, and I will sell you Joseph's horses." The white man returns to me and says, "Joseph, I have bought your horses, and you must let me have them." If we sold our lands to the Government, this is the way they were bought.

There has been far too much stalling over our outstanding land issues. Many Native leaders have grown old and died poor while sitting at negotiating tables listening to more promises about the "nation-to-nation" relationship. The endless talk goes on while the forests continue to be logged, rivers and oceans continue to be over-fished, and more dams and pipelines are built on unceded Indian land. Government and corporate income goes up every year while most First Nations are fed breadcrumbs and apologies—cheap words with no sustainable dollars behind them.

My people have been demanding "Canadian justice" for more than one hundred years. In the early 1900s, the old Chiefs, who grew up not speaking or reading English, challenged the "Honour of the Crown" in meeting after meeting. In a declaration to Prime Minister Sir Wilfrid Laurier in 1910, the Chiefs of the Okanagan, Shuswap, Couteau, and Thompson tribes sought a "just and lasting resolution to the land question."

These Chiefs set out their positions on Aboriginal Title and Rights:

. . . The Whites made a government in Victoria. Perhaps the Queen made it. At this time, they did not deny the Indian Tribes owned the whole country and everything in it. They told us we did. We trusted the whites and waited patiently for their Chiefs to declare their intentions to us and our lands. What have we received for our good faith, friendliness and patience? Their government or Chiefs have taken every advantage of our friend-liness and weakness and ignorance to impose on us in every way. They treat us as subjects and force their laws on us. They say they have authority over us. They have broken down our old laws and customs. They laugh at our Chiefs and brush them aside. They have taken possession of all Indian Country and claim it as their own. They have never consulted us in any of these matters, nor made any agreement, nor signed any papers with us. They treat us as less than children and allow us no say in anything . . . We never accepted these reservations as settle-ment for anything nor did we sign any papers or make any trea-ties . . . We condemn the whole policy of the B.C. government towards the Indian Tribes of this country as utterly unjust, shameful and blundering in every way . . .

Back in 1910, the Chiefs from the southern interior of British Columbia were speaking of the same injustice felt by all other First Nations throughout the continent. As I read those hundred-year-old words and feelings today, they remind me of my recent dealings with some of the staff in Canada-Indigenous Relations and Northern Affairs and other government bureaucrats. The more things change, the more they stay the same.

I have had young, ignorant and highly paid bureaucrats call my Rez "Her Majesty's land." I have had them tell me that, according to the "fiduciary responsibility" of the Queen, we can or can't do this or that with Osoyoos Indian Reserve land. I told those young ivory-tower Indian agents that no member of the Osoyoos Indian Band has ever said that our land belongs to their Queen. I have told more than one staff member from Indian Affairs or Aboriginal Affairs or Indigenous Services Canada to take their fiduciary responsibility and Her Majesty's empty promises straight back to England. The time when white Indian Affairs staff, being paid by "Indian monies," can still oppress us should be long over!

Recently, I attended a gathering of First Nations and British Columbia cabinet ministers in Vancouver. The organizers had a big board set up where the Chiefs and council members could write on a small round piece of sticky paper and answer the important question, "What does reconciliation mean to you?" I almost puked when I saw what other Chiefs and council members were writing, meaningless fluff words like "respect," "understanding," "healing," "mutual respect," "truth," "harmony." I had trouble finding even one statement that I could apply to my Rez, one statement that would create a single good-paying job or build one house or pay for all the costly programs (health/education/recreation/language and culture) on which the Osoyoos Indian Band currently spends millions of dollars.

Read the bleak history of the poverty First Nations have lived under in Canada and the United States and you will see that words like "respect," "truth," "recognition," "healing" and "wellness" have been used and said a thousand times by government and past Chiefs, going back a hundred years. Chief Joseph also heard many good words from government back in the 1870s, when his people were being led by gunpoint to the Colville Indian Reservation. This was his response: "Good words will not give back my children. Good words will not make good the promises of your government. Good words will not give my people good health and stop them from dying. Good words will not get my people a home where they can live in peace and take care of themselves."

All the old pre-Rez Chiefs heard good words that didn't amount to a damn thing except more broken promises and poverty. In my own territory, the Chiefs of the Spences Bridge wrote to the head of government in 1914. "We have spoken to you many times already in various ways," they told Prime Minister Robert Borden. "We have related our grievances to you, and asked for redress. . . . what we consider to be our rights as the original occupants, possessors and sovereigns of this country . . . and see that we obtain justice." They received none.

I don't want any more touchy-feely words. I want our original reserve lands back. I want all existing reserves to get back to their original size. Rez leaders should not be falling for this trick of colonial good words (the "pat your Indians on the head" kind). Reconciliation must translate into land justice and economic freedom for all First Nations. Reconciliation must translate into words that deal directly with the land and creating jobs and money for First Nations government coffers.

Genuine reconciliation also means recognizing First Nation hunting and fishing rights in a modern context. I want to give a shout-out to all the past Native leaders whose work and sacrifice we benefit from today, and a salute to those who stood on the front lines of demonstrations and organized marches and rallies and sat face to face with government at First Ministers meetings. When Canada sought to patriate its constitution from Great Britain under Prime Minister Pierre Elliott Trudeau in the early 1980s, Native leadership demanded Native rights be included. They made demands, not useful words of healing and respect, and forced section 35 into the Canadian Constitution. I am forever grateful for the leadership we had back then. Chiefs Bill Wilson, George Manuel, Billy Diamond, Ed John, Stewart Phillip, Elijah Harper and so many others fought the reconciliation fight and got into "good trouble," as all civil rights leaders do. Native leadership had to kick open the parliamentary door—and they did.

Non-Native governments always need more and more money, therefore true reconciliation must move First Nations away from financial dependency to being truly independent financially self-supporting nations. A recent and obvious example of true reconciliation is the Treaty Land Entitlement program. This federal program was established to settle land debts owed to those First Nations that never received the reserve land they were promised under the original treaties. We know and we can prove that many First Nations were ripped off when it came to their original Indian reserve land allocations. First Nations involved in these negotiations with the federal government were laser-focused on reconciling a past injustice, and the issue was not open to fluffy word interpretations. And this time it worked. The injustice was confirmed and the federal government admitted the wrong and provided over $400 million in compensation. Many First Nations used the settlement funds to purchase back some of their original reserve lands. In many cases, the Rez had lost its very best economic development land through those early rip-offs—as Osoyoos did. Had we been allowed to keep the land treaties were signed on, history might have been profoundly different.

Part of the reconciliation was that "urban Indian reserves" could be created. In many cases, First Nations reserves were established on swamps and flooded lands, with little chance for the community to create jobs and establish a viable economy. Now, however, they could purchase land under Treaty Land Entitlement in municipal boundaries. To date, some thirty-three First Nations have acquired more than 2.7 million acres of land. Many urban reserves have been created and are generating new jobs and new revenues.

This creation of urban Indian reserves is real reconciliation in action. It is action to be celebrated. Now, if we could only skip the nice words and support the re-establishing Indian reserves to their original size. No mayor and council should ever oppose additions to Indian reserves or the creation of an "urban Indian reserve."

I'll say it once more in simple, logical, non-political, non-BS language—real reconciliation must start with addressing the outstanding, century-old injustice of Indian reserve land thefts.

CHAPTER 13

BE A LEADER, NOT A POLITICIAN

"The sad truth is inescapable; much of the blame for our current unhappy situation rests with our own people . . . To put it bluntly, the Indian people are still in one hell of a mess. It's not enough to put the finger of guilt on Ottawa; that finger points at us as well. We're in a hell of a mess because we allowed ourselves to get in a hell of a mess."

—Harold Cardinal, *The Rebirth of Canada's Indians*

Back in the late 1960s and early 1970s, when Native organizations were being set up all across Canada, Harold Cardinal, a Cree, gained a great deal of experience at every level of government from the Rez to national politics. I find it both ironic and satisfying that, more than forty years later, some of his observations match mine. What's the saying? "Great minds think alike"? Yeah, forty years later most Rezes are still in a hell of a mess because we continue to allow ourselves to get into a hell of a mess!

I admit that when I first got elected I did a lot of finger pointing at Indian Affairs. My inclination was to blame Indian Affairs for many of our problems. It took about a decade for me to realize that the finger pointing also has to be done internally—right here on the Rez.

After being involved in more than a few elections I know first-hand how dysfunctional and downright nasty Rez politics can be. So many individuals are elected to office not because people wanted to vote for them, but because the voters wanted to throw the existing Chief and council out. The end, however, doesn't always justify the means. It's like a hockey coach getting angry at his players and benching the first line to play the fourth line—and thereby losing the game. Rez politics frequently doesn't have much logic or business sense going for it. Too often, it is politics based on pettiness and hate, not progress.

It took me a few years in the trenches of Rez politics to realize that our biggest obstacles are not off the Rez—they are right inside our own house. Rez politics is a "blood sport." It can be downright brutal, and Facebook and Twitter have made it even worse. How we talk to each other on the Rez, how we treat each other, how we disrespect each other is our biggest challenge. The legacy of poverty and dependency on foreign systems has caused all sorts of internal dysfunction. Our biggest challenges exist among our own selves, and that is where the greatest gains or losses will be realized, depending on how we deal with this reality. Are we a house divided or a house united?

Native societies were never perfect, although most Natives like to think they were. Greed existed among traditional tribal societies long before Europeans arrived. Inter-tribal warfare was common. In my tribe's Coyote stories, which predate colonization by centuries, there are lessons about greed and other bad human traits. No different from the Europeans, tribes fought and killed each other over territory. When the fur trade started with the French and English, Native people fought each other over a bigger share of that new economy. Yeah, we have to admit that we are as human as anyone else when it comes to greed. Today, our Chiefs and councils play a huge role in who gets what, when, and how—which is the basis of politics everywhere.

In today's fast-paced internet world, where a wealth of information is always at your fingertips, I still hold to an old saying on leadership: "Leaders are readers." In the book *Rebuilding Native Nations: Strategies for Governance and Development*, edited by Miriam Jorgensen, there is an excellent chapter entitled "What Do Leaders Do?" The author talks about visiting an American Indian nation and talking with the people there about their challenges. "There was a discussion of failed enterprises on this reservation, the lack of jobs, the hardships associated with long-term poverty, and the difficulty of changing things," she writes. "People had diverse views about what was wrong and what could be done about it. Finally, one of the participants exclaimed, 'What we really need is a good leader!' Several others nodded their heads. 'Right,' they seemed to say, 'That's the problem.'"

I have asked many people (Native and non-Native) the same important question: "Why are so many First Nations still messed up today?" Yes, there are the historic reasons having to do with racism and abuse, but if we're talking about today, the answer I most get is "lack of good leadership." I was listening to one of my Zig Ziglar CDs recently, one where the author talked about the difference between being "interested" and being "committed." A lot of people are "interested" in getting in shape but not "committed" to getting in shape. A lot of people are "interested" in their job, but are they "committed" to their job? A lot of people are "interested' in being elected but are they "committed" to running for and holding office? Being "interested" in getting in shape, for example, means you'll focus on it when it is convenient, when you have time, or when you are in the mood. If you are "committed" to getting in shape, you will go to the gym when you don't feel like it, and you will run when you would rather walk. In Indian Country we need candidates who are committed to leadership, not merely interested in it for personal, selfish reasons.

We need candidates who are *committed* to improving the quality of life on their Rez, not just casually *interested*!

I love the quote: "Leaders Change the Conversation about Governance, Development, and the Future." So true! At the Osoyoos council table we start most meetings with a language lesson. We put our disappearing language at the top of our agenda and have one of our language speakers come in. Only then, after that language lesson, do our discussions move to operational issues and economic development. As one B.C. Chief put it, "On the Rez we need to change our conversation and stories to opportunity and success—not blame and failure."

As I have said before, I believe in the power of quotations and messaging. Drawing on my readings over the years, I have put many "quote signs" up around my Rez. Some of the quotations are taken from books. Some, though, are my own:

> *"If your life sucks it's because you suck."*
> *"A real Warrior financially supports himself and others."*
> *"Change your body change your life."*

Good leaders hear all sides before making a decision. Good leaders don't play the blame game. Once you are elected, whatever happens on your Rez during your two-to-four-year shift (term) is on "your watch." Know that, understand that, and never forget that.

I am often asked for advice on leadership, especially by those from all across Indian Country who are running for Chief or council for the first time. After going through nineteen elections and winning eighteen of them, I guess I can claim a 94 per cent success rate, which is a damn good scorecard. I am an ongoing student of Rez politics and have had hundreds of off-the-record talks about Rez elections with those who are about to enter Rez politics as well as those who have been there for years. I have also been to hundreds of Tribal Council meetings and closely observed how other Chiefs and councils conduct themselves around the leadership table.

As a veteran of hundreds of "Rez table" battles, I like to think I have developed a rare combination of "street smarts" and "book smarts." I have seen the good, the bad, and the ugly on and off the Rez. Like many Chiefs I have been in numerous high-level corporate board rooms and in many top federal and provincial government offices. My best leadership experience, however, comes from the more than three hundred Indian reserves and reservations I have visited in Canada and the United States. Based on all of that, I believe I've earned the stripes to offer some advice on Rez elections. I also feel a deep obligation to do so.

Leaders are not just elected people. Anyone who collects a paycheque for doing a job that is responsible for improving the lives of Native people, from daycare staffing to running the tribal office and tribe businesses—all staff—hold an important leadership position. In today's world, you cannot be a leader if you don't read and continuously update your knowledge. And don't just read at your office job—read at home every night and every weekend. Staying in mental shape means forever sharpening your thinking. Too many people, once they leave school or take up a certified trade, stop reading and researching their area of expertise, even if they've been doing their job for ten, twenty, or thirty years. Just as you have to work out every week to remain in strong and healthy physical shape, leadership requires its own regular mental workouts to maintain and update the knowledge needed for personal growth. Others—the ones I call the "slackers" and "fakers"— have one year of experience that they repeat over and over for ten, twenty, or thirty years. They may be showing up at work, but to me, it's still just one year of experience, no matter how long they claim to have been working. But whether it's one year of experience you have or twenty, the big question remains: Are you improving the lives of people in your community outside of your own immediate family?

It is remarkable how often I hear that a particular Rez is politically controlled by a large and extended family. The Chief, councillors, and staff often have close family connections. They have a monopoly on the community or a business—more like the Sopranos than the Waltons! Fortunately, that is not the case in Osoyoos. I certainly don't belong to one of the biggest families on the Rez. In fact, my immediate family is one of the smallest. On my Rez it takes more than one family group-ing to get elected, which is the way it should be. Some people naively think, *I'm gonna run for Chief or council and all my family is going to vote for me, so I'll get in.* First, it's rare that all of your family is going to vote for you, even if they all say they will. And even if they did, it's probably not enough votes to get elected. On my Rez it takes many votes outside of your immediate family to get elected.

We know that those who are successful in business, sports, and pol-itics do their homework. American business writer Jim Rohn has said, "The key word to life change is 'study.' If you want to be wealthy—study wealth. If you want to be happy—study happiness. If you wish to be successful—study success." Obviously, then, if you want to be a leader—study leadership. Why don't most elected people study leader-ship? As Jim Rohn said: "What's easy to do is also easy not to do."

Still, after nineteen elections I consider myself a "student of leadership," and I still want to learn from the best. When I hear a First Nation is not doing very well, my first question is "Who is their lead-ership?" My second question is "How long have they been elected?" In order for things to improve, either the leaders have to become better leaders each year or there needs to be a change of leadership.

"Everything rises and falls on leadership," American author and leadership expert John C. Maxwell has written. When one of the world's most knowledgeable and renowned experts on the subject says something like that you would think most managers, politicians, Chiefs, and councillors would realize he is right, wouldn't you? But do they even know who John C. Maxwell is? Very few managers or elected officials study what they claim to be. They must therefore believe in the absurdity that they are "born leaders"—time to puke!

Peter Brown, a very successful business man from Vancouver, told me: "There is a big difference between a boss and a leader. A boss is often feared and gives orders. A leader seeks consensus and team work and is not afraid to hire people smarter than him. A leader is not feared but respected and often earns affection from his people."

Just getting elected or appointed to a management position doesn't mean you're an instant leader. You might hold a leadership position, but that may be in name only. Show me your library on leadership. I read and listen to some of the best thinkers on leadership, people like Jim Rohn, Mark McCormack, Zig Ziglar, Harvey Mackay. I have to mention one of Canada's best, David Chilton, who wrote *The Wealthy Barber* and was a regular on TV show *Dragons' Den*. I know very few people on any Rez who buy books to study wealth. I not only bought the book many years ago but was honoured to share a speaking stage with Dave. I got another signed book to add to my collection.

I don't take my position or title lightly. My ego is not so swelled up that I can claim to be a know-it-all. Even after more than thirty-five years as a Chief, I still seek out advice on leadership. The sad fact is that most people who run for election on the Rez don't study anything that has to do with leadership. They will study poker, sports, Facebook, and even bingo—but not leadership! Why bother when, too often, all you need is to be part of the biggest family on that Rez or to just make a few costly promises.

An equally sad fact is that some mean-spirited people are able to get votes by throwing mud. Spreading lies and rumours is something real leaders don't do! Yet that juvenile behaviour still exists among a few who run for council seats. Remember, it's not the title that makes the position, it's the person. As the great leader Winston Churchill once said, "Leadership is not something learned in school. It is innate, an indelible mark of character steeped in integrity, courage, conviction, underscored by the moral imperative to do the right thing."

In sports, your performance is on full display; the score measures your success or failure. That is why one of my first leadership questions is "What is your scorecard?" Even kids in minor sports want to know what the score is. You're either winning or losing. You're either moving the yardsticks forward, staying in the same spot, or losing ground. In politics, half of those elected think that carrying a coffee cup, warming a seat, and throwing around uneducated opinions is being a leader. Others see being aggressive and threatening on social media as a display of their high intelligence. What nonsense!

Have you noticed that aggressive people use the phrase "I've got strong opinions" to justify their mean heart? In martial arts, the best teachers and fighters are usually the most peaceful and quiet. Many tribal people have a saying for their leaders; in English, it translates roughly into "those of the nice." Yes, "nice-hearted" people always turn out to be the very best leaders. History has proven that the best leaders are not the meanest and loudest but the most peaceful and kind. We can all take leadership lessons from Martin Luther King Jr., Mahatma Gandhi, and Chief Joseph.

Real leadership—the kind that it takes to be a good teacher or a good coach—requires certain skills and behaviour 24/7, not just during office hours. It requires good conduct and manners at all times, both at work and in the community, and not just at election time. I give an eye roll to those who wave or say "hi" to you only around election time. As for the phony hugs, it's really sickening how hugging spikes only once every two, three, or four years, mysteriously around the same time—election time. Spare me the "I love all my people" BS, please.

Not all Chiefs and council members are created equal. Some are good, some bad; some are hard-working and some are lazy asses! Some are learners and respectful and some are narrow-minded know-it-alls. On the Rez, *all* members are your people, for better or worse! It doesn't matter if they voted for you or not—you treat people the same. Some still say to me, "Why do you help them? They didn't vote for you." To a phony politician, that might matter. To a leader, people in need are not judged on how they voted.

Real leaders lead by example, and to me that example starts with an impeccable work record. Real leaders show up for work and they work hard, every day. They are *dependable*! Off the Rez, anyone who had overdue parking tickets wouldn't get elected; yet on the Rez some people have no shame and will run for office while owing their community hundreds and even thousands in overdue rent. A simple rule is that anyone who does not pay their bills is ripping someone off and therefore should not be able to hold any position of leadership. Your personal credit is also your scorecard.

When it came to mentors or role models, when I was growing up on the Osoyoos Rez there was nobody. Our very humble home was miles away from the next Rez house. I have sat in leadership training sessions where the group is asked questions such as "Who was your role model or mentor that got you started?" Some say it was their dad or mom, a coach or a teacher, or an Elder. I have listened to some really inspiring stories. Sometimes I have felt embarrassed waiting for my turn to answer, because I had no one person or life-changing event. There was no Rez school or gym, no youth programs when I was growing up. I didn't get to go anywhere or see much on and off the Rez in my early years. My family, like most reserve families, was very poor. My dad was never around and my mom had a very tough job looking after me and my brothers and sister. Alcohol abuse was everywhere.

If anything, my leadership skills grew out of sports and my work ethic as a seventeen-year-old—and it happened almost by accident. In the late 1970s, I played what we called "Indian hockey" and "Rez fastball," and it was usually me who put a team together and set up the practices or organized a tournament. People began to notice: "Hey, this kid can organize stuff!" Even the older players began to leave things to me. I'd pick out the uniforms, design the crests, order everything, and look after equipment. I'd book the rink, fix the batting order, or organize the forwards and defence. It's not as easy as it seems deciding who bats in what order, and who sits and who gets pulled when the game is on the line. Most players, even the older guys, didn't want and couldn't handle that kind of management pressure. Sometimes after the games the finger-pointing and arguments would erupt in the dugout, and I'd say, "Okay—next time you make the call." Usually that would shut everybody up.

As a teenager, I also organized fundraising "Rez dances." Everything good cost money, and our sports teams had to raise their own operating costs. There was no grant money and very few band office handouts. The Inkameep Hall dances were our major fundraising events and they became well-known throughout our territory. The best sports-fundraising party was always at the Inkameep Hall! I would get someone old enough to sign the liquor licence. I did it to do it right, not out of any fear that the RCMP would come on the Rez and up to our community hall during a dance. The "Queen's Cowboys" knew better than to check on a Rez dance. The Mounties would need the whole Canadian Army if they wanted to enforce Her Majesty's laws at a Rez dance. Our hockey or fastball dances were where real friendships and lifelong bonds were formed (some "snagging" too!). After a few "pops," the Rez boys were saddled up!

You really don't think about such things as demonstrations of leadership when you're a teenager. I was just better than most people at organizing things and talking to people. I even talked the older ones into pitching in at tournaments. I looked after the team expenses and paid the bills. Thinking about it now, a seventeen-year-old managing sports teams where most of the players are much older is unique. But I was able to prove my organizing skills and deal with team dynamics between the older and younger players. In business that would be called "people skills." I developed a network of sports contacts and arranged for the umpires, the scorekeepers, and the referees, and I made up the schedules. As the old saying goes, "if you want something done give the task to a busy person."

Sometimes leaders don't want the burden of working with others who don't work at the same pace. My brother Arnie wrote in a letter to Chief and council:

A good heart, a good attitude, and good intentions and all that stuff is not a substitute for ACTION. It's just like a Rambo movie. When Rambo went anywhere on any assignment, who went with him? That person needed the same skill level, the same enthusiasm, the same commitment, dedication, focus, knowledge—or else forget it. Rambo did his best when he travelled alone. I don't mind help, but if it does not come in the form of high-level energy directed towards one objective then forget it.

If it's at all possible, keep the politicians away from these discussions, since there's nothing worse than someone who is full
of ideas but hasn't rolled up their sleeves in years.

I agree with Arnie. Sometimes the very best way to lead on a risky,
gotta-get-the-job-done mission is to be like Rambo!

As Steve Jobs used to say, "If you want to make everyone happy,
don't be a leader, sell ice cream." Making decisions is what leaders do.
I have known many people who are good workers, but I would not
want to have them making company or governance decisions. The
first criteria (though not the only one) for being a responsible decision-maker is to be a good worker. Leaders have to lead by example.
Your personal attendance sets the tone, so you must have among the
best attendance records. There are no excuses for not having near-perfect attendance. If it takes more than one hand to count your absences
and late arrivals then your attendance sucks (I'm not talking about
genuine sick days here). You're not dependable, and if you are not
dependable at work—the job that pays your bills—then you can't be
counted on to make good decisions.

We have people in OIB who have not been late or missed a single
day in more than five years. Doris, our office secretary, was one of
my first hires as Chief; and then there's Billy at our golf course—I
commend their attendance records. The older people always seem to
have the best attendance. A few years ago one of my older people,
J.R., told me he had not missed one day of work in over fifteen years
(and he worked outside—*wow!*). Jane needed only one hand to
count the number of times, in over twenty years working at the
winery, that she missed work because she was sick. And not once
did she actually call in sick. When she was sick she still got up early
and went to work. Once she was there, the boss would send her

home when he saw she was truly sick. Jane knows what it means to "Indian up!"

Sick days are often abused these days, as anyone can phone in sick or go get a doctor's note. Ever notice how some people use up every one of their sick days each year, and if they don't use them all they then expect to "carry over" those days into the next year? Some even expect to be paid for sick days they don't use. Anyone who has near-perfect attendance on the job and doesn't abuse sick leave? That's leadership. It's also a matter of trust. People who have poor attendance and abuse sick days can't be trusted.

A good leader—whether a manager, a teacher, or a coach—not only has to show up on time every day, but they also have to demonstrate a high level of performance and a willingness to make tough decisions. You're not there just to warm a chair and stare at a computer screen, or look for meetings to go to where you can yak the hours away. Some people can stickhandle words all day long but can't put the puck in the net when it comes to making a decision. They can talk a good game, but they can't produce a real scorecard that tells you what they accomplished to earn their paycheque. You can have near-perfect attendance every month, but what other performance indicators have you got? How have you earned your paycheque?

You can't be like a Canadian senator and never have to face a public vote, come and go as you please, show up late for work and leave early, and rack up the travel expenses and per diems by attending every meeting you can. It is pure neglect of office to be running all over Indian Country while on your Rez there is poverty and other problems in dire need of your leadership. Good leaders are conscientious about time and selective when it comes to the meetings they attend. Meetings can be a big time-waster and a waste of money, too. With today's technology, many meetings can be done by phone or

Wounded Knee Memorial Motorcycle ride, South Dakota:
my favourite yearly motorcycle trip!

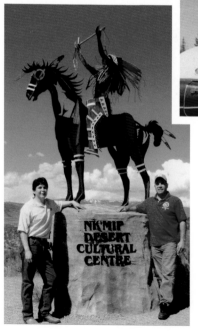

Me with Johnny Blood's Rez bomb, during T.H.E. R.U.N. to Ottawa in 1980. The Blackfoot-organized run was a political demonstration about treaties.

I love Native art. Smoker Marchand and I designed the "Chief" sculpture, and many others, that sit on our resort in Osoyoos.

Native kids should not have to grow up with broken windows and gangster crap!

Rez hockey: Native sports are very important to me.

Have pride in your ride: no Rez bombs! I have a hot-rod heart.

I love speaking about First Nations independence and nation-building. Native people must share our experiences—good and bad.

Speaking in Australia: Aboriginal people worldwide fight the same injustices.

Chief Louie believes tough love and economic development will rebuild native communities.
is Ottawa finally listening?

The first cartoon ever published of me—I love the symbolism.

Former NHLer Gino Odjick loved one of my quotes so much ("Native people have always worked for a living"), he put it on his vehicles.

Rez hockey fundraising dance. A few of the boys!

This election sign should be on every Rez!

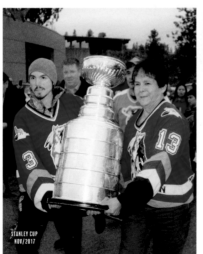

Me and my son, Vern, carrying the greatest trophy in sports.

I love the words and picture that one of our youth put on the board at our youth centre!

Chief and Council: more than 70 years of Osoyoos Indian Band leadership.

One of my "happy places": the gym is where I go for some real healing and wellness.

With our consultant Mel Woolley and our former COO Chris Scott (right). Every Rez needs experienced business people on their team.

One of the best trainings for leadership is to coach a kids' sports team. My son, Vernon, the goalie, and my brother, Arnie (far left).

"Indian Up!" sometimes means doing crazy sh*t!

Iron Horse "Honour Ride" through the Little Bighorn Battlefield.

My "little boss," Zenaya, with her parents and grandparents.

First Rezskin ever inducted into the Canadian Business Hall of Fame (Toronto, 2019).

Some of my family at a personal development course. I love personal development. Front row: my daughters Clarissa and Sarenna (far right).

My grandmother and mom, on Grams' 100th birthday in 2014.

Receiving the Order of Canada in 2017: Any award I receive is really an Osoyoos Indian Band award. I love having my people, from young to old, share in community awards!

My spouse Brenda and me with the Navajo/ Hopi motorcycle honour ride. Notice my Blackhawks jersey!

video conference. There's no need to spend company money on expensive plane tickets when a phone call will achieve the same results. I'm often asked by other Chiefs and councillors about the meetings I might be attending; for example, "Are you going to the Chiefs meeting in Vancouver?" "No," I say, "I got too much work to get done on my own Rez." Besides, there may be Okanagan tribal staff going as well as representatives from other Native organizations to which the Osoyoos Indian Band belongs. If I went to every meeting I was invited to, I'd be gone somewhere every day of the week.

I'm shocked at how much unnecessary travel some elected and non-elected staff do. Don't spend company money like play money. Spend company or tribal money, even if it is funded or grant money, as if it is coming out of *your own pocket!*

One very important question for those looking to lead: "How have you improved the condition of your Rez and the lives of your people each year?" And I mean your "people," *not your immediate family!* If a decision has to be made that involves immediate family, you must abstain from voting. Nepotism and favouritism is still one of the biggest complaints on every Rez. Yes, nepotism is hard to control in small communities, but conflict-of-interest rules and procedures must be put in place to reduce it from happening.

If you are a mature, open-minded decision maker, one who thinks of "we" (as opposed to an immature, narrow-minded decision maker who thinks first of "me"), making decisions is never easy. It can be stressful and time-consuming, as all relevant information and opinions must be gathered. It can also be very emotional. Any time you are making decisions that affect the lives of your people and the land, animals, plants, and water, you must have an open mind and do a lot of thinking and reading. I hate it when at Tribal Council meetings some Chiefs say, "I can't make a decision; I have to bring it back to my community." That might sound nice and noble, but in most cases it's a political cop-out.

And what exactly does that even mean? Bring it back to whom, and how? On the Rez, decisions are made by council or by referendum. Now, bringing some issues to a community meeting where only a small group of voters show up is not the proper way to make decisions. The majority of voters seldom show up at band meetings. This means that if something difficult does get passed by those who do show up, others who are upset with the decision can round up their supporters for the next general meeting and overturn the previous vote. As a result, tribes that make decisions through endless band meetings or general councils tend to find themselves spinning their wheels; not much gets accomplished.

The Harvard Project on American Indian Economic Development has more than thirty years of research on how some tribes are breaking away from federal dependency and poverty. When I first heard about their research, in the early 1990s, I brought Steve Cornell, one of their professors, to Osoyoos to share his thoughts on why some Native communities are successful and others are not. Steve talked about different approaches to successful development. He called the failed model the "standard approach" and the successful model the "nation-building approach." In the standard approach, decision-making is all about the short term: someone else sets the development agenda, and development is treated primarily as an economic problem. This model depends mostly on finding the next federal grant. Economic development on a Rez, therefore, is more of a political problem than an economic problem. The nation-building approach is where success lies. In this model, Rez leadership makes the decisions and mobilizes economic opportunities. Decision-making is strategic, so it is impor-tant that council develops effective governance decision-making. Rules, policies, procedures, transparency, and accountability are all part of any good business, and they are also how a tribal government should be run. The nation-building approach features the following key ingredients for successful Rez development:

- A stable band/tribal governance structure.
- Governance rules that protect day-to-day business and program management from political interference.
- An administration that can get things done reliably and effectively.

Business only goes where it is safe to operate. Legitimate business people will not set up shop in the midst of a "civil war" (Rez leader-ship fighting amongst itself). I was told many years ago that you "don't air your dirty laundry in public." Keep your Rez divisions and disputes internal and out of the local media. In order to attract business people and business opportunities the Rez must develop a "business climate." The community must be pro-business.

Most decisions (especially operational decisions) should not be made through council or community votes. Managers are paid to manage under written policies and operational procedures. Corporate boards don't waste their time on day-to-day business decisions. On the Rez, most everyday operational and employment issues cannot be interfered with by the Chief, the council, or membership. Yes, some issues need to be brought to the membership for a vote, but those important issues should be decided through a proper referendum, not at a band meeting. Chiefs and councils should set up public policies and procedures to reduce political interference and micro-managing.

Office politics exist everywhere. Shop talk, water cooler talk, and coffee break gossip exists everywhere. The Rez is no different. We are not one big happy family. I have to work with people I would rather not put up with, but so does everyone else. I know some would rather not work with me.

"Everyone is entitled to their own opinions," the saying goes, "but not their own facts." Too often, council and band members have only uneducated opinions, and they make decisions based on rumours and not on facts and the truth. Having an opinion based on what you read on Facebook? *Come on*, that's for kids! Having an opinion based on what you read on the internet? *Come on*, that's no better than reading a tabloid! Half or more of what you see on social media is "fake news." Half of what's on the internet is for shock value and for fools. A mature person waits for the truth, waits for facts to be gathered, waits to hear all sides of an issue before even thinking about forming an opinion. Many years ago someone told me, "No matter how thin you slice baloney, there are always two sides."

I have said at meetings many times, "This is my opinion *at this time*, but my opinion may change, depending on new information." Being mature and open-minded means you are always willing to take in additional information and listen to other points of view. A responsible decision-maker will change his or her opinion now and again. I hate dealing with narrow-minded people who refuse to change or alter their opinions. Politicians often have opinions based on who voted for them or who the decision might affect—especially if family is involved. But a real leader takes the names out of the issue and does not let politics or personal interest rule the day. I have often said, "It doesn't matter who said it. What matters is—is it the truth?"

I can't work with people who do not know how to compromise. Narrow-minded people have a "My way is the only way" attitude. In business and in politics I try remember what President John F. Kennedy believed: "The art of politics is knowing when to compromise."

It is said that "the art of being wise is knowing what to let go." I get many complaints each week about people, not issues. Now, I could spend a lot of time and cause a lot of hurt feelings if I followed up on every one of those complaints. And so, I deliberately choose *not* to do so. I listen and then just let it go. Many times, not doing anything makes the issue go away. Sometimes the person lodging the complaint forgets about it; and often what is said in private needs to remain in private. It is a completely different matter, of course, if the complaint is a serious accusation, and the person saying is willing to lodge the complaint in writing. Most people will actually refuse to put their complaint in writing. And so, if all you're doing is verbally complaining about someone else's work performance and spreading hatred, I just let it go.

The way I make most decisions is to have an imaginary scale in my mind. On one side of the sale is a minus sign (-) for negative. On the other side is a plus sign (+) for positive. I list all the negative stuff on one side of the scale and all the positives on the other. Then I put the list down on paper and see how the scale tips. When it comes to most important decisions, there are items on both sides of the scale; it is very rare any decision is all to the good or all to the bad.

It's also worth remembering that many of the decisions a leader makes will upset someone—maybe even close friends and family. But decisions can't be made based on family relations. I have been threatened many times, but when that happens, I try to keep in mind the words of Jax Teller, a character on one of my favourite TV series, *Sons of Anarchy*: "That's how you become a leader—doing the shit that hurts the most."

A leader also has to look beyond a single decision to see how that decision will affect other elements on the Rez. This happened when we had to make that multimillion-dollar decision on whether or not to allow an electrical power line to run through the Rez. The line would go through the mountains and across Osoyoos's environmentally sensitive desert lands. Some of our people were against the plan because of environmental concerns. I had those concerns on my list as well. Some were against it because they felt the financial compensation was way too low. I even got an email saying, "Each Band member should get $1 million each—get that and you will go down as the greatest Chief of all time!" Even though I once read Donald Trump's *The Art of the Deal* (hey! I will admit it), there was no way I was going to be able to negotiate $1 million for each and every band member. All negotiations have to be grounded in reality when financial numbers are being discussed. You can't just pull numbers out of the air and ask for the moon . . . Okay, go ask for the moon—but if you don't get it, come back to Earth.

In order to be successful, negotiations have to reach a state of "win-win"—a place where both sides feel they are walking away with something they want or need. Some of my people say, "But the white man will make a profit, so I'm voting against it." Everyone in any deal or sale wants to make a profit—even you. Think about it: your house, your clothes, your food, your electricity, your gasoline all involve people (yes, white people) making a profit off of you. For every item you own, purchase, or wear someone made a profit on you (yes, even your underwear). Do you really think the groceries you buy every week are sold to you at a loss? That Walmart you love is a multi-billion-dollar company because of profit. That's called the free-enterprise capitalist system. There is nothing wrong with anyone making a profit, just as long as it is within reason.

I have been involved in many multimillion-dollar negotiations and, of course, I always try to get the most out of any potential deal for my Rez. Before any major settlement, we hold a community referendum on the project and, as happens in all Osoyoos Band votes, some vote yes, some vote no, and some choose not to vote at all. That's called democracy. There will always be some "no" votes, and that's fine. Perhaps consensus was possible when a community spoke one language, practised one religion, and were all raised with the same core beliefs. But today, with intermarriage and different religious beliefs, Natives from the same Rez do not look through the same lens. Heck, today we even argue on how to do a Sweat House ceremony.

In my early years as Chief I made the mistake of trying to please everyone. A few years ago, I was having a ceremonial sweat with a war veteran, Charlie Horse, and I asked him about tough decision-making. Charlie said, "Don't wait for things to be perfect. Most things are not perfect, and you can't keep on waiting around for a better deal." So true. Don't wait around for the "perfect deal," which might never happen. Don't let the perfect be the enemy of the good. Sometimes during your term you will only get to "better." I have learned to have the "little-bit-better philosophy." I always hope to make things better this year than last year. Will this decision make things better? As one of our long-serving Chiefs in the Okanagan, Grand Chief Stewart Phillip from Penticton Indian Band, once said: "As a leader, sometimes you gotta say—this is as good as it gets. Our responsibility is not about making everyone happy, our responsibility is to get results."

Another piece of advice for leaders? Be extremely careful of the "scorpions" among your people (and in your camp). Those who aren't happy even when they get 90 per cent of what they want, and who won't accept anything unless they get 100 per cent of what they want.

Those who will kill a deal even if it hurts them and their own community. Remember the fable of the scorpion and the turtle:

> *The scorpion needed to get to the other side of the creek and called over Turtle. "Can you give me a ride to the other side of the creek?" Scorpion asked.*
>
> *Turtle said, "I don't trust you. If I let you on my back you will bite me."*
>
> *Scorpion said, "No, I won't. Don't be silly. If I do we will both drown."*
>
> *The turtle thought, "Yeah—you won't do that to yourself." So he let Scorpion on his back and headed across the creek. Halfway across the creek Scorpion bit Turtle.*
>
> *As they were drowning Turtle said, "I trusted you and now we will both drown—why did you do that?"*
>
> *Scorpion said, "I am a scorpion—I always bite."*

Every Rez community has some scorpions—and things can get really dysfunctional when they are elected to council or appointed to management. It's like trusting that one day the government will provide enough funding. Or that one day a different developer will walk into our office and offer us a better deal. There is always the illusion of a better deal. There is no perfect deal, just as there is no perfect program or service. If we're waiting on perfect, we might as well shut down all the treatment centres and hospitals, as none of them come close to sobering up or curing 100 per cent of their clients.

Some elected people have no clue about how to move at the speed of business—there are too many plow horses and not enough race horses. Too many council members operate from the "funded" or "grant" mentality. Some would rather scare away business opportunities and just continue the dependency model and hand out welfare cheques. Business is a risk-reward proposition, and it's hard work on top of that. Some leaders don't want to hire consultants or experienced people and get it done right. There's a saying—"A boat is safest in the harbour, but that is not what a boat is for." That says it all.

Back in 2000, we made our very first off-reserve business purchase: a cement plant. We had no experience in operating a cement plant, and the purchase was a huge risk. I had a core group of business advisors, and our chief operating officer, Chris Scott, had come from the real business world—not the grant-funded world. Even after one does a feasibility study there are still a lot of best guesses. We could have "what if-ed" that risky business purchase to death. We could have pushed for a better deal, and pushed ourselves right out of contention. The deal was not perfect, and I sweated that million-dollar business decision for many years after we bought the cement plant.

Once you buy something, though, the real work starts. Now you have to make it operate properly and pay its debts, year after year. Fortunately, buying that cement plant has turned out to be one of the very best risky decisions I have ever been involved in. It was a team effort, and it wasn't easy for our team to deal with all the negative thoughts on the Rez and still sign the purchase agreement. But it worked out just fine—so far (fingers crossed).

Having business-minded members on council is critical to decision-making. Long-term council member Tony Baptiste played a major role in the cement plant purchase. I remember one of our very best business contacts, Don Triggs (from Jackson-Triggs wines), telling me years ago: "In business there are times you just gotta pull the trigger! Take a shot."

In most decision-making, I operate on the "future is now" principle. Your people need services now. Your community needs infrastructure now. Your Rez needs more money now. We need to buy more land now—not wait. The more you wait the more costs will go up. On that power line project, I had to consider the good-paying jobs my people would have access to during construction and the community capital improvements that would follow. Sure, the power line is a bit of an eyesore for anyone crossing our beautiful desert lands. There were certainly some negatives. But the positives outweighed the negatives. Every time I see that power line I have mixed feelings: I wish it wasn't there, but then I change my negative thoughts to positive thoughts of our youth centre and fully paved Rez road.

As a Chief, I realize that important decision-making always involves a team effort. Sometimes, outside consultants are needed (and it doesn't matter what their skin colour is). Even so, most often the public expectations weigh heaviest on the one sitting at the head of the table—the Chief. The extra scrutiny and expectations go with the position. If you can't accept that this is part of the job, you shouldn't have the job. I take a lot of comfort in something Bruce Lee (my first hero as a teenager) once said: "You will continue to suffer if you have an emotional reaction to everything that is said to you. True power is sitting back and observing everything with logic. If words control you that means everyone else can control you. Breathe and allow things to pass."

When I was in the Native American Studies program at Lethbridge in the early 1980s, a Mohawk cultural leader named Tom Porter told us: "Native Leaders need to have skin seven layers thick. Because some people will try to hurt you with sharp words to penetrate your heart. Some people, and even your own people, will say bad things about you when you are tired from a long day's work and travel. But you can't let those negative words reach and hurt your heart. Therefore your skin as a leader must be seven layers thick. Don't let those sharp words get to and hurt your heart."

Forty years later I still remember that part of Tom Porter's speech. It has helped me every day that I have been a Chief. My skin has become seven layers thick. The gossip, the negativity, the bad words still hurt and bother many of my close family and friends, but I remind them not to let it bother them because I refuse to let it control me. I believe in the "asshole rule"—don't let assholes control you.

Some community members—the "haters"—still try to play cheap-shot politics. The truth is, when it comes to politics some people do need a "bannock slap." Some of my buddies from the prairie Rezes have told me that some of the so-called traditionalists on their Rezes will try to hurt each other with "bad medicine" at election time. I don't believe in "bad medicine." I do believe that some Rez people are bad-spirited and mean-hearted. Even in this day and age, some Rez people believe they have spiritual powers and can take a piece of your clothes or hair and sing a song or wave their magic wand and actually physically hurt you or a member of your family. I don't believe they have any "power." It's true that, as the expression goes, "some people light up the room . . . by leaving it." I prefer that those folk leave and take their bad medicine with them. My attitude is, "You're no medicine man or woman—go smudge yourself!"

I read once that what a person does in their private moments, when there's no one around to see, reveals their true character. Would you lie? Would you steal? Would you cheat to win? Would you blame someone else? I remember one such private moment vividly. I was barely old enough to read, but I loved reading comic books. I was left in a car by myself on the main street of a small town in the Okanagan Valley. I got bored and went into a store and found a comic book rack. I had no money. I picked up many comic books and put them back.

I walked around the store aisles but always came back to that comic book rack. I was nervous as I planned how to steal one of those books. Eventually, I left the store with a comic book under my jacket. I got back into my mom's car and read that comic book over and over. I knew I was safe and would not get caught, but as I held that comic book it didn't feel right. No one was going to know I stole a comic book, but I would know.

My internal voice got to me (and I was just a grade-school kid at the time!), so I put the comic book back under my jacket and went back into the store. I remember being more scared trying to put the comic book back than I had been trying to steal it. The store clerk was watching me more closely now, as she had seen me come and go. I thought about just getting out of that store with the comic book still under my jacket. But I eventually returned the book without getting caught and was relieved to get back to the car. I've never told that story to anyone—until now.

In business and politics, trust is so important. I have learned to trust some people through defining moments, where they showed me true character I didn't know they had. People who watch your back, who show kindness and fairness and consideration in private moments. People who are loyal to you.

I can't respect someone I don't trust. We may disagree on some issue; we may vote differently. But as long as we can trust each other we can still work together and respect each other. When you work for the same company, when you belong to the same Rez, you are part of the same team. In sports, some players may not like each other or the coach, but when the puck drops everyone has to do their part to achieve success. Real leaders can set personal feelings aside for the greater good of the organization. There's a good quote: "A team is not a group of people who work together. A team is a group of people who trust each other." As author Annette Verschuren wrote in *Bet On Me*: "Your network is your net worth. Every leader needs a personal advisory board. Most don't make networking enough of a priority. The reason? I think it's because they are operating under the mistaken belief that success and effective leadership is all about what you know. Effectiveness as a leader is all about who you know."

Good leaders are always looking to expand their network and get to know and learn from successful people—like when I met Daryl Carter.

Daryl is a founding member of Area 27, the club racetrack that is on the Osoyoos Indian Reserve. It's a 228-acre land lease and the track was designed by Jacques Villeneuve, Canada's most famous race car driver. I had supported the land lease because I saw spin-off benefits for our other businesses, as well as awesome networking opportunities. The track would bring tourists and successful people to small-town Oliver, and some, it turned out, even bought houses at our golf course. Daryl was often around the track, and I got to know this experienced money and securities manager and sometimes business coach. World-class athletes still need coaches, as do most successful people.

Daryl told me about Dan Sullivan, who has a program called "Strategic Coach." What caught my interest were Dan's rules: he said he could not work with you if you broke any of them. I asked what the rules were:

1. Be on time.
2. Do what you say you're going to do.
3. Finish what you start.
4. Say please and thank you.

I love those rules—there's just so much common sense in them—and it sucks that most of us have to put up with people who are constantly breaking them not just in business but in life. I got the first three rules right away, but I wanted to discuss the fourth. "Is it really that important to always say please and thank you?" I asked. Then I remembered what many Native traditions talk about when selecting a leader: that leader must be "of the nice."

I am learning that some of the best rules for business and politics come from moms and grandparents. We need the teachings of our moms! My daughter Sarenna has taught my "little boss" (my five-year-old granddaughter) a variation on Rule #4. When Zenaya wants something, she says, "Please, I love you and a hug." On the Rez we all gotta learn to say, once in a while, "Please, I love you and a hug!" I want to make this my own version of Rule #4.

And to add one more rule: I can't work with anyone who doesn't do some work on evenings and weekends. As I have said many times, "Don't work like a grant-funded bureaucrat lazy ass who only works the easy Monday-to-Friday grade-school hours." Business is seven days a week every week of the year. I can't work with anyone who doesn't take calls, emails, or texts seven days a week, holidays included.

There's a commercial on APTN that says, "The quality of your life depends on the quality of your circles." That's networking—the Rez way. Every individual has a few circles of friends. Successful people have many circles. I have many diverse and different circles of friends and contacts—hunting buddies, sports buddies, politics, business, motorcycle buddies. And now, grandparent buddies. To be successful in business and politics you have to have more than the basic circle of friends that you hang around on weekends or evenings. Your family is obviously your most important circle, but I would say you can never have enough buddies in your business and political circles. The more circles you can develop, the better a leader you will become. If you keep on hanging with the same people year after year and don't expand your network, you're not growing and you're missing out on opportunities.

I encourage youth to get involved in a variety of different activities. Be careful who you choose to hang around. Hard-working people usually hang around other hard-working people. Athletic types hang around active people. Drunks and druggies hang around people who drink too much and take too many drugs. Lazy people hang around lazy people. I tell youth that if they want to make more money, have more things, and open up more opportunities, they should stay away from the lazy asses and find some hard-working people to hang around. There is no good future in hanging around bums and the "go-nowhere crowd"—*even if those people are your cuzzins!*

Remember: "If you're the smartest person in the room—you're in the wrong room." That's a quote leaders should keep under their pillows and read at the start of every day. A smart person finds smarter people to hang around. You want to be a better hockey player, then skate with better hockey players. If you want to learn how to make money, hang around people who actually make money.

My election campaign has not changed in over thirty years. My platform has always been one sentence: "I'll create more jobs and make more money for the Osoyoos Indian Band than anyone else." Rez jobs and band/tribal income are two scores that are easy to track. Every Rez should be keeping count of the number of jobs in their community and the amount of money—especially the amount of self-generated revenue. Remember: it is money, not good words or promises, that pay for all needs on a Rez. Cash must be on your scorecard, and self-generated money determines if your Rez is an independent or dependent community.

I never want the Osoyoos Indian Band to be dependent on government grants, as we once were. I don't want to walk the hundred-year-old trail of failed promises and broken treaties left by the federal government. Economic independence and regaining our heritage and culture in a modern context is and continues to be my leadership goal.

Many years ago, as I crossed the U.S.-Canada border at Osoyoos, I noticed a plaque that had been erected by the Rotary Club. I now make sure to read that plaque every time I cross, as it contains a few simple, common sense rules have really helped guide me in my decision-making. I love the Rotary Club's "4 Way Test":

> The 4 Way Test . . . of the things we think, say or do
> 1. Is it the Truth?
> 2. Is it Fair to all concerned?
> 3. Will it build Goodwill and Better Friendships?
> 4. Will it be Beneficial to all concerned?

On the Rez, we need to ask ourselves that first question. We need to get to the truth before we make decisions or even form an opinion. We don't need someone's Facebook BS, rumours, or politically jaded opinion. Everyone has an opinion. Not everyone has the facts. I still sometimes make the mistake of jumping to conclusions upon hearing only one side of an issue. Leaders have to remember to not make the mistake that so many adults make in believing the hearsay that's going around. Always ask for the truth. Always say, "Hold on, let's gather up the facts and listen to all sides before we even try to have an opinion, let alone make a decision!"

Mature, experienced people know there is a big difference between opinions and facts. Facts and truths stand on their own and don't belong to anybody, whereas an opinion belongs only to that person offering it. And a wise person's opinion should be subject to change based on new information, facts, and truths. Politics (or your backers) should not control your thinking. Only the truth should control your thinking. As John Lennon, one of my all-time favourite musicians, wrote: "gimme some truth."

CHAPTER 14

REZ ELECTIONS

"Vote for your cousin or vote for someone who knows what they are doing!"

—cartoon caption

Before there were reserves and reservations, we did not have elections to pick leaders. Tribes had different systems: some used the hereditary system, some had clans, some had a family head system, and some leaders rose up naturally through great deeds and accomplishments. Some had multiple Chiefs. Some leaders were defined by their special expertise, such as medicine or hunting. Some became War Chiefs. In my tribal area, we had Salmon Chiefs who were in charge of the fishing grounds.

Under the federal government, Rez elections became part of the assimilation and civilization policy. On both sides of the border a two-year election cycle was put in place. In Canada, the Indian Act of 1876 called for each First Nation to elect one Chief and a council member for every hundred people, up to a maximum of twelve council representatives. In the United States, Congress enacted the Indian Reorganization Act of 1934, which called for tribes to adopt constitutions based on the U.S. corporate board model.

For decades First Nations in Canada and the United States have been allowed to customize their elections. Now First Nations can set the elections to three- or four-year terms and can elect any number of council members. Some use different terms for Chief, such as "chair-person" or "president" or "chief councillor." Different titles, same job.

Today, elections are a very important part of the Rez culture. This foreign system of deciding leadership was instrumental in breaking down traditional roles and responsibilities and in causing political dysfunction and mistrust among Native people. Indian agents and missionaries purposely used elections to cause divisions and political unrest. Whenever any level of government wanted to use Rez land for a right of way, or swindle away Indian land for settler purposes, the conniving Indian agents and missionaries aligned themselves with Chiefs and council members who were less hostile to government demands. Scratch my back and I'll scratch yours.

Divisions among tribal leadership go back to the early years of treaty talks, when our people couldn't speak English and the unbeliev-able pressures of starvation and foreign diseases ravaged our villages. In Lakota territory, Chief Sitting Bull was against selling the Black Hills and the reservation land allotment, yet the Indian agents and mission-aries created political unrest that led leaders from the same villages to fight against each other. That still continues to this day. In the early years, the majority of tribal people refused to vote or participate in elections that were run by forked-tongue Indian Affairs agents.

After more than one hundred years of this "Rez culture," First Nations communities are not one big happy family. Like in all towns and cities, there are deep divisions on Rezes across Canada and the United States. Like in all neighbourhoods, there are some neighbours who won't talk to each other—and some who just plain hate each other. Today, elections are necessary as we seek to gain more inde-pendence to govern the affairs of our communities. I have been through nineteen elections in Osoyoos and have observed and studied many local, provincial, and national Native elections. I have read many custom election codes and hundreds of campaign letters. It is depressing to see Native elections becoming so much like white elections. Natives like to call down "white systems," yet in this most important area of picking our leaders, many Natives have crossed over to "dog-eat-dog, win-at-all cost" white politics.

In *Descendants of Warriors*, Saulteaux/Cree author Kamao Cappo wrote:

> With the elective system in place, the reserves have become divided amongst ourselves. I think it is safe to say that on every reserve there are three groups of people at any given time. There are those who think the present Chief and Council are the best and are doing a great job. There is another group who think the incumbent Chief and Council are unfair and only care about themselves. The third group of people couldn't care less one way or another about who is the Chief and Council. These groups also change positions intermittently in regards to opinion depending upon who is elected as leaders of the community.

Our ancestors would be disgusted by how Rez elections are now mirroring off-Rez elections. Many Natives forget that, first and foremost, we are a people, with a shared bloodline. On the Rez there should be no political parties, no "us and them." Rez elections should not follow the cheap-shot, money-rules campaign ways of white elections.

One of my supporters in my very first election told me they were going to put up signs saying *Vote Clarence for Chief*. I told them, "Don't do that—and if you do I will take them down myself." I told them that's what white people do in town and we don't need to be doing that on the Rez. Our Rez election is *our* business. We don't need to have signs up for the general public to see. The local newspaper and radio station asked me for my platform and I told them it was none of the public's business. I talk to many OIB voters personally, face to face whenever possible. That's the Indian way: no signs, no campaign letters, no tweets, no Facebook. If I can't meet members face to face, then the telephone will have to be used, but otherwise I stick to the Indian way. I have never written a campaign letter to my membership. I don't come from a Rez of thousands of people. Our community is small enough that I can still have direct personal contact with the majority of my people.

Now, as Rez populations grow I know it's becoming more difficult to sit down one on one with most of your people. In most tribes, membership is scattered on both sides of the border. In many First Nations, 50 per cent or more of the membership lives off the Rez, mainly due to lack of jobs and housing. So today, campaign letters— by mail, email, or Facebook—are becoming part of the Rez culture, no matter how much some of us (old-school types) dislike it.

I tell Native youth not to vote for anyone that gives the usual "I care speech." That is the easiest and most common speech to make: *"I care about the people—I care about the land—I care about the Elders—I care about the youth—I care about our language and culture—I care about housing—I care about education—I care about health programs—I care about drug and alcohol abuse—I care about fairness and equality for all members—I care... I care... I care..."*

I'm still amazed by how many voters get conned by this kindergarten—political promises talk. I once read that the two top emotions in politics are hope and fear. Every calculating politician today plays on people's "hopes and fears," and they will lie through their teeth to spread whichever suits their purposes, even when there may not be cause for either. It's easy to claim you care. What's not easy is to come up with the money to pay for everything you claim you care about.

Education and health care are not free. Programs for Elders and youth are not free. Environmental projects cost money. Housing is not free and neither are language and cultural programs. The war on drugs and alcohol is not free, either—treatment centres and counselling are expensive. Everything has a price tag. Real leaders know talk is cheap but governing is not.

Unlike off the Rez, the Rez's elected leadership really does affect everything for its membership, from cradle to grave. Therefore, voting and electing good, honest, hard-working, experienced leadership must be a priority of every Native community. If your Rez is plagued with economic and social problems, look at who your leaders are! Every election is a chance to improve your community's socio-economic situation. If your community scorecard sucks, quit electing the same people who keep making the same teary-eyed—but unfulfilled—"I care" promises. Leadership isn't about advancing yourself. Leadership is about advancing your people.

If bad, self-serving people are being elected to council, it's partly because good, reasonable people are not voting. As George Jean Nathan wrote: "Bad officials are elected by good citizens who do not vote."

I receive many emails and phone calls from young Native people asking for advice on running for Chief or council. So, here is my advice to all future Native Rez leaders. Start by always being a genuine leader and a hard worker who pays their bills, and not another phony politician. Leaders lead by example and tell the truth. Leaders don't spread lies; politicians spread lies. On the Rez we should never act like politicians in white elections, where one side calls down the other side. If someone has to call down another in order to make themselves look better, take a closer look at the one slinging the mud: there's probably something

corrupt there. On the Rez we are a *people*—the *same* people—not political parties in opposition.

A leader should always be in good financial standing. As I mentioned earlier, anyone who owes the band or tribe money should not
even be allowed to run for office. If you can't balance your own
chequebook, why should membership trust you to look after a community's finances?

And here's some advice for those doing the voting: only the very
best workers should be elected—not the best yakkers or complainers.
Don't elect slackers! Don't elect people who don't hold a full-time job
(unless they have retired and earned their rest). Don't elect people who
show up late and do nothing more than carry around a coffee cup.

How a person spends their personal time is also very important. If
the community's elected leaders are good, hard-working people,
what do they do with their personal time? Do they attend evening and
weekend meetings and cultural gatherings? Do they support youth
programs? I call evenings and weekends "leadership hours." As Sam
Walton, the founder of Walmart, once said; "It's during the week you
keep up with your competition but it's on evenings and weekends you
get ahead of them!" Real leaders work evenings and weekends. They
attend community gatherings to show real support; they don't just
show their face around election time (eye roll).

The greatest hockey player of all time, Bobby Orr (sorry, Gretz),
once said, "You have a level. I have a level. We all have a level." Just
because you're a good player does not mean you would make a good
coach or manager. The fact is that all-star players very rarely make
good coaches or managers. Maybe being on council or working as a
boss is not your level. Some good workers can do good work outside
their specialty field and some can't. Some can handle stress and others
cannot. Sometimes there are too many Chiefs and not enough Indians.

Most people, including me when I was young, do not understand the "smoke and mirrors" of phony politics. Tribal politics can be brutal, and the scars can last for decades. Those who grow up on the Rez have personal opinions about each other and at election time those opinions can get out of hand. I know Facebook and other social media platforms can be used for the good, but on the Rez I have seen and heard about how much they can also be used for the bad. There are too many "keyboard warriors" who won't call you down to your face but will sure feel brave while on the internet. It's really sad that some people can win and lose votes based solely on the gossip and slander that gets spread. That's not Indian; that's white electioneering.

A university-educated friend of mine in Alberta ran for council once, got elected, and never ran again. She told me: "I was twenty-four, idealistic, and was blindsided by the amount of corruption in people I thought were honourable and good people. I was angered by the old guys who took every opportunity to travel and never pro-duced anything. People I held in high esteem were basically phony and really didn't care about making things better. They just wanted to spend money. Being on council is like walking in a minefield. I am happy with my work in the hospital. I can say what I want and do what I want without being scared of being fired or losing an election."

Another very qualified friend from Ontario told me she got elected to council once and won't run again. "Our Chief and council were not interested in business and economic development or supporting our culture," she said. "No one read or did the homework before our meet-ings. They argued with band members and with each other. It was toxic."

Yes, elections are a democratic necessity and we Native people have to learn how to get through them while keeping our traditional values of honesty and respect. We have to remember that, as band and tribal members, we are a people for life. "All my relations" is not just a throwaway expression. "All my relations" is a code used at spiritual ceremonies, an Indian code of honour and respect! "All my relations" is something real Rezskins need to remember and practise at election time!

Just as in every family, there will be times when we disagree. Only on the Rez will you see siblings, or a parent and child running against each other for Chief. On one Rez, a father and son ended up in a court battle after the election. All Rez families have disagreements on important issues, but the mature families will still love and support each other. I know a few Rez couples who at election time discuss the candidates list for council and, after a mature discussion, vote for different candidates. Now that is the "Indian Way"—the mature, respectful way to vote.

I still hear about "mafia" crap happening in some Rez elections—ridiculous promises of jobs, housing, and cash. Real leaders don't make promises that can't be kept, never threaten anyone, and never pay for votes. A Chief back east recently wrote a letter to his community saying that he will not run for Chief again because of threats of violence against his family. No candidate's spouse or kids should ever be threatened by anyone. A Mohawk Chief once told me, "You can threaten me, but never threaten my wife or kids—or I'll blow your head off." Another Chief from Ontario has had enough of the "Rez thugs"; after the "Facebookers" spread lies about her owning a house in Arizona, she's decided she won't run again. As she told me, "Today, some band members have no shame in lying on social media." In a recent Osoyoos election, one of these phony "Facebook warriors" spread lies about me owning shares in a pipeline. It's sad what some lowlife Rez members will do and say to steal a few votes.

Land-lease and settlement votes are just as important as election votes. Every Rez needs income each year to pay for all its programs and services, or else a decline in those services will happen. It's up to leadership to bring in that money. Real leaders take all votes personally and don't take a casual or lazy approach to voting. Real communication doesn't happen only on Facebook, or in newsletters and membership meetings. Real communication also means "working the vote"—which means talking to as many people as you can, one-on-one, in person or over the phone, up to and including on voting day. Remember, your community's future is in those votes—so get out there and *earn* them. In my one-on-one conversations with people, I'm always surprised when someone says, "I didn't know that. That's not what I was told by others—and I'm sure glad we had this talk, because now I understand what the vote is all about."

I have presided over eighteen Osoyoos Indian Band councils, I have chaired more than seven hundred council meetings, and I have worked with seventeen different elected Osoyoos Band members over my thirty-five years as Chief. When I think back on and look at pictures of my past councils, I am very proud of each and every one. Some of those elected members were, and still are, political opponents, and some are my close friends. A few have also been elected many times and been involved in much of Osoyoos's success. Tony Baptiste and Ronny McGinnis have both served for more than twenty years. The Osoyoos Chief and council has the same important factor that most successful Native communities have—continuity of leadership.

Some of those seventeen past and current council members didn't vote for me and I didn't vote for them. But that's fine; that's democracy. The main point is that in every Osoyoos council I have been part of we have been able to work through our political differences and still get Osoyoos Indian Band business and governance done. As Winston Churchill once so wonderfully put it, "democracy is the worst form of government except for all those other forms that have been tried from time to time."

The bottom line is that Chiefs and councils are elected to improve the standard of living of their people and provide better cradle-to-grave services. Important decisions have to be made by resolutions. In some years the Osoyoos Indian Band council will make well over one hundred Band Council Resolutions, which are formally voted on. We make many tough, emotional decisions. We try to reach a consensus, of course, but if that fails we go to a vote—because, like it or not, a decision has to be made. Of the hundred or so Band Council Resolutions enacted each year, the vast majority (80 to 90 per cent) have the signatures of the Chief and all council members. A score of 80 to 90 per cent is a very good scorecard in most business and political fields.

Furthermore, good leaders should always act like their community's youth are in the room, like their kids are watching and listening. I love having kids in the council chambers or at band meetings. Many times council women will bring their babies to an all-day meeting. Children's voices—their laughter and cries—remind me of why I sit around the council table. As part of a school project, the grade school kids on our Rez came up with a list of what constitutes proper conduct for their school and classroom. They called it the "Essential Agreements." Here are a few rules from Osoyoos Indian Band kids that every Chief and council can learn from:

> Be good communicators by listening, thinking, and being open-minded.
> Be respectful toward others, yourself, the land, and our surroundings.
> Ensure that the Okanagan culture and language are at the forefront of our decisions.

Listen before responding.

Have a weekly "drop everything and tidy" time.

Be respectful of each other and our differences.

Imagine if all Chiefs and councils could learn from our kids and follow their grade-school classroom rules at all our meeting tables. The simple fact is—the Rez kids are right!

At Osoyoos, our council spends the majority of its time on the Rez, as would be expected. We concentrate on looking after the home base, our own backyard. We concentrate on creating jobs and making money for our programs and services. Yet all over Indian Country I hear an ongoing complaint that the elected leadership travels too much, and that Chief and council members are away from their local Rez duties too much and never around.

I realize national and provincial issues are important, but that is why we have a National Chief being paid the big bucks and overseeing a big staff. Further, we have provincial Regional Chiefs also being paid the big bucks, and overseeing still more staff. Now add the Tribal Council wages and staff. Aren't there enough paid political Indian leaders and bureaucrats whose full-time job is to look after provincial and national issues? If those being paid to protect and advance Native issues off the Rez are not performing, then get rid of them. There should be no need for any Chief or council member to spend so much time away from their home base.

After nineteen elections I still have one of the lowest travel budgets of any Chief in the country. Over the last few years my travel expenses have averaged around $7,000 a year. Yes, that's accurate. Most Chiefs run up travel expenses well above $20,000 a year—every year. Heck, the senior staff on most reserves spend more on travel than I do. I was on a plane once sitting next to an old Native woman who had just visited her Rez, and she told me her people dislike how often their Chief and council members travel. They have a saying: "Our council are never there—they are always in the air."

Yes, there are many off-Rez title and rights issues. And yes, we need to continue to fight the federal, and provincial and state governments. But that is why we elect and pay for Native political organizations at the Tribal Council, federal, and provincial levels. There are meetings every week all over Indian Country, on many issues. It is easy to send a proxy to represent you. I always give my proxy to another First Nation that's asked for it. But as a Chief I was elected by my people to first and foremost look after the immediate and pressing local needs of my Rez.

At Osoyoos, we also don't have the rule that elected people can't hold a job in the community. We don't believe that being elected to Chief or council means you have to give up your job. I believe those who hold jobs, especially senior department or management positions, should be that Rez's "A-team." If one of your people currently holds an important position for your community and is doing a very good job in that role, they shouldn't have to quit their job to represent their people on council. Under that rule, some of the best candidates will not run for council because, obviously, there is no job security in Rez politics. I say let them hold on to their regular job and also get elected. At Osoyoos it would cost roughly $500,000 a year (all costs included—salary, travel, phone, office space) to pay six full-time council members. That's $1 million every two years, every election. I can think of a heck of a lot of better things to spend a million on.

It's true that I've heard a few council members justify a less-than-stellar performance by blaming their job: "I had a full-time job to do and didn't have enough time to deal with council issues." What about your weekends and evenings? That's why you get an honorarium. We meet two times a month (twenty-four times a year) during office hours. Our system is not perfect, but neither is a system where elected people can take a leave from their full-time regular job to be on council, and if they get voted out they get their old job back.

If your Rez population is in the thousands and your business growth warrants it (let's say $50 million or more), then yes, there may come a time when some or all of your council should be paid a full-time salary and take up office space as elected leaders. If you want to attract your best and hardest workers to run for Chief and council, then yes, they have to be paid, but paid fairly and properly. I have seen some bands and tribes overpay their council members and others underpay. No Chief should be paid more than a prime minister, president, or premier. No Chief or council member should be paid more than the mayor of a major city. I don't care how much money that nation brings in—the wages have to make sense. On the other side of the ledger, a few bands and tribes have not caught up with real-world wages; they pay their elected leadership so little that the best talent from that community won't run for office. Why put up with job insecurity and political bashing for next to nothing? There is an old rule in business: "You get what you pay for." Chief and council members have one of the toughest, if not the toughest, jobs on and off the Rez and they need to be paid properly and fairly by their community.

Back in the 1980s Osoyoos didn't have a chief financial officer, a chief operating officer, or a human resources department. But as we grew, completed more transactions, and took on more duties and responsibilities, our organization chart added more full-time positions. It's important, though, to think carefully before making these kinds of changes. Never spend more money or add more positions without first doing a cost-benefit analysis. The Osoyoos council system has changed and will continue to change as we grow and evolve and face new challenges and opportunities.

After thirty-five years as a Chief, I know I don't have thirty years on council left in me. I know I don't have another ten years left in me, and neither should I! I have been blessed to have served over three decades in a role of the highest honour and responsibility on a Rez— being a Chief. I was first elected Chief at the age of twenty-four, so I have been a Chief in my twenties, thirties, forties, fifties, and now sixties (it sucks getting old). I remember partway through this run, after ten years or so, I decided I wanted to match or beat my great-grandfather Manuel Louie's record of being Chief for sixteen straight years and being elected eight times in a row. Now I have far surpassed that. And at the time that it happened I didn't even notice the milestone. I was too busy trying to create more jobs and bring in more revenue to the Osoyoos Indian Band.

The word "Chief," even though it is English, is a meaningful word to First Nations. In Indian Country in Canada, we use the word Chief. In the old treaties and in old Indian Affairs documents, they used the word "Chief." The word "Chief" is what white government officials called our village leaders. If I used the Okanagan word for "Chief" (I'lmiux) most people wouldn't understand what I was saying. If a Mohawk speaker used the Mohawk word for "leader" I wouldn't know what they were saying. So, we use the word "Chief." I was in the Australian Outback a few years ago and was introduced to many traditional Aborigines. Many spoke almost no English, yet when they heard the word "Chief" I noticed right away a different look in their eyes. Same thing in New Zealand. The Maori people are very strong in their own language and culture and yet the word "Chief" means a lot—far more than other English titles.

In tribal societies, the title of Chief means far more than "Mayor," "Governor," "Senator," "Chairperson," and, yes, even more than "Prime Minister" or "President." A real Chief is not a politician and does not act like a politician. On the Rez, the duties and responsibilities of the "Chief" truly encompass cradle-to-grave care for the people, as well as duty to the tribal lands. An Elder at Osoyoos told me many years ago, after an election: "In your hands you hold the lives of our people." I have not forgotten that sentence.

On some reserves and reservations the word "Chief" has been replaced with "Chairman" or "President." Indian Affairs policy in the 1930s tried to modernize and model the Rez council after a corporation board. Still, on those reservations I never hear anyone say that they are a descendant of a past chairman or president. They say, "I'm a descendant of Chief Joseph," or Chief Sitting Bull, or whatever Chief their tribe once had. Old-timers on Osoyoos always ask for "the Chief" when they come into the band office. Younger band members tend to use my first name and very seldom referred to me as "Chief." I am fine with that. I don't need a title in front of my name. When business people ask how they should address me I always tell them to call me "Clarence." But often, even after I tell business or political contacts to use my first name in and outside of meetings, they still address me as "Chief." When the local white old-timers talk to me about my great-grandfather they always say, "The old Chief Manuel . . ."

Today, I still get a jolt when youth on my Rez call me "Chief." I see them in the gym lifting weights and when they leave, they say, "See ya later, Chief." Or when I walk around our grade school, I hear the word "Chief" from the little people. It is so neat when I pass them in the hallway and I can hear their little voices tell their little white buddies, "There's the Chief." It's not an ego thing with me; it's an ancestral respect thing. I don't own that title. It does not belong to me. That title in my language goes back thousands of years. Even the little white kids have a look of respect when they hear the word "Chief." I don't think that look would be there if I was referred to as "Chairman" or "President."

The thing that means the most to me about being a Chief can be summed up in a simple but very powerful sentence that I've heard from more than a few band members over the years. It took many years for some of my people to say this to me, to see enough in me, to look me in the eye (sometimes with water in their eyes) and say, "No matter what—you will always be my Chief!" The first time I heard that it really hit home, and it still does! For most Osoyoos Indian Band youth today—at least those under the age of thirty (which is the majority of Osoyoos Indian Band members)—their only memory of an Osoyoos Band Chief is me. That realization tears me up. I know what my Rez had when I was growing up. Every day I see the businesses we have now that we didn't have when I was a kid, as well as the new and better community buildings and houses my people now live in. Kids do not have to grow up four or more stuffed into one small bedroom (like we had to in my family and in so many others). Kids don't have to go to school hungry anymore. Our Rez school has a very good breakfast and lunch program. Kids have more recreational programming. We have good community playgrounds.

At our youth centre one of the kids drew our Osoyoos Indian Band logo and wrote under it, *Rez life is the best life.* That made me so happy. Rez kids have more job opportunities and actual career choices these days. Yet I still wish I could have done better for them (my "little-bit-better" philosophy), provided a safer, cleaner Rez with better facilities, a bigger gym, and more educational and recreational programs and services. I wish we had more Okanagan language use and stronger evidence of the Okanagan culture. I wish that as the young become teenagers they could have better summer job opportunities. And, as they become young adults, more housing and career opportunities. I wish we could have bought more land to add to the reserve so the youth would have more economic and cultural opportunities in the future.

Our Rez is still more than four thousand acres smaller than it should be. My Osoyoos ancestors settled on a thirty-six thousand-acre Rez in 1877, one that was then reduced to thirty-two thousand acres. As I look back, I am so grateful for the awesome workers and team members I have served with in all Osoyoos Indian Band operations. It is so true that everything that happens to the good on a Rez requires a good team of good people to get done. During my time as Chief there has been no such thing as "I did this" or "I started that." To me there is only "We did this" or "We started that." I have been part of a team (of consultants and council members) that has built and accomplished many things we should be very proud of.

When I look at the old black-and-white photographs of my people and my Rez, I imagine how tough it was for my ancestors back then, not having electricity or running water, and how hard working our people were. Families grew up in very small houses with wood stoves to keep warm and a cold walk to the outhouse in the morning. My mom and many others had to pack water to cook and clean. It's important that we remember the past and don't forget that our accomplishments today are on the shoulders of our people who suffered through the hard times. I say thank you (*limlmt*) to them every time I am in a ceremony.

I believe in what I call "the cycle or circle of leadership" on the Rez. The time is near for younger people to take over the seats around the Osoyoos Indian Band council table—just as others and I did back in December 1984 when I was twenty-four years old. Osoyoos, like every Rez, has some awesome young leaders: Sammy, Leona, Taylor, Sonja, Justin, Nathan, Myra, Eddy, Tara-Lynn, Jenna, Mandy, Lindsay, and so many others I trust will carry on the hard-working Osoyoos tradition. I hope they will take what we have done to a higher level by carrying the best of the past into the future.

Over the last few years, the younger people on council have brought many great ideas and have led many positive operational changes. As I get older and realize my leadership time is coming to a close, I know my Rez will be in capable hands and that Osoyoos will have great future Chiefs and councils.

I will always be there to lend a helping hand—or a good kick in the rear—in person or in spirit.

I love what leadership expert John C. Maxwell had to say on the duty of experienced leaders: "The job of a real leader is to create other leaders, not followers."

CHAPTER 15

"LISTEN TO THE WIND"

Traditional Decision-Making and Leadership Lessons

On rare occasions, First Nations leadership has to make major decisions that lie outside of contemporary business and politics. That's when we must incorporate some traditional spiritual practices to guide us. We must look back into our ancestral practices in order to go forward. These are tough decisions that carry with them the weight of our ancestors. First Nations have thousands of years of experience making tough decisions on these lands. There was a time we didn't need lawyers or consultants.

A few years back an ancestral grave was dug up on Osoyoos Lake, in a provincial park called Haynes Point. The park was named after the settler who stole more than four thousand acres of the best Osoyoos Rez land in 1877. I was back east when I got a phone call from the RCMP letting me know that an old Indian grave had been dug up by a BC Parks contractor. When I got to the site, archeologists had been called in and some members of the Osoyoos Indian Band had been hired to help carefully sift through the hole (gravesite) left by the backhoe.

As I stood above the hole and asked questions about the find, one archeologist told me the bones had been disturbed and the skeleton broken up, and that according to the material found with the bones the grave was very old. I stood there with the BC Parks representatives and some of my people and silently watched the archeological workers sift through dirt. I asked, "What is that small building close by?" The park staff said it was an outhouse. The backhoe had been digging a new septic field when the operator noticed that some bones had been dug up. I was lost in my thoughts.

I don't recall what the RCMP or the park staff might have been saying at the time. I ignored their words and kept looking at the hole where one of my people's bones were being dug up. I just know the others wanted those archeologists to keep on sifting through the dirt, to collect the bones and let the backhoe get back to work. Then they would allow us to bring the bones back to the reserve for reburial. I had been through this before, on a different site. I remember thinking, *They want us to be good little Indians and not disrupt their plans for this tourist campsite. They want to dig up the remaining bones of my ancestor and get them out of the way of their provincial park toilet.*

"Move the Indians." For well over a century, that has been the standing colonial policy of pioneers, settlers, and governments when it comes to the "Indian Problem." Every time Indians are in the way of white progress the solution is to move them: move their reserve somewhere else; relocate them to a flood plain, a swamp, or up against the rocks. And now—even in death, when the government needs the land where my people are buried to use *for a toilet*—the solution is to move the bones, to relocate the Indian graves again and again.

I remember getting more and more pissed off as I stood there watching the gravesite of one of my relatives being dug up for a septic tank. All of a sudden, I said, *"Stop! No more digging!* I want that struc-ture torn down!" I didn't ask permission from BC Parks or the RCMP. I didn't ask for a negotiating meeting. I didn't care what the white so-called responsible authorities were going to say. I just wanted the digging to stop and anything near that grave to be torn down.

"This site is a historical ancestral grave and it will be respected as a grave," I told them. "All the non-Natives here, go tell your bosses in government and the RCMP at the highest levels the Osoyoos Indian Band is taking control of this site and we will protect our ancestor's resting place from this day forward. Do not bring your machinery back here or you will cause a standoff that will escalate into something very costly and ugly."

I remember one of the white archaeologists looking at me and saying something like, "Let's get ready for a standoff. I'm up for a fight."

I told the Osoyoos Band members who were there, "This is our burial site now to protect, don't let anyone disrespect it." I knew right away that I needed to call on a few traditional knowledge keepers, not university-degreed Indians. I needed to consult Okanagan language speakers to figure out proper next steps. There are times a university or college education is valuable, yes, but there are also times when traditional education and knowledge are more important. As the days went on, band members continued sensitive archeological work on the entire Haynes Point Provincial campground. And we prepared the bones for reburial on the exact same spot where our ancestors had buried our relative more than a thousand years ago. The B.C. government quickly organized high-level meetings because the local mayor and council were getting public pressure on the question, "What are the Natives going to do with this important public tourist park?" The provincial campground, obviously, is a very important part of the local economy.

At the first meeting I had with a B.C. cabinet minister on this tenacious issue, I listened to the usual government textbook response: "We are very sorry and very concerned and want to respect Native cultural protocols and desire a peaceful outcome that's good for all British Columbians." As I sat and listened to the minister give the token opening statements, I thought of the Oka conflict and the Ipperwash conflict—both also involved ancestral gravesites. Then I asked a very simple but very important question: "How many years have to go by for white people before the graves of their family members are no longer important?"

The provincial minister looked shocked. For a moment, she was lost for words, but then she tried the usual "reconciliation" talk— political, useless rhetoric. The minister did what every government politician does: she didn't answer my question but spoke around it. So I told the cabinet minister to go ask the premier the same question: "How many years have to go by before the graves of your family are no longer important?" To this day I have not received an answer from any government leader to that simple but most important question.

All the government wanted to know was how much more time we needed with the gravesite. They promised it would be protected while we sorted things out. I told them I didn't need the government or the RCMP to protect an old Indian gravesite. I told them that Native people had been pushed around long enough and had our best lands taken by settlers for over one hundred years. "And now you want to push our ancestor—one of my people—out of their final resting place? Not this time!" I told them I didn't care what their legal authority was—the Okanagan ancestral grave was not going to be moved. I told them protecting the ancestral gravesite was not a government responsibility but the responsibility of the Osoyoos Indian Band.

The government also wanted to know our conditions for allowing the park to be reopened, as the tourist camping season was coming up quickly. We set no date for a future meeting and agreed to nothing except to put the dug-up bones back as respectfully as possible. A few weeks later there was another meeting with local government officials, as they were getting public pressure about the reopening of the campground. Protecting the graves of our ancestors is not in the Canadian or American business or government handbook. It's not in the Native business handbook either; it's just something we know in our heart and soul.

As the weeks passed, I found out the burial site was one of the oldest recorded in our territory—more than one thousand years old. I called for a men's Sweat House ceremony to be held there. Again, I didn't ask for government permission. For the first time since the 1870s, when the government forced us onto reserves, my people built a sweat house on that site. A group of us held a traditional ceremony on that strip of land only a few yards from that ancestor's grave to help us with decision-making. Other Okanagan Chiefs, councillors, and cultural-knowledge people joined me in that ceremony. That felt so good and so powerful. It was one of the best ceremonies I have ever been involved in.

Sometimes, as Native people, we need to get away from the paper, get away from the office, get away from the corporate talk, get away from the lawyers, get away from the modern comforts—and get our butts into a traditional ceremony. To me that is one of the best decision-making tools we have—ceremony! Sometimes we as Native people have to look to our past in order to figure out how to go forward. It's weird that no one ever taught me that.

A few months after the Sweat House ceremony the municipal and government representatives wanted an update. They pressured me for a meeting. I had developed a personal relationship with some of the local government reps, who told me privately that many local people were upset about how long it was taking for me to put forth a position on reopening the well-used provincial park. I told them I would agree to a meeting but that I didn't want any media in the room. Further, I indicated that what I was going to say at that meeting wouldn't be for the media, and that it must be kept "in-camera."

When it came time for that meeting, they all sat around the table looking at me, anticipating a list of demands or the usual tough political speech. I told them I was having a very difficult time with this issue and that it was weighing very heavy on me. One of them asked me if they could help in any way, which I appreciated. Over the years, I have built a very good working relationship with the mayor and councils of Osoyoos and Oliver, as well as with the local member of the Legislative Assembly in Victoria. I knew these people genuinely wanted to help me. But I also knew that this decision was above corporate Canada's and government's way of thinking. I shook my head and told them in one sentence what I was going to do.

"I'm going to go down to the site soon," I told them, ". . . and listen to the wind."

They all looked at me, stone-faced; they didn't know what to say. I didn't ask for any studies to be completed or stakeholder meetings to be held. I didn't ask for reports or future meetings with some committee. I stood up and told the non-Native leadership that on this very tough and complex issue I was simply going to go down to the burial site and "listen to the wind."

Someone in the room asked, "How long before you come to a decision?"

"I don't know," I said. "As long as it takes."

The meeting was short, and all the non-Native leadership there respected my decision. I didn't feel any superior colonial attitude. I left that meeting and did exactly what I said I was going to do.

A few days later I drove to the site, walked silently around the ancestor's grave a few times and sprinkled some tobacco there. I walked down by the water and listened to that great sound of water lightly pushing up against the rocks on shore. I love the sound of water. I grew up right next to the Okanagan River and our little poor Rez house had no air conditioning, so half of the year our bedroom window was open and I fell asleep and woke up listening to the sound of the river.

The sound of a light wind ruffling the leaves and pine needles in the trees is also one of the greatest sounds on earth. As a Native leader, sometimes the best thing you can do is go out on the land and listen to the wind. Listen to all the sounds of nature. I don't know how long I walked and listened, sat and listened, closed my eyes and thought about many things and asked the ancestor for help. I didn't want an escalation of any type, but I also knew we had to "Indian Up!" and protect the ancestral gravesite.

Days later, I was thinking about who I could call in Indian Country to give me some advice. A smart leader sometimes has to go outside of their circle and seek advice from different sources. Years ago, I had read about the Ipperwash standoff that happened in southern Ontario in 1995. It was a situation where several members of the Stony Point First Nation occupied the provincial park to assert a claim to nearby land that had been expropriated during the Second World War. The land that was taken also held traditional burial sites. During the violent confrontation, the Ontario Provincial Police shot and killed Dudley George. Through negotiations with the province, Ipperwash Provincial Park was eventually returned to the Chippewas of Kettle and Stony Point First Nation.

A few weeks after we shut down the provincial park at Osoyoos I got a call from an Ontario Chief who wanted to meet with me. There was nothing unusual about that—I often get calls from Chiefs and council members who want to stop by and "go to school on Osoyoos." So we met for lunch. During the meal I told him I was struggling with a decision outside of normal business and asked if he knew the Chief from the band that was involved in the Ipperwash Crisis. He gave me a strange look and said, "I *am* the Chief of that community that stood up to the province." I was astonished. The person who likely had the best understanding of the situation I was having a tough time dealing with was on my Rez, sitting right across from me. Yeah! "Indian Magic" can happen anywhere, at any time! I went to school on the Ipperwash Crisis. I also contacted one of the best Chiefs in B.C.—Miles Richardson, who was president of the Council of the Haida Nation from 1984 to 1996. I call Miles a Chief because he knows how to act like one, as he stood up to the province and the forestry companies who were over-logging his traditional territory, the islands now called Haida Gwaii.

We eventually told the province that the only way the campground was going to reopen is if the Osoyoos Indian Band was managing it. We also told the province that the colonial name that the settlers gave that area had to be changed. The provincial park bore the name of a rich white settler (Judge J.C. Haynes) who had stolen over four thousand acres of our best reserve land back in the 1870s. We wanted our Native name for that important area brought back—and the name of the thieving white settler removed!

Like all First Nations, the OIB has, in our traditional language, place names for all of the significant areas in our territory. The name "Osoyoos" comes from the word *sw̓iw̓s* and is a very important place name in our language. It means "the shallow area—crossing area" (meaning an important crossing area for my people on foot and horse-back). Which is exactly where the burial ground was found. We told the government our conditions: we wished to take over the management of two provincial parks near our Rez and to bring back the original Okanagan Native names for those two sites. The other provincial park in OK Falls was original Osoyoos Indian Reserve land that the joint federal/provincial McKenna-McBride Royal Commission had stolen in 1913 under settler pressure.

Months later, I was called to a B.C. provincial government session and asked to bring some of Osoyoos's few language speakers and students to stand in the legislature and read out the name changes to the two provincial parks. On March 16, 2016, our grade school's language teacher had a happy heart and tears in her eyes when she read the Okanagan words for the official renaming of the two parks. The official name changes—the former Haynes Point Provincial Park to *Sẅiẅs*, and the former OK Falls Provincial Park to *Sx'ex'nitk*—meant that, after more than a century, the names our ancestors used to describe those two small pieces of land would from now on be officially used by all people who visit those parks. Canada has to "reconcile" and tell the truth that this country has more than two official languages (English and French). Those who want to change the use of Native names in logos and sports should realize it's more important to change the colonial oppressive names of mountains, lakes, and streams.

There is still an unsettled land question on both of those sites. The final chapter has yet to be written. It will one day require "genuine reconciliation" between the Osoyoos Indian Band and the B.C. provincial government. We want both sites back to what they should have been—Osoyoos Indian reserve land.

We have to stand up for our Indian hunting and fishing rights. Supreme Courts on both sides of the border have ruled that we have inherent rights. Back in the 1960s, the fisheries wardens would come to the Okanagan River—where my people, including my dad, still fished salmon for food, as members of the Osoyoos Indian Band had done for thousands of years. The wardens would try to get my people to sign up for fishing licenses. One time, the warden showed up and asked my dad, "Where is your licence to fish?" My dad rolled up his sleeve and with his other hand pointed to his brown skin and said, "This is my licence." The warden got mad and said, "All of you need to sign this licence to fish here!" My dad and a few other Osoyoos Rezskins grabbed the warden and threw him in the river. When he got out he drove away and came back with the RCMP. Again the warden told my dad and others they needed to get a fishing licence to fish for food. By then the Osoyoos Indian Band Chief had showed up. He told the RCMP and the warden that the Okanagan Indians have inherent fishing rights and would not sign any fishing licences. The warden and the RCMP then left the Okanagan River fishing grounds.

In 2020, much the same story was unfolding on the East Coast. First Nations were being forced to defend the old treaties and their fishing rights for lobster. The Mi'kmaq Chiefs were merely asserting their Supreme Court of Canada treaty right to fish for a "moderate livelihood," yet many white lobster fishers opposed this, sometimes with violence.

All tribes, all First Nations have laws and protocols in their traditional language and ceremonies. There are times we need to be guided by them in order to make the right decision. On the West Coast, the Potlatch ceremony was used. On the prairies, the Sundance ceremony was used. Back east, the tribes had longhouse ceremonies. In my territory, we have Winter Dances, Sweat House, and *Captikwł* (our stories).

Canadians and Americans have preached to us "savages" for over five hundred years about how relevant and real their Bible stories are. Those words—which in truth are printed words written by a handful of "wise men"—that come from somewhere over the Atlantic are somehow supposed to be the ultimate "truth" for all races of people, which are supposed to be followed without question. Ridiculous. Every First Nation has the equivalent "word of God." Our stories—our Bible—can be found in the oral history stories of our ancestors, who were just as smart as anyone's "wise men." And our stories used animal figures (not Joseph and Mary). In one of our *Captikwł*, a little mouse helps big Grizzly Bear:

> At a winter dance mouse sang and Grizzly Bear gave mouse a
> long tail—mouse said—one day I will help you, even big people
> need help—Grizzly Bear said—you're too small, you could never
> help me—the animal people found Grizzly Bear sleeping and tied
> him up—mouse knew Grizzly was in trouble and went looking
> and found him tied up—Grizzly asked for help and mouse climbed
> on top of Grizzly and chewed the bindings—Grizzly got free and
> stood up and thanked mouse and said—If it had not been for you
> I would have died. From now on we are always friends.

In such stories are life lessons. Everything matters; even small things can help. No matter how big you are, how wise you are, someday you too will need help.

There are sacred tribal sites all over Canada and the United States. In 2001 I was involved in the return of Spotted Lake (kłlilx'ʷ) above the town of Osoyoos. Spotted Lake is a one-of-a-kind lake: it has 365 white-rimmed circles that appear on the lake bottom most of the year, and it was used by the Okanagan Nation as a healing and spiritual lake for thousands of years. Spotted Lake was one of our "churches." When it fell into private ownership and the non-Native owners tried to develop the lake into a spa and dig out the mud to sell, my people protested and demanded that the sacred lake not be commercialized. Every time the owners tried to develop the lake, my people were willing to set up roadblocks and fight to preserve the natural beauty of the lake as spiritual grounds. Throughout North America, First Nations are the only race being forced to set up road-blocks to uphold their religious beliefs and protect their places of worship. Where is the reconciliation in that?

In the late 1990s I was given a newspaper clipping by our golf course manager about another proposed commercial development of Spotted Lake. At the next Okanagan Tribal Council meeting I brought up the proposed mining of our spiritual lake with the other Okanagan Chiefs. We wrote letters and got our lawyers involved and eventually got to Minister of Indian Affairs and Northern Development Robert Nault and then Prime Minister Jean Chrétien. This time the federal government actually practised genuine "reconciliation" by putting their money where their mouth was. They found the funds to buy out the "non-Native title to the lake" and return the lake to its rightful caretakers—the Okanagan First Nation.

I keep on saying that reconciliation must start with First Nations getting their old reserves and sacred cultural sites back. Spotted Lake is a prime example. And now that that lake is out of private ownership, all people—including non-Natives—have better access to the sacred site. This shows that "real" reconciliation with the original people of this land—the First Nations—makes business and religious sense for all Canadians and Americans!

I think of my gramma when I tell people it's possible to mix traditional ways and beliefs with non-Native ways. My gramma was one of the few on my Rez who held a Winter Dance, which is one of the most complicated ceremonies my people do, and was also a devoted Christian. In her house there were many church pictures on the walls, as well as many Native religious items. My gramma proved that you could hold two radically different beliefs and be devoted to both. In the same way Natives, if they use their common sense, can be both pro-business and traditional.

I don't believe anyone is a pure socialist, capitalist, or environmentalist. We all love to flick on the switch (electricity) and drive our vehicles (oil and gas), and we all want clean water and healthy food. Most would agree we need some sort of free-enterprise system. We don't want government controlling everything, and we need individual entrepreneurship with checks and balances. But we also need government environmental standards and health standards. We need government employment standards. We need government to build roads, bridges, and other infrastructure. But we need a common sense balance between individual freedoms and public responsibilities. When it comes to politics, a wise person once said that reasonable people stay in the middle of the road—don't go too far to the left or you will wind up in the ditch, and don't go too far to the right or you will also wind up in the ditch. On most business and social issues try to stay in the middle of the road; incorporate some left *and* right politics in your decision-making or traditional and contemporary thinking—I keep hearing the words "balance" and "holistic" among Native people.

First Nation leadership should never become so corporate that it fails to put into practice one of the founding principles of being Native—sharing. Canada was founded on Native people sharing. The pilgrims would have starved to death if the Indians did not share food with them. Same with the French in what is now Montreal. I have been told by countless tribes that all First Nations come from a sharing society.

And yet today pipeline companies get First Nations to sign multi-million-dollar "non-disclosure" deals, and Native leadership tells other Native leadership that we can't share our agreement. I call that out. Can't share with your cuzzins? That's corporate blackmail. Native leadership should not fall for that corporate/legal "trick or treaty." There should be no secrets in Indian Country between nations. At Osoyoos we will always share information with other First Nations— that is the traditional/ancestral way!

I call on many First Nations in Canada and the United States to share all sorts of information on how they run their corporate and governance business. I ask for settlement agreements, and most do share those with me. Many Rezskin relatives call on me to share our stuff—and I am always honoured to help out and send them our agreements. But today some of our bands and tribes are getting too bureaucratic: "Oh, we gotta check with our lawyer." It's sad that some of our people have forgotten how to send "smoke signals." There are Indian ways to share corporate information and get around non-disclosure agreements. Come on, Rez leadership, don't be naive—*think!* Those corporations (mining companies, pipeline companies, etc.) are very sneaky. Behind their highly paid lawyers, they are finding "off the record" ways of sharing non-disclosure information with each other.

In the Okanagan, we are so lucky to have had a Native-led educational institute of higher learning since 1979, which is very rare. It's headed by Dr. Jeannette Armstrong, a traditional/contemporary professor. The En'owkin Centre offers Okanagan language- and cultural-based learning while partnering with the University of British Columbia and the University of Victoria. Many of my people (including me) have either worked there or taken courses there. (I am its current president.) The En'owkin Centre has taught me and many of my people the value of traditional thinking.

The Chief of all Chiefs, Sitting Bull, said, "I have advised my people this: when you find anything good in the white man's road, pick it up;

but when you find something bad, or that turns out bad, drop it. Leave it alone."

Outstanding land issues are a priority with First Nations and we must use both modern and traditional knowledge to reconcile the injustices of the past. On major cultural and governance decisions, Rez leadership must go back to ceremony and find a quiet place out on the land or near water, take a walk, get on a horse, or in a canoe...and truly take the time to listen to the wind! As a Native American proverb says: "Tell me the facts, and I'll learn. Tell me the truth, and I'll believe. But tell me a story, and it will live in my heart forever."

CHAPTER 16

THE TERRIBLE TRUTH ABOUT CONSULTANTS, LAWYERS, AND ACCOUNTANTS

"Good judgment comes from experience.
Experience comes from bad judgment."

—common saying

Every Rez has them. Every Native organization has them. There are over six hundred federally recognized First Nations in Canada, and over five hundred federally recognized tribes in the United States. In Canada, there are also over eighty Tribal Councils and forty provincial Native organizations. Also in Canada, there are upwards of eight hundred Indigenous organizations of various types. Taken together, that amounts to thousands of consultants, lawyers, and accountants who get paid a good wage to improve the lives and conditions of Native people.

The term "Misery Industry" is often associated with all the funded money spent on First Nations communities. Year after year, despite all the billions spent, despite all the consultants and social service "experts," the cycle of poverty continues.

I love the title of the book *Dances with Dependency*, written by Calvin Helin, a Tsimshian from northern British Columbia. The book calls out the "cost of poverty" and the millions of dollars spent on keeping Native people poor. The APTN First Nations television network even produced a program titled *Is There a Misery Industry?* The program pointed out that "Lawyers, prison guards, doctors, social workers, councillors, INAC bureaucrats . . . it seems a lot of people make a living off Aboriginal dependency, the business of keeping Aboriginal people poor—and sick and perpetually in need of others."

Millions of dollars are spent on these experts. Sometimes they are necessary; sometimes they are useless. All are expensive and all will tell you they are the best. But beware: not all "experts" are created equal. For First Nations throughout North America, some experts have turned out to be the second coming of the churches or the cavalry.

It angers me how much Native organizations spend on lawyers. Take a look at how much your band or tribe spent on legal advice last year. It will shock you. Some Chiefs and councils are so timid and lacking in confidence that they feel everything they say or do needs to be reviewed by a lawyer. Lawyers and consultants love Rez leaderships that lack confidence, as that means more phone calls and meetings they can attend. Everything a consultant does is billable. Like Indian Affairs (now Indigenous Services Canada), the federal Department of Justice is an "Indian fighter," always afraid of being sued by pissed-off Indians. Quit pissing us off and the Crown won't have to worry about being sued.

In the United States, many tribes have in-house legal counsel and some council members won't agree to meet unless an attorney is handcuffed to their wrist. No Rez leader should be controlled by a lawyer or consultant. Yes, we all need legal advice now and then, but real leaders don't walk on eggshells worrying about being sued and refusing to make a deal unless it's deemed perfect—according to a lawyer. There is no such thing as perfect, so don't wait around for perfect! Every entrepreneur knows business is risky; most lawyers have never started a business in their life and are not business people.

One of my "teachers" in business was Mark McCormack (who also happened to be a lawyer), the legendary sports agent who founded International Management Group and represented the likes of Arnold Palmer, Jack Nicklaus, Charles Barkley, Derek Jeter, Chris Evert, and many other professional athletes. In his book *The Terrible Truth about Lawyers*, McCormack wrote:

> Lawyers formalize the deal. They shouldn't *do* the deal. Often because a lawyer wants the language to be perfect they often kill what could be a good deal.
>
> Many lawyers pretend they are business people, usually they are not.
>
> A client should always demand a complete and detailed bill from his attorney.
>
> Keep the lawyers out of the early stages of a deal.

Like doctors, lawyers are not experts at everything. A good doctor will refer their patients to specialists if needed. No doctor specializes in all medicine. It follows, then, that no lawyer is an expert in all law. Every First Nation should use multiple lawyers. Stay away from lawyers or legal firms who claim to specialize in everything. And don't let an experienced lawyer shuffle your important work off to junior lawyers in their firm. Lawyers, like all contractors, treat you like a long-lost friend until you stop using their services or until a bigger contract that pays them more money comes along.

I'll say it again: be proactive in keeping up with political and business news. Don't use the same lawyer for every issue. Ask for references and research the big cases those lawyers have won. Seek out the winners! Remember that legal advice is just that—advice. And their expensive clock is always ticking.

I am the first to concede that accountants and timely financial data can be critical in government and business. Leaders require the right numbers in order to make an informed decision. When a business is up and running, it's the financial numbers that give leadership the necessary heads-up on any action that might be needed. As successful businessman Harvey Mackay says, "The first hire after yourself . . . is your bean counter. Entrepreneurs are always going broke because their dreams ran ahead of their numbers."

Every two or three years put your audit out to a competitive quote. Competition is usually good, as it keeps billings in line. When I hear of a band that is now in third-party management—meaning Indian Affairs has taken over financial management because of serious deficits—I often wonder, *Who were the accountants and the in-house bookkeepers that let that happen under their watch?*

Good financial staff supplies a paper trail of warnings to Chief and council. But sometimes the Native leadership doesn't listen to the financial warnings—even when they are there in black and white. Remember, real numbers don't lie! Some Rez leaders care more about political favours than about protecting the community's bank account. That's not leadership. In my book, it is a serious neglect of duty and responsibility.

Once, on a reserve in Alberta, I sat in the crowd while the accountant told the membership their community was going to be broke in ten years if they didn't stop spending their one-time multimillion-dollar land claim settlement. That settlement was being spent by one generation on too many costly per capitas, leaving nothing for the generations to come. The Chief was standing with the accountant, but very few of the membership seemed to care.

When it was my turn to give advice to the community, I told them, "You've got to protect and save what's left of that land claim trust money. Look at the numbers and think generations ahead—not just of current needs but future needs." I know many of the members ignored those audited numbers, though. At the next election the Chief and council members who wanted to reduce spending and save the land claims money were voted out. So much for seventh-generational thinking (*eye roll*).

I have observed that some of my own members don't care about the "financial strength" of the Osoyoos Indian Band Development Corporation. They just want bigger per capitas, bigger raises every year, and more free programs and services, and have no consideration for spending or budgets. Responsible leadership needs accurate numbers in order to make an educated decision. It can't just spend, spend, and spend some more!

In the business world, income and expenses must be tracked every day. I've noticed that many grant-dependent organizations have a casual attitude toward their funding and show a lack of respect for money. Most organizations that belly up to the funding trough treat grant money like "play money." When you don't have to earn—by selling or producing a product—as you must in the business world, getting a funded cheque creates bad habits. Natives must have devoted, knowledgeable bookkeepers and accountants who can "red flag" misspending or overspending. Checks and balances must be built into tribal finances!

The financial accountability of First Nations has grown over the years to a point where most now require a full-time chief financial officer or in-house accountant. The leadership on the Rez must spend a lot of time with their top financial staff in order to be knowledgeable about their community's financial standing month by month.

The financial staff must also never be frightened to bring up concerns. The earlier financial concerns are brought up to council or managers and department heads, the quicker overspending and deficits can be avoided.

Any time something goes over budget and creates a deficit, the manager or council should be the first to blame. But right beside them must be the bookkeepers of that business or department. Bookkeepers/accountants have a responsibility to warn of all inappropriate transactions, and they must do so in writing. Anyone can spend money; but it takes hard work, discipline, and structure to make money. And you gotta have the backbone to say "No" to some of the weekly requests to spend money, as there are endless causes in every community.

In every successful business off the Rez, good financial staff are praised. But on the Rez a good, tough bookkeeper is often looked at as the "bad guy" and called down because they must report overspending or voice concerns about spending policy. Someone has to start saying "No" when the money becomes short, and the first person to blow the whistle should be the accountant. There is a rule about money: "Stop the buck before it stops you."

Bookkeeping positions must be filled by qualified and experienced number-crunchers. In business, bookkeeping is your scorecard. Bookkeepers and accountants will either save your ass or sink your organization. You can't have the usual "Hire me because I'm a band member" approach. Don't hire your cuzzins just because they're your cuzzins!

Architects and engineers are also necessary experts from time to time. These are both very technical and specialized fields—but don't let these experts run your project. They often get paid on a percentage basis, so the bigger the budget the more they pocket. Don't let them talk your Rez into building something too big or too complicated. I have seen many fancy drawings of huge buildings that never got off the drawing board because the Rez leadership couldn't figure out a working budget and didn't know where they were going to get the money required to build. Yet the architect still got paid for those fancy drawings that are collecting dust. Design what you can afford, not what you would like to have.

Remember, every extra square foot costs thousands of dollars— not only to build but also to maintain. I have been on some reserves where a nice hockey rink or community building is shut down. It was overbuilt and the Rez could not afford to maintain it or even keep the lights turned on. Remember, whatever you build you will have to have the money to feed it each year, or your dream project will soon be an eyesore! The money wasted on a failed dream project could have built houses or gone into much needed social services.

Natives often forget to get their top accounting staff in the room with the architects and engineers. Sure, it makes sense to build a bigger road or water line for future growth—but again, don't overestimate your growth and overbuild. Your top financial staff must double check all projections and estimates. At Osoyoos, our finance staff have caught consultants putting in management fees when they don't manage the project, as well as trying to get away with double billing us. Don't let consultants rack up travel bills without providing detailed backup for their invoicing. Make sure, as well, that there is always a specific, detailed contract before hiring a consultant. Again, do your homework: call other tribal leaders to get reference checks on architects and engineers.

Is your Rez just surviving, not thriving, on underfunded government grants—barely eking out an existence? Does your Rez have unemployment over 30 per cent? Is the biggest employer on your Rez the band office, school, or social services? Is welfare your community's biggest budget line? If so, then it's time to get some business advisors or a business consultant and, most important, to elect a business-minded Chief and council. Because your Rez is obviously suffering from "dependency syndrome."

Sometimes having outsiders look in makes a big difference. There is truth to the old saying that some people "can't see the forest for the trees." A new perspective can improve a situation. I have a collection of self-help audiotapes on various business topics—most are old cassettes—and one of the best lessons I learned was from a group of successful Canadian business people who were asked what they wished they had done sooner. At the top of the list was "Hire some advisors!"

Think about it. All successful business people have advisors—legal, technical, financial. No one is a know-it-all, though many sure act like they are. Hiring advisors is one of the most important decisions a leader makes.

As a leader, what you read says a lot about you. The sad fact is most Native leaders don't regularly read business books or newspapers, or watch the news. I am always interested in what is happening in Indian Country or the business world. (Okay, sports as well. I keep up on my teams—the Habs, Redskins, and Blue Jays!) When I hear about a company or First Nation that has done something good, I want to find out more about it. I want to "go to school" on the success or failures of others. Sometimes a simple phone call with the right people can have a major impact on your community.

Back in 2000, I read in a Native newspaper about the St. Eugene Resort on the St. Mary's Indian reserve in British Columbia. I knew the Chief there—Sophie Pierre. I called up Sophie and asked her a few questions about their very impressive multimillion-dollar resort project. One of the questions I asked was "Who helped you on the project—did you hire a consultant?" Sophie did what all good Chiefs do—she was very accommodating; she answered all my questions; and she took the time to pass me on to the right people. She gave me the name of a consultant she used and I made one of the very best phone calls I have ever made. Today, twenty years later, I can report that not only has Mel Woolley from Calgary helped Osoyoos put the puck in the net a few times but has also hit a few grand slams. A few years ago we calculated that he and a few other consultants we used had brought more than $25 million worth of economic development to the many business enterprises on our land.

All good Chiefs push their Rez to be the best it can be, but the top-performing Chiefs also want to share their success with other Native communities. Unfortunately, not all Rez leaders share information or take the personal time to help out their cuzzins. Others are too "*Summa-choot*" (an Okanagan word that means "to act like white people") and come across like pompous, elected royalty. They're too important and busy to be bothered helping out another "Skin." It makes me sick when I see how quickly some Native leaders will adjust their calendars and trip all over each other to get in line to talk to a high-ranking white politician. Yet they won't even return a phone call or email from another tribal leader? It makes no tribal sense. As Native people, our goal should never be to become "corporate fat cats" or "elitist" but to get back to "inter-tribal trade." Any time Native leadership from one village asks another for help or advice, especially regarding something that Rez has accomplished, that help should be forthcoming. Sharing information is one of our highest duties and responsibilities. We must help out our relatives—that's the "Rez code."

I want to recognize another Native business leader who, like Chief Sophie Pierre, has not forgotten the Indian way of doing business: Chief Leonard George, from the Tsleil-Waututh First Nation in the

North Vancouver region. Back in the 1990s, I read an article in a business magazine about a multimillion-dollar condo project on a British Columbia coast Rez. I was determined to "go to school" on that Rez, so I called up the Rez office and asked for Chief Leonard. He not only took my call right away but, without hesitation, set aside some time for me to visit his project. I took along a council member and we spent the whole day being shown around by the Chief himself. He took us for lunch and we talked business.

As we headed for the airport, Tony, the Osoyoos council member I'd brought along, asked me a question: "Did you notice what happened today?" I didn't know what he was referring to. Tony said, "That Chief just spent most of his day with us." I didn't pay much attention to this at the time—being a young Chief then I thought that's what all Rez leaders did—but I later realized how precious time is and that "time is money." As Native leaders, we must make time to support each other and carry on old-fashioned "Native hospitality"—just as our ancestors did. I have never forgotten the "Rez leadership" lessons Chiefs Len George, Sophie Pierre, and Manny Jules taught me. No matter how rich or poor our villages are, we should always make time for one another and share our experiences, good and bad. That's a fundamental ancestral Rez rule!

Back in 1995, we decided to do a "visioning project." We held community meetings over many months. We brought in some consultants and facilitators and organized into three groups—youth, adults, and Elders. We produced many documents and a wish list of activities. As an organization grows and takes on more and more, it's very important to hire new positions. So we decided we needed a chief operations officer. We hired a businessman named Chris Scott. Chris had never worked on an Indian reserve, but he was a hard worker and brought great personal business experience. Chris and Mel became a great team and "put the puck in the net" time and time again. I loved the business talk with those two. When we met with Indian Affairs in Vancouver or Ottawa, or with other funders to compete for economic funding dollars, our presentations were always among the best! I learned a lot from those two business consultants who have both gone on to help many other First Nations. Like I said above, Natives must at all times be willing to share our business successes—and our failures. We have to tell the truth, not offer phony political excuses and blame everyone but ourselves. We have to own our conditions!

An important thing to remember about all contractors is to never let them run the Rez. By all means take their advice—especially technical advice—but never forget that no one's advice is perfect. I have told consultants that I don't want to work with people who act like Indian agents, treat us like wards of the Crown, and demand that we follow and listen. I'll go "hostile" on any advisor who talks like some colonial government or corporate know-it-all.

In Osoyoos, our advisors and consultants have been a huge factor in all our accomplishments. A few times, of course, we have been given the wrong advice. There are a couple of businesses we should not have invested in. One was in California—a zip line, of all things. In my office I have pinned up a piece of paper. It is a picture of a pig on a zip line—a reminder that, yeah, the Osoyoos Indian Band Chief and council got talked into investing in a carnival ride in another country. Yes, we did an internal business analysis. Yes, we were shown a detailed business plan and our top financial staff vetted it. Yes, we had our lawyer review all documents. And yes, most of the advice we received proved not to work in the real world of business. We blew it.

But, like every team that hates losing, we didn't stay with the same team. We eventually fired our lawyer and CFO, just like happens in sports. Sometimes after a losing season, someone has to get fired.

I read somewhere that in real military combat those who win are those who have a good Plan B, or a good Plan C—because when the bullets start flying and the real action begins most Plan A's get blown to pieces. We had neither a Plan B nor a Plan C for the zip line. The lesson I took away from that failed investment is that I need to stand up to advisors and council more and quit always going along with the majority just to show consensus. I had a gut feeling about the project, and I refused to travel to the States to look at other zip lines as some council members did. Eventually I told council and our COO that if they were so sure the numbers were right, they should buck up your their own money to invest in the project. The COO and one member of council eventually were willing to put their own money where their mouth was. I like it when someone digs into their own wallet and backs a project with a six-figure investment to show their financial commitment.

But council got too greedy! They said that if we were going to let two people invest then we should be going to all band members and giving them a chance to invest too. Come on! Most band members don't have savings, and those who do should not invest serious cash into a zip line, in another country, no matter how good the numbers look. Council got dazzled by the money the project was projected on paper to make. I had two people willing to share in the risk, but council didn't want their money (*Can you believe that? Big eye roll*). I eventually went along with the majority. Not long after, the project ran into trouble and the numbers projected by our own consulting team went down the tubes. Remember, a feasibility study doesn't involve real numbers based on past facts—it is a best guess.

The lessons are obvious. If you invest in another country, get legal advice from a lawyer who works in that country or state. I realize business is risky and no one bats .1000. No successful business person is without a few failures. And yes, it's better to try and to fail then never to have tried at all. But that was one we should never have tried. We should have been smarter.

At Osoyoos today, we use a range of advisors and consultants. Most governments have a two- or three-quote rule on contracts over a certain amount. Rezes should do the same. Another Rez rule: Don't become too friendly with consultants, as those friendships may affect your ability to deal with them. I remember a time when we wanted to get tough with one of our contractors. He had worked for us for many years and had previously done a decent job, but we were increasingly upset about his recent performance. So, as always, we huddled before a meeting with him and we all agreed that he should be fired. Then we called him in. At the beginning, we stuck to our plan. Then we let him talk. Our mistake. Like most Rez Indians, we can often get sucked in by a sad story, as we grew up with many sad stories. On the Rez we give our people more chances than we give to non-members. The contractor told us of his personal problems. He went on and on about his hardships and we bought it hook, line, and sinker. At the end of the meeting, he walked out with a raise (*another big eye roll!*).

Another Rez Rule: Don't listen to sad personal stories from consultants!

All Native organizations promote and give their members special considerations. We have replaced many good outside-hire employees with members of the Osoyoos Indian Band. And we're very proud of that. All First Nations make hiring band or tribal members a priority. In Native newspapers I see job ads with "Tribal membership preference." At election time, all candidates promise more jobs and benefits to members. The terrible truth is that Native organizations, like Indian Affairs, have some "bad apples" that have a detrimental effect on Rez growth and success.

Many of my own people have asked me to fire other band member staff—"Fire so and so and hire some white people. At least the work would get done." That may be true in some cases, but then I also hear, almost every month: "Why do we have non-members holding that job? That job should be held by a band member." The issue of member/non-member staff will always be a hot topic on every Rez. Rez politics will always play a role in hiring staff.

The terrible truth about hiring consultants is "You're damned if you do and damned if you don't."

As American business writer Dick Grote wrote in *Discipline Without Punishment*, "It's not the people you fire who make your life miserable, it's the people you don't."

CHAPTER 17

HEREDITARY CHIEFS VERSUS ELECTED CHIEFS

"Let's get ready to rumble!"

— UFC ring announcer Michael Buffer

In 2020, the issue of hereditary Chiefs' jurisdiction and elected Chiefs' authority gained national attention during the discussion of major pipeline projects in northern B.C. The question came down to who, exactly, represents a First Nation both off the Rez and on traditional territory. (The vast majority operate under the elected system. A few have elected and hereditary chiefs.) Many times I have been asked for my view of the conflict between the elected chiefs and Council and those that still have hereditary chiefs. I have tried to avoid answering, as I simply do not understand the protocols of how some clan systems and hereditary chief systems are set up. Remember, it's not wise to have an uneducated opinion.

As an elected Chief and an ongoing student of leadership, I am very curious about the circumstances that lead any First Nation into a dispute between hereditary Chiefs and elected Chiefs on major projects. I wonder about the politics behind the scenes. And I wonder why the conflict wasn't worked out long before it became front-page news for everyone to read and puzzle over.

One of the best elected Chiefs I have gotten to know is Sophie

Pierre of the Ktunaxa Band. She had this to say about all Chiefs, elected or hereditary: "When you become a leader you don't become all powerful. There is more 'responsibility'—not 'power.' If you have certain skills, people will follow you; if you misuse them, they will no longer follow you. Therefore you must have the ability."

I understand that some tribal groups in Ontario operate under a very difficult and complicated system of governance with elected leaders and traditional leaders. First, let us be clear that in the elected Chief and council system a Chief does not act like a dictator or royalty—and neither should hereditary Chiefs. In Canada's parliamentary system, the prime minister or premier is the head of their party; they control who sits in cabinet and what gets voted on, and the party typically votes as a group. On the Rez, a Chief has one vote around the council table, just like every other elected council member. At Osoyoos, I can be—and have been—outvoted on numerous issues. So, when I hear that an elected Chief supports a pipeline, I know it's not just the Chief. The majority of council would have to be in support, through a proper band council vote. In fact, it is even possible that the Chief was outvoted on the issue and was actually against the pipeline. Yet it is still the Chief's responsibility to respect and support the decision of council and the community. That's how most Rez democracy works.

On major decisions—leasing Rez land, land claim settlements, or major off-reserve deals such as the construction of a pipeline—elected Chiefs and councils must bring those matters to full band meetings and often have another vote (a band referendum) that involves the full membership. Not all First Nations govern themselves under the same rules and procedures. At Osoyoos, the Chief and council would have had many membership meetings on a proposal such as the pipeline that concerned the Wet'suwet'en. Council would then have prepared a public document that would have been reviewed by our lawyers before bring brought to a discussion at a full membership meeting. The issue would then be put to a referendum vote involving the full membership of OIB. All those eighteen years of age or older can vote, and polling booths would remain open from 9 a.m. to 8 p.m. to ensure everyone has the chance to register their vote. Osoyoos Indian Band members living off reserve would have had ballots mailed out to them with enough time to allow them to return their votes for counting. Each vote cast would carry exactly the same weight as any other vote. An information package on the issue would have been mailed or emailed to members living throughout Canada and the United States. Today most First Nations also have a community Facebook page or website where information documents are posted.

The main point here is that a major decision such as a pipeline would have involved not just the elected Chief and council but the entire voting-age membership. As happens on all issues decided this way, some would vote yes, some no, and a few wouldn't vote at all. Once that membership vote is in, however, Chief and council are obliged to support the membership's decision. It doesn't matter if you are an elected Chief or a hereditary Chief; the membership vote is the decision.

Now, I don't know how or if the full membership in those northern B.C. communities voted on those pipelines. That's the most important question for me: What's the membership's decision? Not, what's the position of the elected or hereditary Chiefs? On Osoyoos Rez and in most Okanagan First Nations the word "hereditary" very seldom comes up. As discussed, elections were not part of our traditional culture.

The memory of our elected Chiefs at Osoyoos goes back to the early 1900s. As for how traditional Chiefs were selected before our Rez was created in 1877, no one knows exactly. Some may give their best guess and say, "I know as our ways were passed down to me." I shake my head when I hear some of our older people say they know the old ways—and yet what they say is different from others who also claim to know the old ways. Often I don't know which old person to believe. Like many tribes, we had Chiefs for different things. It is no surprise that much of that knowledge has been lost.

In my non-expert opinion, before the late 1870s, when the "Rez culture" started, my people spoke only one language and practised only one religion (spirituality). There were no outside influences and their traditional governance obviously worked for thousands of years. Today, my people have for generations (150 years) been educated and raised in many different ways. Some were adopted out, some went to residential school, some accepted the Bible, some were raised by their grandparents, some were raised off reserve . . . the differences go on and on. Very few of my people speak our Okanagan language and fewer yet participate in traditional ceremony. As well, intermarriage has been happening for generations, bringing all sorts of different cultures to the Osoyoos world.

For all these reasons and more, we have for generations used the elected Chief and council system. I'm not saying it's better. It's what works for us and what we have become accustomed to. To me, under the "Rez culture" we no longer share the same heartbeat or speak the same language or believe in the same God—let alone practise the same politics. The contemporary reality is that some of our old traditional system would not work today. The Osoyoos of the 2020s is not the Osoyoos of the 1820s.

Not long ago, one of the Okanagan bands in my territory tried to go back to a governance model based on the "family head" or clan system. At community meetings the elected Chief and council were getting bashed (keep in mind that most community meetings are not attended by the majority of voters). Those members who did attend wanted to take control of business and governance affairs from the elected Chief and council and institute a more traditional system. Meeting after meeting took place, many very emotional sessions, and eventually that community went to a "family head" system of governance. It didn't last long. Once decision-making goes from the majority rule of an elected Chief and a small elected council to a large group of twenty, thirty, or more people trying to reach a consensus, it becomes impossible for the band to move at the speed of modern business.

It was "chaos," many members from that band told me. Documents were not getting signed. Essential band programs and services were interrupted or ground to a halt in a whirlwind of family politics. Many of my relatives on that Rez spoke of the infighting going on at every family head meeting. Meeting agendas were not structured and political grandstanding took up a lot of the time. I'm not saying all "traditional councils" are dysfunctional, but I don't know how effective councils that operate in this way can be. I just know there are not very many traditional councils or recognized hereditary chiefs left. That one family-head system of governance in the Okanagan lasted less than a year. They are now back to an elected Chief and council handling community affairs.

Traditionally, leadership activities started at an early age, not when you turned eighteen and were old enough to vote or run for council. Like all First Nations, my people had very serious youth rituals and ceremonies, some starting when the children were only five years old. We had puberty ceremonies where kids were sent up to the mountains to stay overnight by themselves, fasting and seeking a vision that would help them find their "animal spirit."

Today, very few Okanagan Natives practise those traditional leadership ways. Then, you had to *earn* your "hereditary" title from childhood on. Now, any band or tribal member eighteen or older—with no leadership experience, and perhaps with no real work experience—can run for office and get elected. The leadership qualities of traditional leaders were known long before they turned eighteen. They had been trained and watched from their earliest years. People knew they were special.

At the Arizona State Museum, I saw this write-up about Chiefs on the San Carlos Apache Rez: "Apaches valued personal leadership. Chiefs were chosen on the basis of charisma exemplified by their ability to inspire confidence, allegiances and respect. Like most Indian leaders, they lacked the powers to coerce followers and governed solely on their skills at achieving consensus." I like that.

In one of my favourite songs, "God," John Lennon wrote that he didn't believe in kings. I also don't believe in kings—or queens. I don't believe in royalty of any sort. I don't believe that just because you happened to be born into a certain privileged family that your family blood is more special than mine. Today, no one in my First Nation territory is raised much differently than anyone else. We are all equal. Today, most every Rez Indian claims "Chief bloodlines." I stopped counting many years ago the number of Natives I have met who claim Chief bloodlines.

I was gassing up my Harley in South Dakota a few years ago. I have a portrait of Chief Sitting Bull painted on my bike and a few of the local Rez boys were looking at it. All of them told me they were the great-great-great-nephew or whatever of Sitting Bull. I told them, "That's very nice"—but I thought, *Why are you telling me?* Chief Sitting Bull is one of my heroes (his picture hangs right beside me in my office), but even his bloodline doesn't make you any smarter or better than anyone else.

I have not and will not forget that kings and queens, in the name of God and empire, killed off millions of First Nations people all over North and South America. Most Canadians and Americans forget that their ancestors fled Europe and the feudal land system to come to the "New World" for personal freedom and the promise of land ownership. No sane person today wants to be governed by kings, queens, or authoritarian dictators. I don't expect anyone to ever bow for me (Chiefs, elected or hereditary, are *not* royalty), and I sure as hell will not bow to anyone whose only accomplishment is to claim they are royalty because their bloodline is "hereditary," which is simply birth by chance.

Some First Nations have developed governance rules whereby hereditary chiefs sit with the elected Chief and council. They get one vote, just like everyone else. That's mixing the old with the new. Other First Nations have protocols that the hereditary or traditional leadership govern anything to do with culture and ceremony, but the modern business issues are left with the elected Chief and council. Major issues are taken to the whole membership for a referendum vote.

I remember my grandmother saying, "You want to talk about language and culture and traditional stuff come to me, but don't come to me for advice on business. I have never run a business in my life. You get business advice from those experienced in business and it doesn't matter what race they come from." I still hear you, Gramma!

Roy Fox is an elected Chief and also a hereditary chief of one of the biggest First Nations in Canada, the Blood Tribe in Southern Alberta. He has some wise words on the issue:

> Elected Chiefs and councils have been described as creatures of the Indian Act, accountable only to the Federal government. . . .

These mischaracterizations have given space for protesters and even cabinet ministers to pick and choose which Indigenous peoples—and especially which perspectives—they will acknowledge. I don't think any elected chiefs pretend they are perfect... As elected Chiefs, we are faced with the cold realities of poverty and dependence every day. Our people come to us for housing . . . They come to us when they need to cover the costs of a funeral . . . to pay tuition . . . Imagine these realities, and understand how inadequate it would be to tell a young mother with hungry kids and no food in her fridge that . . . we are going to keep on passing on major projects and opportunities in our territories until something that matches our high principles happens to come along.

It's wrong and immature to call elected Chief and councils creatures of the Indian Act, or to label them as "sellouts," or "greedy or corrupt" when development projects on their Rez or territory were voted on by the whole membership. Those few First Nations with elected and hereditary Chiefs or clans or family-head systems have to figure out among themselves an inclusive system of governance that works. Do it now! Do not wait until the next big project or issue comes up.

As the 1987 Harvard Project on American Indian Economic Development argues, all First Nations must work on "Nation Building" or "Rebuilding": "When Native nations make their own decisions about what development approaches to take, they consistently out-perform external decision makers—on matters as diverse as governmental form, natural resource management, economic development, health care and social service provision."

There is nothing wrong with combining some traditional leadership with elected leadership, as long as the terms are clearly spelled out on paper. In today's world, we can't have unwritten rules. Whatever governance system a First Nation uses, it must be voted on by full membership. As well, any changes can only be made with the involvement of full membership.

A Chief does not sit above the people but with the people. A Chief must, in decision-making, have the support of the majority of their people. If a majority say, after much debate and thought, "This is the direction," then no Chief can act like a colonial monarch and treat their people like peasants whose voices do not matter. In most systems of traditional governance there are ways of removing a Chief. Yes, even hereditary Chiefs can be removed. Mohawk historian Doug George-Kanentiio says that Mohawk tribal leaders "were nominated by the clan mothers and were subject to ratification by their respective clans. They served for life unless impeached by their clan for violations [such] as insanity, greed, assault, rape, treason, and incompetence, among others. The clan might also indicate they have no confidence in a leader or he/she might by their own actions commit crimes which violate their oath of office thereby removing themselves from office."

In the Indian way, it is the majority who rule. And they do so through a governance system of honour, caring, sharing, and respect. They do so through ceremony and ancestral teachings that need to come back to every leadership table on the Rez.

The ongoing conflict of hereditary chiefs versus elected chiefs—or, if you prefer, Indian Act councils versus traditional councils—can descend into an argument over whose chief bloodlines are better, or "my Elders are smarter than your Elders." Reminds me of a book I read in high school—George Orwell's *Animal Farm*—where a leader proclaims: "All animals are created equal . . . but some animals are more equal than others!"

CHAPTER 18

"THAT HURTS THE EARTH, PAPA!"

"When the last tree is cut down. The last river poisoned. The last fish caught. Then only will the white man discover that he cannot eat money."

—Cree proverb

We were on the Navajo reservation that straddles the border between New Mexico and Arizona in May 2019, on a break from the Navajo Hopi Honor motorcycle ride. I had noticed smoke stacks in the distance and figured they were some sort of power generation plant. As I found out later, those big smoke stacks were for burning coal. I was sitting beside my three-and-a-half-year-old granddaughter, Zenaya, and heard her make one of the most amazing observations. "What did you say?" I asked her. I thought I had heard her right, but I had to ask her to repeat it. She lifted her little hand and pointed toward the distant smoke stacks.

"That hurts the earth, Papa."

My granddaughter (like so many young people today) is so Earth-smart and environmentally sensitive—far more environmentally sensitive than those I grew up with in Osoyoos. I gave Zenaya a big hug and placed my head on hers, lost for words as we both stared at those coal-burning smoke stacks. I thought, "Yeah, baby girl, you are so right—and so smart for noticing something most adults don't even give a serious thought to."

I am as guilty as anyone of not paying attention to daily pollution. When I was younger I never thought about "Mother Earth" or what I could do to reduce energy waste or recycle. This moment with Zenaya was a real kick-in-the-rear moment for me, and one I will never forget. The teacher becomes the student. Yeah! Sometimes adults gotta start listening to what kids are saying! It's their future, not ours!

When I was in grade school or high school no one brought up environmental issues — *ever!* There were no discussions about pollution or conserving energy. The teachers never brought up recycling programs or used "blue boxes." Today, our Rez school kids have made presentations to Chief and council on their "blue recycle bag and box" program and the importance of recycling. Youth are challenging the Chief and council at Osoyoos to make sure we implement environmental measures. Our school and our offices now have blue boxes and recycling bins throughout our buildings. I personally have smartened up and now recycle my household plastic and paper.

We have become a "throwaway society." Use something once and throw it away. Just remember: Your garbage, what you use once and throw away, has to go somewhere. Start paying attention to the daily and weekly number of plastic bottles and cups you throw away. I now look for recycle bins everywhere I go, and their presence has a lot to do with my first impressions of a place or a Rez. Everyone can make a daily commitment to recycle and use less energy. If you can turn on a switch, you can also easily turn it off. Make a daily contribution toward the health of Mother Earth!

Before Canada and the United States came into being, the traditional territories of First Nations were not polluted or infested with foreign weeds, plants, and trees. Today, the property outside my mom's little house next to the channelled Okanagan River looks nothing like it did only forty years ago when I was growing up. In less than one lifetime there has been major environmental damage in my own backyard. The Okanagan River dike is now covered with Russian elms, a weed tree that is growing out of control. In many places, the landscape that was once bare and had only small native plants now features a full canopy of invasive trees and plants. Other foreign weeds (baby's breath, spear grass, puncture vine) cover the side of every road in the Rez.

I have to tell First Nations people who come to see my territory that this is not how our land, river, and lakes looked even fifty years ago. The settlers brought with them not only foreign ways but also foreign invasive plants from overseas. In many areas the noxious weeds are not only an eyesore but dangerous to wildlife and kids. My granddaughter calls the sharp pain she gets from the burrs that hurt her feet and hands "pokees." I warn her and other Rez little ones to stay away from those foreign plants. But foreign plants are every-where and our kids' natural playgrounds—the ones I grew up loving—are overrun with "pokees" that make kids cry when their bare feet and hands touch them.

Our lakes and river are infested with a European weed called mil-foil. In some areas the green, feathery weed is so thick that people cannot swim there. Worse, our salmon cannot swim there. Local municipalities spend thousands each year to send a special weed machine out on the lakes to rip out the milfoil, but it just grows back quickly. It is, sadly, here to stay.

I often wonder what our land looked like before the Europeans invaded our territory. I imagine the natural beauty of the Okanagan before the first fort or church was built. Osoyoos and Okanagan Lake are not pristine anymore. Now boats are checked for a mussel that is invading our waterways. The sad truth is that the original natural beauty of my territory can now only be seen in old photographs.

My people are a salmon people; historically, some of the world's best salmon runs were in my traditional territory. But the dams along the Columbia River destroyed many of our salmon runs. For thousands of years, my people had Salmon Chiefs who regulated the catch, and the historical record is there to prove that the salmon numbers were healthy and strong.

A few years ago a Department of Fisheries and Oceans bureaucrat showed up at my office and we got into an argument over declining salmon stocks. He told me: "Our agency is the responsible authority over Okanagan salmon." I told him, "Really? You should be ashamed to say such an outright government lie! Before your so-called responsible authority our 'Salmon Chiefs' were in control, and the salmon were plentiful for thousands of years. Yet in one lifetime your agency has put our salmon on the endangered species list. How is that '*responsible* authority'?"

Look at the declining salmon numbers all over North America. Wild salmon stocks are suffering. The year 2020 proved the worst on record for the Fraser River's sockeye salmon. While returns of adult sockeye had averaged 9.6 million between 1980 and 2014, the Pacific Salmon Commission predicted just under a million would return in 2020. That prediction, it turned out, was vastly overconfident, with barely a quarter of a million of the fish expected to return by season's end. When it comes to wildlife management, provincial and state governments have all failed Mother Nature!

One of my best childhood memories is going salmon fishing along the Okanagan River. All the Rez kids loved to go along with the adults and watch them food fish the old way, with dip nets and gaffs. When we were old enough to hold a dip net or a gaff, we loved to spend hours and hours food fishing. (Not trophy fishing or recreational fishing. *Food* fishing.) We would often pedal our bikes along the dike to the few fishing areas where the government would allow Native food fishing and pedal back home with our catch of the day draped over our handlebars. We didn't have a freezer, so my mom would often tell us to not catch so many salmon.

Salmon season was one of the few times my people gathered in big numbers to fish together. There is a small dam north of the Rez off of which our community would fish. The salmon were forced to jump because of the constructed dam. It was wonderful to watch them jumping. Generations of my people fished there. As I got older, the local water authority restricted access so that there could be no more Native food fishing at the dam. The government water district eventually put a fence around the whole area. Many of my people would climb the fence to continue food fishing. One even lost a finger climbing the sharp fence to food fish to feed his family.

In my opinion, government agencies get a failing grade in all animal and fish protection. Through their colonial policies, they have put hundreds of species on the endangered list. My people, through the Okanagan Tribal Council, have forcibly taken over the enhancement of salmon stocks and now have Native fish hatcheries on both sides of the border. What government says about managing fish and animals is one "lie." When it comes to the natural environment, the other government "lie" I keep hearing is about "clean energy." It's like the main drug dealer in the movie *Scarface* saying, "I always tell the truth—even when I lie." I have told BC Hydro staff, "There is no such thing as clean energy—only *cleaner* energy." I see huge wind tower turbines built out of metal—that's mining. I see solar panels built out of metal—that, too, is mining. And how clean are solar panels once they are thrown away? Industry and government are lying when they use the words "clean energy." Electricity is not "clean energy"! Don't believe it for a minute.

The massive $9 billion Site C dam in northern B.C. is the latest in a long line of hydro projects that have caused huge environmental damage in First Nations hunting and fishing lands. Treaty 8 First Nations have identified hundreds of sacred sites in the planned Site C flood zone. Ask the James Bay Cree about "clean energy"; they fought Quebec's 1971 "Project of the Century"—the largest hydroelectric project in North America.

In many First Nation territories, including my own, electric dams have caused the loss of salmon runs, the flooding of ancestral village sites and grave sites, and the loss of thousands of acres of natural land, now under water. The Grand Coulee Dam in Washington State is located in my traditional territory and is one of the biggest hydroelectric projects in the world. It was, unbelievably, constructed *without* fish ladders, which led to the cultural loss of food and ceremony for my people. Before that dam was built (1933–41), my people had lived their lives for thousands of years around the yearly migration of the great salmon runs up the Columbia River. Once the dam was finished, my people went to their ancestral camps along the river, just as their parents and grandparents had done, to await the salmon run— only to find out there were no salmon. The fish could not get past the enormous dam. The United States Army Corps of Engineers has estimated the annual loss at over one million salmon.

It is heartbreaking to think of the physical, mental, emotional, and spiritual hardship my people had to go through because a dam ("clean energy") was built. Thousands of acres were flooded along with thousands of gravesites. Native village sites that had stood for thousands of years had to be relocated.

There is a black-and-white photo of my people—some in Chiefs' headdresses—standing on a hill overlooking that huge dam that destroyed a big part of our culture. The photograph was taken during the U.S. government's opening celebration of the dam and, of course, the Federal Indian agent would have demanded that the Indian leadership be there in regalia. In the photo, you can't see the faces of the Chiefs, only their backs. But I can see the devastation, the sadness, and the bitterness from their body language. The grand opening of the Grand Coulee Dam was no celebration for my people. Instead of a celebration, my people—who had now been placed on the Colville Reservation—held a different gathering. They called it the "Ceremony of Tears."

Plastics is another environmental concern. As I wrote earlier, we have to reduce and recycle plastics. Like many of us, I am now paying attention to the damage plastics are doing to our creeks, rivers, and oceans. I have seen the photographs of our water relatives suffering from the tons of plastics being thrown in the waterways. It is good to see that some corporations have stopped using plastic straws. Some cities are also putting their bylaws where their mouths are. Most talk about protecting the environment, but few actually act on it. The city of Vancouver has banned single-use plastic bags and straws and is also banning Styrofoam cups and containers. Even so, you cannot help but notice the lack of respect we show for our lakes and rivers.

All over North America, forest fires are an increasing threat. With all the new types of transportation (side-by-sides, ATVs, motocross bikes) and easy road access from logging operations, more and more people are heading into the woods. More people, unfortunately, are also showing less respect for the danger of forest fires. In the Okanagan Valley, we have been covered in smoke for parts of the summer, from both local fires and from those outside the province. It was particularly bad, and particularly alarming, in the summer of 2019, when I began working on this book.

The summer of 2020 saw the worst smoke ever from wildfires in the Okanagan. We also had smoke coming up from California and Oregon, which only goes to prove that climate change in one area of North America will affect everyone. The smoke was so bad that Osoyoos Lake could not be seen from the main highway.

It is past obvious that logging practices have to change and access to the woods has to be more restrictive. Climate change is real, and it is having a real effect on the forests. My people are battling with Weyerhaeuser, the huge multinational forestry corporation that has been logging in our backyard for more than half a century. Over the last few years the company's clear-cutting has expanded and caused massive flood damage to creeks that run through the Osoyoos Indian Reserve. We have held many emotional meetings with Weyerhaeuser and the B.C. Ministry of Forests in an effort to reduce clear-cutting and the annual allowable cut.

Our hunters have noticed a sharp decline in the deer, moose, and elk habitat. The forests in the Okanagan are a very important part of our heritage and culture. Trees are used in most of our spiritual ceremonies. In our Winter Dances, a fir pole is set up and our cultural Knowledge Keepers hold on to that pole. The Osoyoos Indian Band members are understandably very upset about the amount of logging going on in our backyard and the yearly increase in forest fire threats. We must act!

In 2020, the world began dealing with a new global threat—COVID-19, a novel coronavirus pandemic. Many Native prophecies have warned about disrespecting Mother Earth. The warning is that humans will eventually cause too much sickness to the land and water. And once the land, animals, and water are sick, great sickness will spread to humans. Humans cannot overpopulate any region, pollute and pollute for decades, and not suffer the consequences. Natives know what happens to the land and water when animals overpopulate an area. Eventually, some sort of disease inflicts the herd. And when humans overpopulate an area and resort to taking shortcuts (saving money) on animal storage and animal food harvesting, that's a guaranteed recipe for sickness.

Now, throw in the reality of that mostly ignored pandemic: climate change. To me, there are glaring factors that connect the dots. COVID-19 is not just about a virus that came from overcrowded "wet markets" in China. It is also about a direct line, not a dotted line, to climate change. Too many people (overcrowding) . . . too much energy needed to support those people . . . too much animal and human waste . . . not enough land left in its natural state . . . natural water tables being compromised. The list of environmental damage indictors goes on and on. Too much pollution of the air, water, and land in one place will always lead to disease.

We all need to do a better job of protecting the wild animals, fish, and plants, and in keeping our rivers and oceans clean. Who protests and marches when an animal or plant is on the verge of extinction?

Hundreds of thousands of people died from this virus before governments started telling their people to take COVID-19 seriously. Sadly, it took economic suffering to finally force world leaders to connect some of those dots. First Nation traditional knowledge keepers have been telling governments for more than a hundred years that everything on Mother Earth and in Father Sky is interconnected. COVID-19 must be looked at holistically with all the connecting factors. It is time for those same prime ministers and presidents to tell their people to take the root cause of global warming seriously.

Our population continues to grow exponentially. As I write, we're nearing eight billion, and it's estimated that by 2050 that figure will reach ten billion. How do we feed that many people without damage to our natural backyards? The sad reality is that every human (no matter how small) causes pollution.

Native people have known for thousands of years that humans are interconnected with nature and must respect nature and live with nature in a balanced way. We can't over-hunt, over-fish, over-log, or over-pollute the waters or land. The words of Chief Seattle were right over 100 years ago : "The earth does not belong to man, man belongs to the earth. All things are connected like the blood that unites us all. Man did not weave the web of life, he is merely a strand in it. Whatever he does to the web, he does to himself."

CHAPTER 19

"WHO'S YOUR FAVOURITE INDIAN?"

"What treaty that the white man ever made with us have they kept? Not one. Where are our lands? Who owns them? What white man can ever say I stole his land or a penny of his money? Yet they say I am a thief . . . . What white man has ever seen me drunk? What law have I broken? Is it wrong for me to love my own? Is it wicked for me because my skin is red? . . . Because I was born where my father lived, because I would die for my people and my country."

—Chief Sitting Bull, from the book *Touch the Earth*

In the movie *Smoke Signals*, a drunken Indian father asks his little son over and over, "Who's your favourite Indian?" The son replies: "Nobody, nobody, nobody . . ."

One of my tribal area monthly newspapers, the *Colville Tribune*, ran a letter to the editor on Indigenous Peoples Day (Columbus Day). It was written by a Native youth, RaShawn Lemery, who reflected on that rarely asked question, "Who's your favourite Indian?" That most important question is never asked among my race. How sad, I thought, for Native youth not to have heroes and role models from their own race. Colonialism (which is another word for racism) taught Indian youth to look elsewhere for role models.

That question reminded me of my first trip to New York City a few years ago. I distinctly wanted to go to Harlem. I didn't realize why at the time, other than because that's where people of colour lived. I had so many Black heroes in sports, music, entertainment, and politics. On the streets of Harlem, I found what I was looking for: "Black Pride." Many street vendors were displaying Black Pride merchandise, and I bought pictures of Muhammad Ali, Martin Luther King, and Malcolm X, as well as several CDs of famous Black musicians.

Harlem made more sense to me than the glamour and glitter of Manhattan. I connected with Harlem and loved seeing Black people's pride in their own race. They were showcasing their champions. Most Black people can answer the question "Who is your favourite Black athlete or singer?" As Reggie Jackson said, "As a young Black, I was ashamed of my color. I was ashamed of my hair. Ali made me proud. Ali helped raise Black people in this country out of mental slavery."

I love the question "Who's your favourite Indian?" Maybe it's because I can answer it. Not with "nobody," but with many, many examples. Our race has gone through the theft of our lands, broken treaties, cultural genocide, residential and boarding schools, the Sixties Scoop, termination and relocation assimilation programs. Native kids during my youth went to movie theatres all over their traditional territories and became ashamed of their ancestors. Native youth saw movie after movie where the Indians are always the bloodthirsty savages. Native girls had to sit in public theatres and hear the word "squaw" used over and over by famous Hollywood actors. Hollywood made millions depicting Indians who were defending their lands and way of life as the bad guys who always lost. Always.

Not that many years ago, most kids still played "Cowboys and Indians" in every public school playground. Not so many years ago, during my gramma's time, members of the Canadian and American governments and even the president and prime minister used the term "Indian Problem," as if nothing more needed to be said about the Indigenous First Nations of North America. They were a "problem." Not many years ago the churches viewed Indian reserves as unholy and filled with a race of people that needed soul-saving and to be converted from "Devil worshiping." The white people's leadership called First Nations people "hostiles" and "savages."

Little wonder why, in my lifetime, First Nation people avoided the question "Who is your favourite Indian?"

Today, however, I can easily and proudly answer that question.

My favourite Indians are:

- those contemporary Chiefs who organized the modern Indian movement in every province and state (Union of B.C, Chiefs, National Indian Brotherhood [Assembly of First Nations], National Congress of American Indians, American Indian Movement, etc.);
- Sitting Bull and Chief Joseph, whose pictures hang above my desk;
- Crazy Horse and all the leaders of the "hostiles" who refused treaty and defended their Indian way of life;
- those who speak their language (even if only a few words);
- our language teachers, Modesta and Sherry;
- those who practise their people's religion and ceremonies;
- those who sing their people's songs (we have some awesome young drummers, like Kick);
- those who go to school—not for themselves, but for their people and their Rez;
- those who hold a job, any job, and earn their daily wage (no slackers);

- those who are never late and know that real "Indian time" means getting there early and pitching in;
- those who pay their rent and keep their credit good and put their money where their mouth is;
- those who participate in cultural events and practise culture;
- those who don't play a dirty, cheap-shot modern politics of lies and rumours and that treat everyone the same—even those who vote the other way;
- those who hang around Indians, visit every Rez they drive close to—no matter what town they are—and seek out and hang around "the urban skins";
- those who keep their house and yard clean (your yard is a true reflection of your Native Pride of ownership);
- those who hunt and fish responsibly (don't overfish, and don't overhunt or overpick);
- those who don't leave garbage behind;
- those who don't rip up the land with their dirt bikes, quads, side-by-sides, or trucks;
- those who don't sell drugs or bootlegs and will identify all those who do criminal activity in our communities (even their own family);
- the drunk and homeless Natives who have gone through hell and are still fighting the fight and are not a threat to anyone (I still give them a wave and some money to get them through the day);
- the contemporary Native musicians who include in some of their songs lyrics of Rez life and Rez struggles (XIT, Floyd Red Crow Westerman, Willy & Jess, and our own Jim Boyd);

- those old Indians who realize that becoming a "True Elder" is about far more than reaching a certain age;
- those who speak against bullying and violence and uphold the peace;
- those who organize Native sports;
- First Nation school teachers like Helen, Val, Celina, and Ryan;
- Native business conference organizers like Jennifer Wood;
- the Native media, who tell our side and stick to the truth and give our people a kick in the rear, a wakeup call, a bannock slap, but also a pat on the back (verbal hug) for all the good in Indian Country;
- all the Grams and Papas who pitch in every week to raise their grandkids and give them a better childhood than they had;
- those who aren't "know-it-alls," who believe in personal development, and who continue to read the books and attend conferences; and
- my Native motorcycle family—those organizers of all Native Motorcycle Honor Rides (Run to the Rez—Apache; Trail of Tears—Cherokee; Navajo/Hopi Honor Riders; and of course the Wounded Knee Memorial Run).

As you can see, my favourite Indian is all over Indian Country, on and off the Rez. Ultimately, my favourite Indian ranges from the uneducated to the very educated, from the everyday alcoholic to the sober, from the very quiet to the outspoken. And, when it truly counts, my favourite Indian knows when and how to "Indian up!"

As Mi'kmaq leader Anna Mae Aquash so perfectly put it:

The whole country changed with only a handful of raggedy-ass Pilgrims that came over here in the 1500s. And it can take a handful of raggedy-ass Indians to do the same, and I intend to be one of those raggedy-ass Indians.

CHAPTER 20

DAMN, I'M LUCKY TO BE AN INDIAN

"The Indian way of life, you don't separate education, you don't separate it from the home life, you don't separate it from your spiritual life. The way you live your life every day is your religion. It's not something that has a special day and that's it!"

—Madonna Thunder Hawk in the documentary *Warrior Women*

It was 1979, Native Awareness Week at the University of Lethbridge. I was nineteen years old, sitting in a lecture theatre listening to a great speaker, a faith keeper from the Iroquois Confederacy. He said something that has guided me daily now for over forty years, especially whenever I am down, in need of a lift or a reminder of where my roots are and why I work so hard—and he said it in one sentence:

"Damn, I'm lucky to be an Indian!"

I was literally a "starving student" from a poor Rez at the time. I had no monetary support except my underfunded Indian Affairs education allowance. I was in a university filled with middle- and upper-middle-class white students. I'd left a Rez where there was a lot of poverty and alcohol abuse. But—damn, I missed being back on the Osoyoos Indian Rez! Just like in senior high school, I was barely hanging on, barely staying in university, but the Native American Studies program was reminding me how lucky I was to be an Indian.

I remember the faith keeper saying something like this:

Our identity and our Native rights are not dependent on the United States or Canada. Sometimes I'm walking down the streets of a city or town, surrounded by white people in a cement jungle. I'm the only Indian, far from my Rez. I'm wearing a "Native Pride" baseball cap or shirt or something Native, feeling out of place and receiving those slight *Who is this guy?* glances from people I pass on the street. I'm thinking I could take off this Indian stuff and just try and melt in and accept defeat to the ordained, dominant race. I'm tired of fighting all the land and social injustices against Native people, tired of being oppressed, tired of trying to save my language and culture, tired of the nightmares from residential/boarding school. I'm tired of the anger and bitterness built up inside of me from the broken treaties and land thefts. I'm disgusted when I go back to the Rez and see the poverty, alcoholism, drug abuse, violence, and daily family struggles of my tribe while in this city the whites enjoy all the modern comforts on my ancestor's land—Indian land. Do I give up the struggle? Then I think . . . after all the injustices done, after all the racism and hatred and outright massacres and killing of Indian people on our own soil by the English and French, as I walk alone in the city I give my head a shake. Stand up straight and look the passing strangers in the eye and think with 100 per cent conviction, *Damn! I'm lucky to be an Indian!*

The first time I heard those words I thought, *Damn right! Me too!* Back then I was reading everything I could about First Nation issues and researching the historical truth of the British and French imperialism that created Canada and the United States. I, too, got angry and sad every day over all the past and current injustices (still do!). But long before I got to university it was my "Okanagan Native

Pride" that kept me going! All through grade school and high school in Oliver, B.C., the kids from the Osoyoos Indian Reserve were far outnumbered by the white kids. There were only a handful of us in the public school in any given grade; we even had our own "Indian bus" that picked up the kids on the Rez and took us to school in town.

I don't remember much racism toward me in grade school. I participated in sports at recess and lunch, usually street hockey or football, and sports put me in the same circle as most of the white kids. The white kids picked on the few other minorities in the school—kids with East Indian or Portuguese backgrounds—but rarely did they pick on Indians. They knew that, even though we were vastly outnumbered, Rez Indians wouldn't back down. Indians would always fight back. Just as we have been fighting since 1492. In grade school, I saw Rez boys stand up to and back off lots of white kids. During my time in grade school and high school there would be the odd scrap, a few fist fights, but the white kids had a sort of "street respect" for kids from the Osoyoos Indian Band. Even though our numbers continue to be very small in high school, my people have still managed to hold sports records for hill running (Ron), most push-ups in one minute (Shawn), best hockey goalie (Narcisse), and MMA champ (Marlin).

Yet racism still affected most OIB kids back in the 1960s and '70s. There was once a provincial—and racist—rule that First Nation kids were not allowed to attend public schools. It was only in the early 1960s that Osoyoos kids were allowed to attend public schools, which I guess makes me one of the lucky ones. Most Rez kids dropped out of school by grade eight or nine. Later I would hear that racism was a key reason why so many hated school and eventually dropped out. Kids know when they are not welcome. Kids can sense when they are excluded by the majority. It happens in the classroom and it happens especially in the playground. A few times I was asked by white kids in grade school, "How come you're not like the other Indians?" I can't remember the full context of the question or how I answered it, but I do remember saying, "I'm no different than the other Indian kids—no one likes being picked on or left out." In grade school and high school there were no Native boys in my grade, but I kept my Rez identity and my white buddies knew that and respected it.

It's so sad that most Rez kids quit high school early back then. With the racism in public school and the poverty and alcohol abuse back on the Rez, and very little in the way of programs and services, most Native kids didn't stand much of a chance. Even so, the generation in which I grew up, like the generations that went before us, was a generation of damn hard workers who were a proud people. This included those who quit school and got a labour job right away. I believe that, no matter your circumstances, you can still make a successful and fulfilling life if you find a job—a job you love—and you work hard at that job. Most of our OIB dropouts became damn good, dependable workers. Sure, many still drank too much, but most had a "work hard and play hard" ethic.

Like most reserves, Osoyoos didn't have much when I was growing up. Most adults did manual labour: you worked in the orchards, apple-packing houses, vineyards, or in forestry. The lucky ones got a job in the Band office. Like half the families on the Rez, I was raised by a single mother, as my dad was never around (unless he was drinking). There was a big alcohol problem in most families. Not all, but most. Our family was one of the many where little kids witnessed alcohol abuse at an early age. The effects of residential school are multi-generational, and I witnessed a lot of lateral violence and hatred among my people. In B.C., Indians were not allowed into the public bars until the mid-1950s. Maybe that's where a lot of the problems came from? Growing up, I often heard stories of white guys boot-legging to people on the Rez because it was against the law for Indians to go into liquor stores.

I have not been able to cover all aspects of Rez life and culture. Rez life is complicated and unique. Many of those who grew up on a Rez share the same tough upbringing, but they also have some different and very special experiences. Some experiences are only told in the sweat house ceremony or within our own inner circles. My own experiences have of course shaped my opinions. Others have different stories to tell. I have to respect that.

There are only two countries in the whole world that have federal Indian reserves or reservations, two countries that simultaneously boast to the world about their commitment to justice and freedom: Canada and the United States. So, even though tribal nations can be so different, our Rez experiences and Rez life are what bind us. My people, the Okanagans, are like all Native people in that we have an ancestral attachment to our territory that the colonial governments could not break. There is nowhere else on Mother Earth that Okanagan people can go and be Okanagan. The English can go visit their ances-tral Britain. The French can go deeper into their heritage by experi-encing their ancestral France. For all First Nations, identity and culture is tied directly to traditional lands. But their "ancestral home" is now called Canada or the United States.

Chief Crazy Horse was once asked by a white man, "Where are your lands?" Chief Crazy Horse pointed and replied, "My lands are where my dead lie buried."

Every time I go to the Wounded Knee Memorial Motorcycle Run, I travel through southern Montana, right past the famous Little Big Horn Battlefield National Monument. Like most "Rezskins," I had heard about how the Indians massacred Custer and made that name famous. Of course, that is not the truth—it's just more "colonial white history."

In 1876, the U.S. government declared "any Indian not confined on the reservations be declared hostile." They sent out thousands of soldiers to bring them back to the reservations by force. In June of that year (the same year Canada forced the Indian Act on First Nations), the Lakota, Cheyenne, and Arapaho were practising their hunting rights (summer buffalo hunt) and their religion (the Sundance). The First Amendment to the United States Constitution clearly promises "freedom of religion." But when General George Custer attacked the Indian village, the First Amendment was nowhere to be found. It did not apply to Indians, and neither did the words in U.S. law that claim "We hold these truths to be self-evident, that all men are created equal . . . "

Custer and his soldiers swore an oath to uphold the United States Constitution, but 99 per cent of that Constitution didn't apply to the first peoples of North America. As is usually the case when the army attacks a Native village, the first casualties at Little Big Horn were women and children. Most Americans don't think about the terror Native women and children went through when Custer attacked. I do. Going to this sacred site where First Nation people were protecting their way of life and forced to fight for their freedom was always on my bucket list—and now I do an "honour ride" through the battlefield on my motorcycle each August.

It is such a powerful, spiritual place. I look at the land there and think, *This is the very land where two of my heroes—Chief Sitting Bull and Crazy Horse—were still free and had to literally fight for their freedom and protect their families from United States bullets.* Many times I have slept on the ground not far from the battlefield, where I know many of the last free and independent Indians walked and rode. What a spiritual feeling of Native Pride at its highest level.

There are hundreds of Native traditional spiritual sites all over North America that make me very proud to be a (hostile) Indian!

One of our leaders passed away from cancer the other night. He was not only a past council member, but he also started one of our hockey teams and was one of my hunting buddies. I will miss him terribly.

All elected leaders go through the joy and pain of Rez life. Every year new members are born, and every year we bury some of our own. I know I am in the last quarter of my life and that I don't have many sunsets left. I was reminded of this when I visited my very sick friend. He was so weak he could not talk when I looked into his eyes and shook his hand for the last time. And once again I witnessed the pain of family members watching a loved one, a leader, struggling to breathe.

One of the toughest questions I get asked is about my legacy. It is an important question, for as we get older we should take time to reflect on our life's accomplishments and, more important, our hopes and dreams for future generations. Whatever we have done in our work and social life will affect those around us for many generations. In 2019, I became the first Native to be inducted into the Canadian Business Hall of Fame. I told the Hall I could only accept the induction on behalf of the Osoyoos Indian Band. I am not an individual entrepreneur; I am not a sole business owner; and I have never owned one business. I did not invest my own money into any of the Osoyoos Indian Band's businesses. I am elected by the majority of my people every two years to work for my Rez. It's the band, it's the community that owns those companies, and I am part of the team of people that helped those businesses either continue to grow and created a few new businesses.

The recognition I have received is not about me; it's about the First Nation I work for and represent. If I were not the Chief—entrusted by the majority of my people to represent their business interests—I would not have made anyone's award list. So you can appreciate my discomfort when asked the usual question put to those being inducted into a Hall of Fame: "What do you want your legacy to be?" What a tough question. I had never really thought about it before. My work has never been just about me or my family. A Chief's work is about and for the whole community they belong to and also extends to their tribal nation and the rest of Indian Country.

At first I could not answer the question. And then, when I did try to answer, I got pretty emotional about it on camera. I actually asked that the interview be stopped while I wiped the tears away and said, "Let's skip that question and move on to others." When I think about that important question, I think about all of my people, so many of whom have passed on, who put their trust and the future of their kids in my hands as they voted for me—eighteen times—to be the Chief of the Osoyoos Indian Band. That weighs heavily.

The extraordinary honour of this call to duty is hard to explain. And I don't know if I can even talk about such a thing as "my" legacy. My thirty-five years of work on my Rez is truly about "we," not about "me." It is so easy to give the "I care" speech. It's not about that. As a continuing full-time student of Native issues, I know I was born into a great race of people. I was born into a very special First Nation with a very special territory. And, like all First Nation people, I must be aware of our ancestral roots and that "we truly were born on the shoulders of our ancestors." Anything we accomplish must include a strong sense of going back to time immemorial. Our language, our culture, our ceremonies, the land, the water and every living thing, plants and animals, are part of that legacy, our tribal creation stories. That's our true legacy. I now know why I had trouble answering the question "What do you want your legacy to be?" Because my legacy is not about "me"; it's about "we," especially the past! To me, without the past—especially the ancestors the federal government called "savages" and "hostiles"—I wouldn't even have a legacy to talk about!

As for me personally, I hope I have provided a good example of a Chief who worked as hard as our ancestors, who showed up on time— no "Indian Time"—who had near-perfect attendance, who respected the rules of work and told the truth, even when others didn't want to hear it. I have always been guided by the critical importance of truth. My commitment has been to the Osoyoos Indian Band land and people. I have been dedicated to creating more jobs, more opportunity, and making more money for the OIB Rez than anyone else could have been had they held the position of Chief. I have been one of those proud OIB workers who earns his paycheque every two weeks. And I can honestly say those most important words: "I love to hear from my people!" *"I love my job!"* I know I have been someone who worked hard to make OIB a better place to live, work, and play—that's incredibly important to me.

For me, it's a given that we love and care unconditionally for our spouse, kids, and immediate family. Raising kids is the ultimate life responsibility. I wish I had been a wiser and better dad back in my twenties and thirties when we were raising our kids. I was always a good provider, always held a job and paid the bills, but I could have been a much better father. I am so grateful and owe so much to two women, Sam and Brenda, who are such good moms and now grandmas. To my son, Vern, and my daughters, Clarissa and Sarenna: I wish I had spent more time being a father and less time at the office and away at meetings. I have a grandson, Darian, and recently, as happens to most people in their fifties and sixties, I am blessed with maybe my last big personal responsibility and loving every minute of it—"Papa responsibility!"

In 2017, a little person I began to call my "little boss" even before she could say a few words really became my boss. For the first time, I am being called something that, on a personal level more than rivals the word "Chief." I am being called by one little Indian Rez girl . . . "Papa"! My granddaughter, Zenaya, is my new best teacher, my saviour from the emotional drain of Rez politics, my new life energy on and off the business and political battlefields.

When Zenaya was four years old she asked, "Papa, can you play with me?" and for some reason I walked away. She then said something I will never forget: "Papa, you never leave family behind!" As a Chief, I was told that a Chief's family is not only their immediate family but the entire community. I often do things for my people on a personal level that only close family members would do for each other. I go above and beyond my job description, and so should all Rezskins.

I now experience the feelings I saw in other grandfathers when I was younger. How upset my kids' grandfather (Ben) would get when he heard or read the news about abuse against kids. Kids he didn't even know. I now get upset when I read about or see on the news kids suffering. That's grandpa thinking! I have seen grandparents set aside time and cancel their own plans just to do whatever their grandkids wanted to do—which was just to play. That's Papa thinking!

When I was younger and there was a party going on or a hockey or ball tournament, I would try to find a babysitter. Now I would rather stay home and not feel like I missed a thing just to get bossed around by a little girl. That's Papa thinking!

One of my first heroes was the "Champ"—Muhammad Ali—who has left us with so many great quotations, including this one: "The man who views the world thinking the same at 50 as he did at 20 has wasted 30 years of his life." Yeah, I don't view the world or the Rez now the way I did thirty years ago. As we get older we are supposed to get wiser. I believe our inner world thinking changes every ten years. Once we get out of our twenties and into our thirties we shouldn't think or act the way we did in our twenties. Come on! We shouldn't wear the same clothes in our thirties we wore in our twenties (so embarrassing!). And in our fifties we should have more of an inner moral and mental compass that we ever had before. The people we have met and the books we have read and the speeches we have heard should have broadened our thinking and bolstered our ability to filter the good from the bad. Personal growth and awareness should happen every decade.

Yeah, as we get older we are supposed to get wiser, and my "little boss" is bringing me full circle. I am starting to view things with a different lens both personally and in business. Wow! After three decades of negotiating multimillion-dollar deals and meeting many of the top business and political people in Canada and the United States, I would never have thought being called "Papa" by a little Rez girl was going to be my very best teacher and make me a better Chief. I am so "damn lucky."

As an Osoyoos Indian Band member I am so lucky to have been born into a First Nation that has so much. The Osoyoos Rez is not an urban reserve and neither is it a remote community. We truly have the best of both worlds (urban and rural). Being located in the Okanagan Valley, we are next to two small towns (Oliver and Osoyoos); to the west in front of us are the towns (urban) and in back of us to the east are the beautiful mountains and forests (rural). It takes less than ten minutes to drive east up into the mountains, up into the wilderness—our vast hunting-gathering grounds. We are lucky to be near all the modern urban needs—a hospital, high school, ambulance, fire departments, clothing and grocery stores. The closest big "Indian store"—Walmart—is only thirty minutes away. My people do not have to drive hours from their Rez to go shopping or get groceries. And the towns are so close that they are able to address water and sewage needs for our business projects. Our kids don't have to be bussed for hours to get to high school. Some of our youth actually walk to high school from our Rez. When our people are in need of medical emergency, help is close by. The South Okanagan General Hospital is located on our old Rez land and now borders our community. The town fire department is only minutes away and has saved multiple Rez houses. At Osoyoos we have a pretty good community water system—not perfect, but better than most. We seldom have a boiled water advisory. Most of my people are within a five-to-twenty-minute drive to work. We are so "damn lucky."

Our housing on Osoyoos Rez is better than most. Most homes have access to high-speed internet. We have more jobs on the Rez than we do band members. Our people don't have to depend on underfunded Indian Affairs jobs. My people have real career opportunities right on their home turf and don't have to move away to get a job. Our biggest source of income, like many First Nations, is from land leases, which provide the much-needed money to pay for services from "cradle to grave."

Even though we had over four thousand acres of Rez land stolen from us—our best economic land—we still have one of the best, economically strong Rezes in North America. We own several businesses. We own miles of Osoyoos Lake and half of another small lake (Gallagher Lake), and we have two awesome private community beach areas. Our people can still go on horse rides out into the desert or up in the mountains. The "Indian horse culture" still exists on the Osoyoos Rez. We are so "damn lucky."

Our four Food Chiefs are still providing for us—the *Spitelm* (Bitter root), *Seiya* (Saskatoon Berry), *Titlele* (Chinook Salmon), and *Skimest* (Black Bear). Our four Food Chiefs sacrificed themselves for the "people to be" many thousands of years ago. Still, today, most of our traditional foods are either on our Rez or accessible just off. My people still go and pick berries and dig roots. My people are within a short distance of places to hunt deer, moose, and elk, and we still have a salmon run in the summer. We have two creeks running through our Rez and our community sweat houses are on one of those creeks. We are so "damn lucky."

Winters in Osoyoos are not prairie or northern winters. Our winter lasts a couple of months. We complain when it gets down to -8° Celsius (17° Fahrenheit), and we might shovel snow off the sidewalks outside our house two or three times a winter. Yet, because we are in a valley and the mountains are right next to us, we are only forty minutes away from a ski hill named Mt. Baldy. In our language it is called *Spultmentan*, which means "white top." That mountain is so important to us: it's important culturally, but also for food, water, and the modern pastimes of skiing and snowboarding. Many Osoyoos Indian Band youth love the winter sports. And the town hockey rink is only minutes away. Often in March or early April we can golf and ski in the same day. We are so "damn lucky."

Like most First Nations, Osoyoos belongs to a Tribal Council group of same-language-speaking bands on the Canadian side of the border—Lower and Upper Similkameen, Upper Nicola, Penticton Indian Band, Westbank, and Okanagan Indian Band. On the U.S. side of the border the Colville Reservation is traditionally part of our tribal territory. On every one of our Okanagan (*Syilx*) Rezes are very special lands, rivers, lakes, and cultural landmarks. I love visiting and have developed lifelong friendships in all my Nations' communities. Like all tribes (Nations), my people are so fortunate to belong to a group of brother/sister Rez's. When it comes to protecting our First Nation rights and title, Osoyoos is not alone: we belong to an ancestral group of communities that will always have each other's back.

My goal each month, each year, every time I am elected is to make things a little bit better for my people. And I've got the pictures and the stats to prove that. Yes—I know we did strike out a few times. But as a wise person once said: "It's better to try something great and fail—than to do nothing at all and succeed." As a Rez, we still have a lot of improving to do, and I have hope that when I no longer take up a seat in the council chambers that the future Osoyoos Chief and councils will have a measurable scorecard that will outperform my time.

Back in 1877, when the Osoyoos Indian Rez was created, our ancestors had a difficult time coming to terms with being restricted to the small piece of their territory that was now called an "Indian reserve." This concept was totally foreign to them. Yet they did their best to provide a land base from which future generations could survive as a distinct people. Our ancestors suffered through the toughest of times and yet truly left us a near-paradise from which to live, work, and play! The Osoyoos Indian Reserve—as my brother Arnie wrote—is "Where the heavens go to play."

There's a biker saying I like: "Life's journey is not to arrive at the grave safely in a well-preserved body but rather to pin the throttle and skid in sideways, totally worn out, shouting 'Holy shit . . . what a ride!'"

I have been on one hell of a ride. We will all face our last sunset someday, and I know there are many "calls to action" I won't be around for. I want my people, my family and friends to know it has been an honour to represent and serve the Osoyoos Indian Band, the Okanagan (*Syilx*) Nation, and all the Redskins in Indian Country.

I also want it on the record that, when I depart on my "iron horse" for the last ride, I'm not going to any pearly gates or hell, since I don't believe in either of those places. Most Rez Indians have been to hell and back many times, anyway. How could this not be the case, for those raised in poverty, drug and alcohol abuse, domestic violence, sexual abuse, the residential school system, etc.? Many years ago, I was showing a white historian around our Rez. We stopped by the old church graveyard and noticed some mounds outside the fence. The mounds had no markers. I asked the historian why some of our people had been buried outside our own cemetery fence in this way. He told me that, back then, the church would not allow "unbaptised Indians" to be buried in their own community's cemetery. I couldn't believe it. *The priests decided where my people could be buried?* Christian-baptised Indians inside the fence, "savages" outside the fence? If that's where the "savages" got buried—outside the fence—then I, as a "born-again savage," want my people to bury me outside of a fence. No cross, no church hymns, none of those foreign ways. Just bring your traditional drums, Okanagan language, Rez humour, and "iron horses."

No heaven or hell for me. The first place I will be going after my last breath will be a Rez dance hall. The Happy Hunting Grounds can come later. I know my ancestors will allow me to first find that Rez dance hall on some bright star in the sky. There I'll join those I grew up with, friends and family I miss every day: Arnu, Gordon, George, Noni, Tilly, Wayne, TC, Virg, Virgil, Ethan, Dog, Modesta, Rob, and my big girls, Clarissa and TJ, and so many others.

It will be a "payday Friday" because, remember, Rez dances would only happen on paydays. Rezskins often go from paycheque to paycheque. The fundraising dance will be at the Nk'mip Community Hall for our hockey or ball team. It will be breaking daylight; the hat will have been passed around for the second time to keep the sixties and seventies classic rock music playing. The DJ will be playing Loverboy's "Turn Me Loose," loud and proud. The (pop) bar will have been closed for hours, but the dance floor will still be packed with the die-hard Skins from all the Okanagan Rezes on both sides of the border.

Then the last song will be Keith Secola's "Indian Car":

I got a sticker that says Indian power

I stuck it on a bumper—that's what holds my car together

We are on a circuit of an Indian dream

We don't get old we just get younger

When we're flying down the highway riding in our Indian car . . .

It's my daughter Cloey's favourite song. Everyone will raise a fist and give out a Rez *war-whoop* that will sound like the thunder of a thousand drums to remind all the Canadians and Americans unjustly occupying our land (unceded land) that the "Indian Problem" they created is still around.

The Rez dance will shut down well past daylight and outside will be rows of Harleys and Indian iron horses, plus a few Rez bombs with missing windows, dents, rust holes, and broken mufflers. Everyone "still going" will mount up and grab their "old ladies" or "Xs." My kids, Vern and Sarenna, will be on my Harleys. My "little boss," Baby Z, will be proudly holding up the Osoyoos Indian Band flag. All the bikes will start up at the same time. The sound of a a hundred Harleys and Indians will send the wild Rez horses into a gallop and wake up our bros taking well-earned naps under the tables.

The thunder of the pipes will roar down the Osoyoos Rez road. As we pass by other reserves and reservations, more Indian bikers (hostiles) and Rez bombs will join the long line of riders. The awesome feeling (nothing like it) of being on an Indian memorial motorcycle ride encompasses all Rez things past, present, and future.

The throttles are pressed wide open. We are heading to Standing Rock, North Dakota—Chief Sitting Bull's Rez—and then on to the Wounded Knee gravesite on the Pine Ridge Rez, South Dakota, to meet our ancestors who could not speak or read English, who were not baptized, and yet who symbolized the inter-tribal fight for freedom and justice. The nearly three hundred Lakota buried at Wounded Knee remind all First Nations that we will hold on to our language, culture, and ancestral responsibilities at all cost.

That's where I'm going when I close my eyes for the last time. I know I have left a few footprints behind—and a trail. My last thought will be "Bury My Heart on My Rez!"

And my last words will be . . . "Damn, I'm lucky to be an Indian!"

CREDITS

p. ix: Chief Joseph. "An Indian's View of Indian Affairs." *North American Review* 128:269 (April 1879): 412-33.

p. 1: Thomson, Duncan Duane. 1985. "A History of the Okanagan: Indians and Whites in the Settlement Era, 1860-1920." PhD diss., University of British Columbia.

p. 11: "End" from the album *Plight of the Redman* by XIT (1972). Lyrics by Michael Valvano and Tom Bee. Reprinted by permission of Sony Music.

p. 13: Chief Dan George in the film *Little Big Man* (1970).

p. 24: Banks, Dennis. *Ojibwa Warrior: Dennis Banks and the Rise of the American Indian Movement.* Oklahoma: University of Oklahoma Press, 2011.

p. 38: Excerpt from *First Nations Self-Government* by Leroy Paul Wolf Collar. Copyright © Leroy Paul Wolf Collar, 2020. Reproduced by permission of Brush Education.

p. 41: Johnson, Harold. *Firewater: How Alcohol Is Killing My People and Yours.* Regina: University of Regina Press, 2016.

p. 49: Oskaboose, Gilbert. "A Canoe of Fools." *The Nation News.* July 19, 1996. http://www.nationnewsarchives.ca/article /a-canoe-of-fools/. Reprinted by permission.

p. 67: Excerpt from the *Navajo Times*.

p. 83: Excerpt from *First Nations Self-Government* by Leroy Paul

Wolf Collar. Copyright © Leroy Paul Wolf Collar, 2020.
Reproduced by permission of Brush Education.

p. 95: Deloria, Jr., Vine. *Custer Died for Your Sins*. Oklahoma:
University of Oklahoma Press, 1988.

p. 100: *Honouring the Truth, Reconciling for the Future: Summary of
the Final Report of the Truth and Reconciliation Commission of
Canada*. Truth and Reconciliation Commission of Canada. 2015.

p. 100: Milloy, John S. *A National Crime: The Canadian Government
and the Residential School System, 1879 to 1986*. Winnipeg:
University of Manitoba Press, 1999.

p. 103: Excerpt of letter from Duncan Campbell Scott in 1918 to
British Columbia Indian Agent General-Major D. MacKay.

p. 104: George-Kanentiio, Doug. "Failures of Canada's Truth and
Reconciliation Process." *Cornwall Free News*. April 24, 2019.
https://cornwallfreenews.com/2019/04/24/failures-of-cana-
das-truth-and-reconciliation-process-by-doug-george-
kanentiio-042419/

p. 110: Sellars, Bev. *They Called Me Number One*. Vancouver:
Talonbooks, 2012. Reproduced by permission of the publisher.

p. 123: "Tootoo says Eskimos name discussion should centre on feelings
of Inuit." Canadian Press. July 9, 2020. https://www.sportsnet.ca
/football/cfl/tootoo-says-eskimos-name-discussion-centre
-feelings-inuit/

p. 131: Chief Phillip Martin, as quoted in *The Choctaw Revolution:
Lessons for Federal Indian Policy* (1988) by Peter J. Ferrara.

p. 143: Cappo, Kamao. *Descendants of Warriors*. Calgary:
Eaglespeaker Publishing, 2019.

p. 145: Pearson, Noel. *Up from the Mission: Selected Writings*.
Melbourne: Black Inc., 2011.